God and Caesar

Edited by
Michael Bauman
and
David Hall

CHRISTIAN PUBLICATIONS, INC.
CAMP HILL, PENNSYLVANIA

God and Caesar

Edited by
Michael Bauman
and
David Hall

Christian Publications
3825 Hartzdale Drive, Camp Hill, PA 17011

Faithful, biblical publishing since 1883

ISBN: 0–87509–574–7
LOC Catalog Number: 94–72351
© 1994 by Christian Publications
All rights reserved
Printed in the United States of America

94 95 96 97 98 5 4 3 2 1

Dedication

For
Russell Kirk
and the champions of the permanent things

God and Caesar
ed. by Michael Bauman and David Hall

Foreword

Confusing the Visible
with the Certain

I have been involved in ministry since 1942. As I have ministered in the church, the para-church and the Senate, one of my greatest concerns—especially as I have witnessed the effect of evangelicals on government—is that the church is seen by our contemporaries largely (and at times exclusively) as an institution. The impact of the Church on the world is normally perceived only as based on its institutional impact on society.

Rather than considering the external container or institutional measurement of effectiveness, I much prefer to think about how the church of Jesus Christ has truly and best influenced the world in history. How does the church impact culture? Is this institutional influence primarily a product of the few hours a week that the church gathers? Is it not rather that the result of those few hours—not at all to demean the high significance, value and mandate of worship—is marginal, compared to the real impact of the church of Jesus Christ in the world?

Jesus said, "You are the salt of the earth." Salt works on contact. Once the contact is made, the salt disappears. When it is doing its work, it becomes invisible. Jesus also used the analogy of the sower and the seed. Here again,

1

when the seed is effective, it sinks in, takes root, grows and becomes invisible.

I am, at times, absolutely appalled at the minimal impact that evangelicalism is having on culture, the world and on government. And I am an evangelical. No small portion of this failure is the preoccupation with the church-as-institution alone. The people in our congregations wrongly assume that they are having a godly influence on the world only when they are involved in some kind of program, or else when they are employing some marketing technique, or method, supposedly to evangelize or witness—once again, not so much in a personal way, but in an institutional way. In pursuit of the measurable, we have traded our evangelizing and witnessing for a dented porridge bowl of marketing techniques. In fact, "marketing" is often the blatant term we employ.

A senator friend of mine was asked by a Christian broadcaster to help raise money to help air an evangelistic broadcast. The TV broadcaster sold this as a very effective approach. The senator asked how much it would cost to air the program. The evangelist answered: "We estimate that it will cost us [so-much] to *market our product* in this area." I was shocked and so was the senator, to hear a mission field referred to as a market. I fear that we are marketing the gospel, and in the process we communicate that people are only validly witnessing when and if they use a certain marketing technique or method. Witnessing is considered valid only if it is using visible tools or techniques.

The idea of being salt which disappears or a seed that sinks into the ground—both of which continue their effectiveness even if invisible—is largely lost. Some seem to think that we are only being Christian when we are broadcasting or obvious. We do well to recover an emphasis on the invisible and focus less, perhaps, on the more obvious areas. Each of the parables of Matthew 13 is concerned with the hiddenness of the gospel message—the hiddenness of the kingdom, the hiddenness of the treasure, the hiddenness of leaven in the loaf and the hiddenness of a seed in soil. We have become so bottom-line conscious in the institutional church (and para-church, too), that we cannot raise monies or justify ministry unless we can quote statistics, or point to the bottom line to prove how successful we are. Thus, we have to measure immediate results. We want to evaluate the harvest, in the short term, so as to use it to prop up our money raising tactics.

Yet, the real impact of the church of Jesus Christ on the world is immeasurable. As a pastor, I always enjoyed—and was challenged—to gaze on my congregation and imagine where they would be between Sundays. Where is the church in its non-Sunday life? Except for a few meetings and the staff, the church is hidden from the world, hidden by Christ, but still his potent witness.

To understand the influence of the church of Jesus Christ in the world, we must first comprehend that it is hidden, that it is immeasurable, that there are no criteria for measuring the immediate results. If a pastor is doing the job that Paul describes in Ephesians, he is equipping the people to do the work of ministry. That, unfortunately, has come to be associated with programmatic institutions, or marketing techniques, instead of being filled with the Holy Spirit, so as to manifest the Son of God—day in, day out, every minute of every hour of every day.

We also have forgotten to pray for "all those in authority," as Paul enjoins us in First Timothy 2. We may underestimate the value of prayer because it is not very compatible with marketing and its orientation toward quick successes. Rarely, when I visit a church or attend a conference, do I hear our leaders prayed for in a pastoral prayer. We have surrendered one of our best tools. Many Christians criticize the President or the Supreme Court; but few pray for them. A return to this might be a key to the revitalization of our nation and government.

We do well to keep our eyes more on God's Word and its promises—even in the realm of politics—than strictly on the visible, the institutional and the programmatic. God's Spirit is more effective than all of those. God works in ways we do not expect; often invisibly—though most certainly—through witnesses who are faithful to Him.

It is my hope that books and efforts such as this one will call us back, and forward, to those works which our Lord has prepared for us to accomplish. We must begin by recapturing the biblical and historical emphases represented in these pages.

Richard C. Halverson
Chaplain to the Senate of the United States

Preface

*W*hat is worth doing, says the old proverb, is worth doing well. What evangelicals have been doing lately is to make their influence felt in the marketplace and in the public square. They have, in short, become powerful. This book is designed to help shape, direct and inform that power, to aid evangelicals in doing politics and economics not only better but well.

The essays printed in these pages represent some of the best political and economic thinking of one of America's premier evangelical professional organizations, the Evangelical Theological Society, for whom these papers were initially prepared and presented. Some of the scholars who contribute to this volume are well-known and long-established. They need no introduction. Others are fresh voices, eager to be heard and worthy to be heard. Not surprisingly, therefore, the viewpoints presented here are varied. Evangelicalism is not monolithic. If any one idea unites all these contributors, it is that they all take the Bible seriously. These authors are firmly convinced that God is not Someone in *addition* to politics and economics. He is Someone in *relation* to them. To help the church better understand that relationship is the burden and intention of this book.

The editors wish to thank Angus MacDonald of the *St. Croix Review*, as well as Ronald Trowbridge and Lissa Roche of *Imprimis*, for permission to reprint here a modified version of "The Dangerous Samaritans." Our deepest and most enduring political debt we acknowledge in the dedication.

Michael Bauman
David W. Hall

Psalm 101 and the Ethos of Political Leadership
by Daniel J. Estes

Contemporary American society faces a crisis of leadership. In recent years scandals at the highest levels have rocked the business world, the financial markets and the religious community. Added to these regrettable events is an ongoing disillusion regarding political leaders. The questions raised by Watergate, Iran-Contra and Whitewater linger on. The falls of Gary Hart, Jim Wright and John Tower still produce tremors. Disenchantment with the duplicity of government officials has produced cynicism in much of the electorate. Trust and respect for politicians and political institutions remains mired at the bottom of public opinion polls.

Two fundamental questions emerge from this morass: What should a political leader *be*? And, what should a political leader *do*? In short, the discussion revolves around the ethos of political leadership: What is the relationship between the character and the conduct of a political leader? Should a leader be evaluated solely on the basis of his or her effectiveness in accomplishing the duties of office, or should evaluation as a leader also encompass personal character as well?

7

Numerous biblical passages touch upon political leadership. However, nowhere is there stated a universal prescription for those in positions of political authority. Therefore, each passage must be read in terms of the occasion for which it was originally given, rather than being lifted out of its original setting to serve as an absolute axiom.

This chapter will analyze Psalm 101 to discover how it contributes to the question of the relationship between the personal character and the public conduct of a political leader in contemporary America. I will view this subject from three directions. First, I will place the current question within its historical context in the literature of political philosophy and in recent political commentary. Second, I will investigate the salient contributions of Psalm 101 to the question of the relationship between a political leader's values, character and actions. Third, I will develop a theoretical model for evaluating political leaders suggested by the exegesis of Psalm 101.

1. Context of the Question

1.1 Ancient Political Philosophy

Throughout the ancient world there was a longstanding and widespread consensus that the character and the conduct of a leader are necessarily connected. Kaplan asserts that "an interconnection of morals and politics has characterized ethical theory from the outset: whether because, as in Plato, the state is the individual writ large; or because, as with Aquinas, it has a moral aim."[1]

Aristotle was a key contributor to the political philosophy that dominated the Western tradition in the ancient world. He reasoned that humans could only reach their full potential when their human associations were governed by ethics. However, in this view the ethos for each particular political entity grew out of its unique view of what was advantageous and just for its people.[2] A society's ethics did not represent a universal moral standard, but rather what was most useful for its specific concerns. In fact, although in Aristotle's view the *polis* was designed to encourage the character development of the populace, in reality it was limited to only a small elite within the society.[3] For Aristotle there was a direct link between personal character and public conduct within the confines of a political entity. However, there were not necessarily transcendent values by which the ethics of a specific *polis* could be measured.

Aquinas appropriated much Aristotelian thought, but at this point he added the dimension of universal morality. He argued,

> . . . *governmental action involves responsibility and a choice of means, and the means depends on ends that are moral. The people engaged in politics are moral agents, attracted to both good and evil. They are confronted with challenges that go beyond the categories of technical efficiency. Because people are moral beings and need to integrate their world, they will defend their actions with reference to a broader and more abstract conception of reality and will be confronted with an image of what is right.*[4]

For Aquinas, the political leader must be evaluated by more than pragmatic efficiency, or even by correspondence to the norms of the particular society. Instead, an absolute standard of morality must always be the measurement for political behavior.

1.2   Modern Political Philosophy

Although ancient political philosophy has had an undeniable impact upon American thought, more direct influence has been exerted by modern political theorists. Political philosophers such as Machiavelli, Bacon, Hobbes and Locke rejected the classical and Christian linkage of ethics and politics as a misguided utopian notion.[5] For example, John Locke reasoned that Judeo-Christian monotheism, with its insistence on the worship of only one God and the abolition of all other deities, promoted an uncivil attitude toward those who disagreed with it.[6] Because of this fact, traditional Christianity, in Locke's view, needed to be reinterpreted into a form of civil religion. Locke posited that the law of reason, or the law of nature, was more appropriate to a stable society than the law of Scripture. By saying this, Locke undermined religion in any form as a normative standard for political life.[7]

It was this modern political philosophy which directly affected the American Founding Fathers. In helping to compose the Federalist Papers, James Madison was particularly keen to produce a system of government which would be able to survive the deep colonial factions. Viewing the ancient political idealism as encouraging social fragmentation, Madison reduced the scope of politics. No longer was the *polis* charged with character development in accordance with the societal values (as in Aristotle) or universal values (as in Aquinas). Instead, Madison assumed that a carefully constructed set of checks and balances could make use of individual self-interest in order to get the work of government done.[8] Therefore, the American system of government from its inception was basically pragmatic in its design. Diamond evaluates well the significance of this fact:

> *This removal of the task of character formation from its previously preeminent place on the agenda of politics had an immense consequence for the relationship of ethics and politics in modern regimes. The hallmark of the traditional ethics-politics relationship had been those harsh and comprehensive laws by means of which the ancient philosophers had sought to "high-tone" human character. But now, because character formation was no longer the direct end of politics, the new science of politics could dispense with those laws and, for the achievement of its lowered ends, could rely largely instead upon shrewd institutional arrangements of the powerful human passions*

and interests. Not to instruct and to transcend these pas-
sions and interests, but rather to channel and to use them
became the hallmark of modern politics.[9]

1.3 Recent American Political Commentary

In recent discussions concerning the relationship between the personal character and the public conduct of
political leaders the effects of both ancient political
philosophy and modern political views can be discerned.
In the 1992 presidential primary campaign, 80% of
respondents to a *TIME* magazine poll stated that the press
paid too much attention to the personal character of the
candidates.[10] This finding coincides with an historical
study of the American presidents by Thomas Bailey. He
concludes that though the electorate is aware of the ethical shortcomings of their leaders, it does not often register
its disapproval. Bailey summarizes:

> *Clearly an immense segment of the population of voting*
> *age does not particularly care if the president is less than*
> *candid or even dishonest. Otherwise these citizens would*
> *manifest their displeasure at the polling booth or by not*
> *voting. Many of them reason—if they reason at all—that*
> *crookedness is inevitable in politics; that platform*
> *promises are made to be broken; and that all true*
> *politicians, including congressmen and presidents, engage*
> *in some form of deception, chiseling, or graft, usually on*
> *an inconspicuous scale. Such irregularities are commonly*
> *regarded as an inevitable part of political life.*[11]

At the same time, Americans seem to persist in their expectation of the moral character of their political leaders.
However, what is interesting to note is that contemporary
political commentary which links a leader's personal and
public conduct often argues the case on pragmatic
grounds. For example, Sidey says that character is the
basis for marshalling public support for one's policies:
"We may not find a flawless candidate for any public of-

fice. But we should be looking for one with character that is 'good enough' to command the respect and support of the people."[12] This is particularly important for the President of the United States, for his decisions will inevitably have worldwide effects. Character lends credibility, and consequently power, to a political leader. Moreover, if he can connect his policies to moral principles, then his ability to elicit support is greatly strengthened. Goldwin reasons:

> *Moral principle has weight and force in American political discourse. Even if we assume—as we must assume if we remember that men and women are not angels—that people act in politics primarily in pursuit of interests that are advantageous to them, and usually not advantageous, or even disadvantageous to others, nevertheless, in America individuals and groups are greatly strengthened if they connect their cause to moral principles. And if that connection is a true one, and if decent, disinterested people can see that connection readily, the case is strengthened even more, even to the extent that supporters will be enlisted whose interests might otherwise not make them allies, as might otherwise even make them opponents.*[13]

Thus, what matters most in contemporary American thought is the pragmatic effectiveness of a political leader in accomplishing his or her duties of office. The perception of good personal character is desirable because it can elicit trust and support from the populace. In addition, appeal to moral principle can be a powerful lever to encourage compliance with the leader's policies. Although the vocabulary might suggest that leaders are being measured by the norms of ancient political philosophy, in reality the questions are thoroughly modern in viewing political leadership through a pragmatic lens.

2. Exegesis of Psalm 101

Psalm 101 is one of several psalms which address the subject of kingship or political leadership. In Israel there was a rich corpus of theocratic ideology encompassing both the stewardship of the Israelite kings as Yahweh's vice-regents over his chosen nation, and also the expectation of the eschatological rule of the Messiah.

2.1 Psalm 101:1–4

The psalm begins with the objective standard that governs the psalmist's view of his political leadership. He states in verse 1: "I will sing of lovingkindness and justice, to Thee, O Lord, I will sing praises." His personal loyalty to Yahweh leads him to order his life by godly values. Because *hesed* and *mishpat* are the standards of Yahweh's rule (cf. Ps. 89:14), the psalmist resolves to follow Yahweh's pattern in his own leadership. The rest of the psalm spells out how he puts this divine principle into practical action.

Although the precise definition of *hesed* is debatable, its combination here with *mishpat* unites the stern norm of justice with the sensitive approach of kindness.[14] As Yahweh is both holy and loving, so the psalmist aspires to imitate his balance in his own political leadership. He makes clear from the start that his leadership philosophy builds upon absolute moral principles emanating from Yahweh, not on a relativistic base.

In verse 2 the psalmist resolves to live blamelessly in his personal life. This commitment is a conscious choice to align his life according to the way of Yahweh, a commitment which originates in his heart and is expressed in every area of his behavior. The "blameless way" speaks of comprehensiveness in godliness. This *Tamim* was the quality commended in Noah (Gen. 6:9) and enjoined of Abraham (Gen. 17:1). In modern language it speaks of integrity, the seamless quality which unites a person's entire life—attitudes, ambitions, actions—by one central focus.

Tamim supersedes the convenient dichotomy between one's private life and public life. Instead, the person is viewed holistically, his character being expressed throughout every aspect of his existence.

In this light, the question concerning the meaning of *mathai tabo' 'elay* finds its answer. As the psalmist states his aspiration to lead a blameless life, the quality of life appropriate to his political position, he recognizes his own personal inadequacy. Therefore, he appeals to Yahweh for his help, reflecting the confidence of Prov. 2:7: "The LORD is a shield for those who walk in integrity (*tom*)." Only Yahweh can give to him the capability of living in a way that will enable him to rule properly.[15]

The personal commitment of the psalmist to blamelessness in verse 2 is expanded into wider relationships in verse 3. He refuses to contemplate with approval any base thing. He hates that which swerves from God's path and will not let it contaminate him. The psalmist maintains a fixed antipathy and resistance to all that is worthless and debased. He refuses to consider options that lie outside of the divine moral boundaries. Put positively, he has a fixed conscious commitment to consider only that which meets with Yahweh's approval.

Climaxing the first half of the psalm, in verse 4 the psalmist states that his godly integrity puts moral perversion to flight. Not only does he personally refuse to become involved in what is wrong, he takes a clear and unmistakable stand against it. His moral line of demarcation is Yahweh's *hesed-umishpat* (v. 1). His whole-hearted commitment to Yahweh causes him to reject all that is *ra'*, or contrary to God's will.

2.2   Psalm 101:5–8

In the second half of the psalm, the focus moves from the personal character of the leader to his public conduct. In particular, the psalmist stresses the kind of people with whom he chooses to work. Verse 5 highlights the leader's response to two groups of people. He commits himself to totally destroy or silence the one who criminally slanders a neighbor. In addition, he will not endure those who are proud and arrogant in their attitudes. The good political leader exercises moral leadership by confronting evil, rather than joining it, condoning it or overlooking it.

In verse 6 the psalmist states that he chooses people of proven moral character to serve in his government. The standards which he requires are faithfulness and blamelessness. In other words, he is looking for subordinates who will share his values, not just be technically proficient in political administration.

In verse 7 the psalmist refuses to surround himself with those who are deceitful. In his government truth and righteousness are non-negotiable essentials. The psalmist will not let image replace reality. For him, results cannot substitute for right. He selects people of good character who will assist him in ruling in the blameless way.

Furthermore, the psalmist determines to take an active personal position of moral influence in society (verse 8). As he presides at the morning law courts (cf. 2 Sam. 15:2), he brings timely judgment against the evil ones. His objective is to cut off from the city of Yahweh all who do iniquity. He recognizes that as a political leader he has moral responsibility to uphold a public standard of conduct consistent with both his personal character and Yahweh's prescribed criterion.

2.3   Structural Links in Psalm 101

The general thematic progression in Psalm 101 from the psalmist's personal character in verses 1–4 to his public conduct in verses 5–8 is reinforced by several explicit structural links. In verse 2 the psalmist aspires to personal blamelessness when he says, "I will give heed to the blameless way (*bederek tamim*)." This same vocabulary describes those who are chosen as governmental servants in verse 6: "He who walks in a blameless way (*bederek tamim*) is the one who will minister to me."

A second structural link is the expression "my house (*beyti*)" in verses 2 and 7. In verse 2 the psalmist affirms that in his own house, or in his personal life, he will walk in integrity. In verse 7 he states categorically that "he who practices deceit shall not dwell within my house (*beyti*)."

The third link is the prepositional phrase *leneged 'eynay*. In verse 3 he says, "I will set no worthless thing before my eyes (*leneged 'eynay*)." This is mirrored in verse 7 by "he who speaks falsehood shall not maintain his position before me (*leneged 'eynay*)."

Each of these three instances of verbal repetition connects the psalmist's personal character with his public conduct. That is to say, in Psalm 101 there is a definite link connecting what the leader *is* and what the leader *does*. His competence as a leader is measured at least in part by how his personal character is borne out in his public administration.

3. The Evaluation of Political Leadership

3.1 Hermeneutical Issues

In using Psalm 101 for evaluating political leadership, several hermeneutical questions arise. The question of *intention* asks, Who was the original king who is speaking in Psalm 101? The great majority of commentators rightly regard him to be a human king of Davidic line.[16] However, it is interesting to note that Luther interprets the psalm as a "mirror for magistrates" in a more universal sense. He writes:

> This psalm is one of those which praise and thank God for the secular authorities, as is also done in Psalms 127 and 128 and in many others. Together with other psalms, this one has always been sung in the church by the clergy, who claimed that they alone were the church and the holy, favored people of God. But they did not realize or consider at all that in these psalms they were praising the very group with their mouth which they daily treated with utter contempt and practically trampled under their feet.[17]

16

It seems apparent that Luther read into the psalm too much of his own historical context.

A second question focuses on *application*: To what extent can Psalm 101 appropriately be transferred to the American political context? This psalm, like most of the biblical literature, addresses a specific occasion. Unlike rare cases such as Psalm 117, it does not use universal language designed to fit audiences of all times. Therefore, before it can be applied to a different context the interpreter must determine how the original audience and the target audience for application are related. As I have discussed in a recent article, this question must be answered through careful audience analysis.[18]

In this case, Psalm 101 includes several references that place it within the special parameters of the theocratic state. For example, the psalmist addresses the deity as Yahweh (vss. 1, 8), he refers to the "faithful of the land" (v. 6), and he vows to cut off from the city of Yahweh all those who do iniquity (v. 8). The question, then, is whether it is valid to use the standards of this psalm, which is set in the covenantal context of Israel, as a prescription for leaders functioning outside of that special covenantal relationship. It would seem best to view Psalm 101 as yielding general patterns for political leadership rather than insisting upon a high degree of specific transfer from ancient Israel to contemporary America in this case.

The third hermeneutical question concerns *correlation*: How does Psalm 101 fit with other biblical passages touching upon the ethos of political leadership? It is apparent that Psalm 101 was not written as a comprehensive treatise on political philosophy. It was not intended as a detailed response to questions asked in contemporary America. It must be read first on its own terms, and then its message linked with the data drawn from other relevant passages of the Bible. In other words, in our commendable desire to integrate biblical truth with contemporary life, we must guard against hasty, partial and superficial correlation.

3.2 Theoretical Models

Drawing upon the previous overview of ancient and modern political philosophy and the exegetical insights from Psalm 101, I shall analyze three theoretical models for evaluating political leadership.

3.21 Pragmatic Model

The pragmatic model focuses only on the outcomes produced by the leader. In Machiavellian terms, the end justifies the means, so the only factor that matters is the successful public conduct of the leader. In the 1988 presidential campaign, this was the stance taken by Gary Hart when personal character began to dominate the primaries:

> *Gary Hart's exploits with model Donna Rice, Pat Robertson's youthful dalliance and Sen. Joseph Biden's use of unattributed quotes generated national attention and editorial outrage. Returning the outrage, Hart led an angry counterattack on the relevance of what he preferred to call peccadillos, claiming that temperament and personal behavior have little to do with Presidential stature and merely distract the nation from what "really matters": issues and ideas.* [19]

Similarly, in the 1992 presidential debates, Ross Perot dismissed the character issue by branding it irrelevant.

Larry Sabato is even more dogmatic in applying pragmatism to the evaluation of political leadership. In response to the question, should we be judging the morality of our public officials when we go to the ballot box, he gives this answer:

> *Private morality, no. Their public morality should be judged. Most people should be concerned about where can-*

didates stand on the issues and what they really care about. What they are like in the bedroom is purely private and is mostly on a completely separate track from their public behavior. Some people disagree very strongly with this, but many successful people operate on two tracks. Barney Frank is an excellent example. By all accounts, here is a very able, competent, intelligent, accomplished legislator. His professional life is in order and highly successful; his private life is a mess. Well, how do you pick public officials? Do we have to insist that both their public and their private life be in perfect order? You dramatically reduce the pool of good candidates if you do that.[20]

The pragmatic model presents a stark contrast to Psalm 101. In the psalm, the king's public conduct is an outgrowth of his personal character. He does what he does in public because he is what he is in private. The leader's life is of one piece, not bifurcated into separate public and private realms.

3.22   Integrity Model

The integrity model views personal character as intimately connected with public conduct. The biblical concept of blamelessness (*tamim*) reflects the conviction in Psalm 101 that the king's function is to maintain justice both in his own life and also in society. As Johnson says, "the moral realm and the realm of nature are regarded as one and indivisible."[21]

Political leaders are entrusted with a position of responsibility in society. As such, they are, for good or bad, examples to those whom they lead. Therefore, political leaders historically have been expected to provide sound moral leadership as well. Paul Douglas notes this expectation even outside of the Western tradition:

Confucius, who was a prime minister as well as a philosopher, observed long ago that the indirect effects of a statesman's actions were far more important than his

19

direct decisions. If he were corrupt, he encouraged others to be dishonest and hence he seduced them. If he were honest, high-minded and sought to promote the public good, the citizens would try to be like him. Thus the character of the community would be shaped in part by the quality of the men who occupied the leading positions of public honor and trust.[22]

In addition, character is an accurate predictor of how a person will respond under pressure. James David Barber's groundbreaking analysis of the presidential character argues that political leaders bring to their office a well-established pattern for functioning. Public style is forged in the private experiences of the leader. Barber says that "character is the way the President orients himself toward life—not for the moment, but enduringly. Character is the person's stance as he confronts experience."[23] Therefore, he contends, "If we can see the pattern he has set for his political life we can . . . estimate much better his pattern as he confronts the stresses and chances of the Presidency."[24]

The integrity model, then, evaluates in particular the personal character of the political leader. If the leader has a commendable character, then he will be able to maintain a good role model for his constituents as he responds to the unpredictable challenges of office according to the patterns he has already established in life (figure 1).

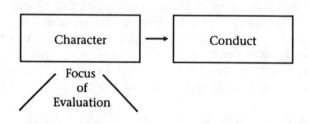

Figure 1

3.23 Values Model

The values model views both personal character and public conduct as being driven by a principled criterion. It asks, What is this leader's world view? What principles are shaping his character and actions? What are his values?

In Psalm 101 the psalmist's moral bedrock is the character of Yahweh. Yahweh's lovingkindness and justice serve as the standard for the king's life and rule. In contrast to other ancient Near Eastern cultures, the king resolved to live under the law of Yahweh (cf. Deut. 17:14–20). As Eichrodt notes, in Israel, "every breach of the law is seen as an offence against God. In every instance it is the divine lawgiver who lays down the law, and the human mediator comes after him."[25] Therefore, the human monarch was continually reminded that "he, too, was under a King who required of him service and honor."[26]

The importance of assessing a leader's transcendent, life-governing values finds widespread agreement. Kaplan demonstrates that social cohesion requires some kind of integrative point. He says that there must be a moral consensus if the political process is to advance.[27] Leaders who live by their own moral preferences can destabilize a society, because their purposes are incompatible with those of their constituents.[28]

The leader's world view,[29] then, is crucial to evaluating who he is and what he will do. How he sees the world will necessarily affect how he views himself, his role, his objectives, his constituents and his policies. A leader whose world view diverges from that of his society threatens social disintegration. A leader whose world view replaces the Sovereign God with some other inferior allegiance will further the cause of spiritual degeneration.

The values model especially evaluates the world view of the political leader. It reasons that over time the public conduct of a leader will be marked by his personal character, which reflects his values. Therefore, the focus of evaluation is placed upon the principled criterion by which the leader sees the world, for this is the integrative center of his life (figure 2).

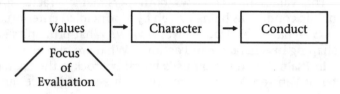

Figure 2

4. Conclusion

4.1 Summary of Findings

This essay has reviewed some key discussions in political philosophy and commentary relative to the ethos of American political leadership. The ancient linkage of ethics and politics seen in Aristotle and Aquinas was disconnected in the modern thought of Machiavelli, Locke and some of the American Founding Fathers. As a result, contemporary American opinion oscillates between pragmatism and the vestiges of ethical idealism drawn from classical and Christian thought.

Psalm 101 relates the ideals of a king who is cognizant of his role as Yahweh's vice-regent over Israel. His moral compass is the character of Yahweh. He then aspires to order his own personal character in blamelessness and to reproduce that character in his public administration. By using three explicit structural links, the psalmist forges a strong connection between who he is and how he rules.

Three models for evaluating political leadership have been analyzed. The pragmatic model considers primarily the public actions of the leader, and does not see a necessary link between character and conduct. The integrity model focuses its evaluation upon the personal character of the leader, recognizing that the leader is a role model for his constituents, and that his established patterns will affect how he responds to the future challenges in office. The values model is the most fundamental approach to evaluating political leaders. It reasons that one's world view is the driving force which shapes both character and conduct.

4.2   Remaining Questions

Exit poll data from recent presidential elections confirm that American evangelicals lack a clear consensus in their evaluation of present and potential political leaders. There seems to be no common standard by which they answer the question, "For whom should I vote?"

In attempting to integrate biblical faith and insights from political philosophy within the context of American political leadership, this paper is more programmatic than definitive. A number of important issues merit further attention. 1. Can the values model suggested in Psalm 101 be validated by other biblical evidence? In particular, on what basis were the political rulers of Israel and Judah evaluated, and how were foreign leaders viewed? There is a substantial corpus of relevant data in the historical and prophetical books of the Old Testament which bears examination. 2. How do the New Testament references to human government coincide with the values model of evaluation? 3. What other insights from political philosophy can illumine the question of the evaluation of leaders? 4. How do other royal psalms develop an ideology which transcends Israel's unique theocratic status? 5. What relative weights should be given to values, character and conduct when evaluating political leaders? For example, should one vote for a candidate who is highly principled but incompetent in the skills of political administration?

Although each of these questions raises points of legitimate debate, one thing is certain: As Christians, we must think *Christianly* about our politics. In the democracy in which God has favored us to live, we are stewards of the ballot. The factors that determine our votes, and the standards by which we evaluate our political leaders, should be marked by the priorities of God's

Word. As God's people functioning as salt and light in this society, we must embody his values, represent his cause, and accomplish his purpose.

Endnotes

[1] Abraham Kaplan, *American Ethics and Public Policy* (New York: Oxford University Press, 1963), p. 8.

[2] Martin Diamond, "Ethics and Politics: The American Way" in *The Moral Foundations of the American Republic* (ed. Robert H. Horwitz, 3rd ed; Charlottesville, VA: University Press of Virginia, 1986), p. 79.

[3] Ibid., p. 81.

[4] Stephen C. Mott, *A Christian Perspective on Political Thought* (New York: Oxford University Press, 1993), pp. 5–6.

[5] Diamond, op. cit., pp. 92–93.

[6] Michael P. Zuckert, "Locke and the Problem of Civil Religion" in *The Moral Foundations of the American Republic* (ed. Robert H. Horwitz, 3rd ed; Charlottesville, VA: University Press of Virginia, 1986), pp. 184–185.

[7] Ibid., p. 202.

[8] Diamond, op. cit., pp. 92–93.

[9] Ibid., p. 83.

[10] Ken Sidey, "A Question of Character," *Christianity Today* 36:4 (April 6, 1993), p. 16.

[11] Thomas A. Bailey, *Presidential Saints and Sinners* (New York: The Free Press, 1981), p. 285.

[12] Sidey, op. cit.

[13] Robert A. Goldwin, "Of Men and Angels: A Search for Morality in the Constitution" in *The Moral Foundations of the American Republic* (ed. Robert H. Horwitz, 3rd ed; Charlottesville, VA: University Press of Virginia, 1986), p. 26.

[14] H.J. Zobel, *TDOT*, 5.51–52.

[15] Aubrey R. Johnson, *Sacral Kingship in Ancient Israel* (Cardiff: University of Wales Press, 1967), pp. 114–115 use a similar line

of reasoning, but he claims without exegetical support that the psalm represents the words of Messiah. This Messianic interpretation reads into Psalm 101 more than the psalm itself can substantiate.

[16] A notable exception is A. Johnson, *Sacral Kingship in Ancient Israel* who regards these words as spoken by the Messianic king.

[17] *Luther's Works* (ed. Jaroslav Pelikan; trans. Martin H. Bertram et al; St. Louis: Concordia Publishing House, 1956), 13.146.

[18] Daniel J. Estes, "Audience Analysis and Validity in Application," *Bibliotheca Sacra* 150 (April–June 1993), pp. 219–229.

[19] Patrick Young, "Presidential Peccadillos," *Psychology Today* 22:3 (March 1988), p. 26.

[20] Gary Bauer and Larry Sabato, "Should Public Officials' Private Lives Matter?" *U.S. News and World Report* 107:10 (September 11, 1989), p. 23.

[21] Johnson, op. cit., p. 13.

[22] Paul H. Douglas, *Ethics in Government* (Cambridge: Harvard University Press, 1953), p. 20.

[23] James David Barber, *The Presidential Character* (Englewood Cliffs, NJ: Prentice-Hall, 1972), p. 8.

[24] Ibid.

[25] Walter Eichrodt, *Theology of the Old Testament* (2 vols: trans. J.A. Baker; Philadelphia: Westminster, 1961–1967), 1.75.

[26] James E. Priest, *Governmental and Judicial Ethics in the Bible and Rabbinic Literature* (New York: Ktav, 1980), pp. 198–199.

[27] Kaplan, op. cit., p. 90.

[28] Joshua O. Haberman, "The Scarlet Letter: The Private Lives of Public Figures" in *Ethics in Politics and Government* (ed. Anne Marie Donahue; New York: H.W. Wilson, 1989), p. 200.

[29] Barber, *The Presidential Character*, pp. 7–8 states well: A President's world view consists of his primary, politically relevant beliefs, particularly his conceptions of social causality, human nature, and the central moral conflicts of the time. This is how he sees the world and his lasting opinions about what he sees. Style is his way of acting; world view is his way of seeing.

Irenaeus and the Kingdoms of the World

by D. Jeffrey Bingham

*E*ach generation must contemplate the relationship between Church and State for itself. The manner in which the early Church perceived the relationship—both in experience and through exegesis of sacred texts—will not suffice, by itself, to address the particularities and complexities of the contemporary situation. But the theological, polemical and exegetical enterprises of the Church in earlier centuries provide material that can contribute to contemporary enterprises. They often inform and enlighten aspects of the problem that the pressing modern agenda may not consider or adequately treat.

In his polemical work, *Adversus Haereses,* Irenaeus, bishop of Lyon, provides a glimpse into the question of the Church's view of the State from a second century perspective. His development of the question is integral to his task as heresiologist and pastor. He writes not to generate debate, but to set forth the foundational elements of the Church's faith. This essay examines Irenaeus' development of the nature and function of the State from a network of biblical texts in order to gain insight into how he views its contribution to the one true faith.

The fifth book of Irenaeus' *Adversus Haereses* (hereafter, *Adv. Haer.*) begins by treating the question of the resurrection of the body (5.1–14).[1] The second part treats the question of the unity of the one God who is both Creator and the Father of Christ (5.15–24).[2] Within this second part Irenaeus dedicates four chapters, 5.21–24,[3] to proving the one God through consideration of Christ's temptation. The portion of *Adv. Haer.* focused upon in this essay, 5.24.1–3, occurs here.

In *Adv. Haer.* 5.24.1[4] Irenaeus begins by stating his major thesis that the devil lied when he tempted the Lord by saying, according to Luke 4:6, " 'All this has been delivered to me and I give it to whomever I will.' " The devil was speaking of the kingdoms of this world as though he possessed them and had authority to dispense them. Irenaeus does not read the devil's words in light of such texts as John 12:31; Rev. 13:2–10, or in light of Jesus' lack of protest to the claim. Such texts and Jesus' silence have influenced others to see a degree of truth in the devil's declaration of authority over the world's kingdoms.[5] Irenaeus, however, sees no validity to the devil's words, and against them he places several testimonies of Scripture. These testimonies argue that God, not the devil, determined or delimited (*determino*) the world's kingdoms.

First, Irenaeus cites Proverbs 21:1, "the heart of the king is in the hand of God." Second, he cites Proverbs 8:15, which he credits to the Word who spoke through Solomon: "By me kings reign, and the mighty administer justice. By me princes are exalted, and sovereigns rule the earth." Third, he cites Paul's testimony in Romans 13:1: "Be subject to all the exalted authorities, for there is no authority except from God, and those which exist have been established by God." Fourth, he cites another word of Paul from Romans 13:4, which speaks of the governing authority as one who "does not bear the sword in vain: for he is the servant of God to exercise wrath on the one who does evil."

This selection of texts from Proverbs and Paul provides Irenaeus with scriptural language that counters the devil's words. God (or the Word) appears as the only one who determines or delimits the world's kingdoms in the sense that he establishes, maneuvers and directs them. Thus, through creating them and exercising providence over them, God exclusively sets their limits.[6] The devil may not make legitimate claim to the authority to dispose of them. After Irenaeus presents his scriptural evidence from God's sole determination of the world's kingdoms, he quickly clarifies what Paul meant when he spoke of authorities. Against the heretics who interpret them as angelic or invisible authorities, Irenaeus insists that Paul has human authorities in mind. He supports his interpretation of Paul by again citing Scripture. First, he draws from the context of the two citations from Paul in Romans 13. He cites Romans 13:6 in order to make the point that they must be human because Paul speaks of them receiving tribute: "For on account of this reason you also pay taxes, because they are the ministers of God devoted to this very thing." Second, in support of his view that these powers are human, Irenaeus alludes to the practice of the Lord in Matthew's gospel where he gave directions to pay taxes to the tax-collectors for himself and Peter (Mt. 17:27). Irenaeus understands Romans 13:6 and Matthew 17:27 to be complementary, each echoing the other, for he again cites Romans 13:6 to justify the Lord's directions. For Irenaeus, the Lord's payment of tribute to the human tax-collectors teaches that the Lord recognizes and submits to the earthly authorities established by God. However, the Lord does not recognize or submit to any governing authority of the (spiritual) devil who tempted the Lord to worship him. Irenaeus' rejection of the gnostic interpretation of Paul's authorities as spiritual functions is a rejection of the devil's claim to have God-given authority.

At this point, Irenaeus has completed the expression and validation of his first argument in support of his thesis that the devil is a liar. The devil does not appoint the world's human kingdoms and authorities; God does. To this, the testimony of Scripture attests. Therefore, the devil is a liar.

In *Adv. Haer.* 5.24.2,[7] Irenaeus develops his second argument in support of his thesis that the devil is a liar when he proclaims himself the appointer of the world's kingdoms. This second argument comes by way of an explanation of the need and purpose of human government in light of God's nature. In Irenaeus' view, humanity has departed from God and has reached the apex of savagery. Humans view each other as enemies; they engage in all types of disorder, murder and greed. In response to this savagery, God imposed upon humans the fear of humanity because they did not recognize the fear of God. Thus, human government originated from God because man had disregard for God. God proposed for humans to attain some degree of justice and mutual forbearance by being subjected to human authority and by being educated through the custodial guidance of human laws. Irenaeus' notion of the nurture of justice through the custodial guidance of human laws is informed by Galatians 3:23–25. As the law of the old covenant was a custodian that restrained humanity until Christ's coming, so civil law is a custodian of humanity's growth toward justice in light of its rejection of God.[8] For Irenaeus, the dread of the sword substitutes for humanity's failure to fear God. In support of this, he once again cites Romans 13:4: "For he does not bear the sword in vain: for he is the servant of God to exercise wrath on the one who does evil."

Thus, in Irenaeus' understanding the State exists as God's creation for the purpose of ordering justice by penalizing injustice. This justice ordered by the State, however, can only be an external justice of outward appearance. The foundational cause of injustice and evil, the failure of humanity to fear God, allows for secret, hidden, internal sins. Humanity, then, under the State, without the fear of God, performs like Cain, not Abel.[9]

Next, Irenaeus briefly addresses God's oversight of even the human authorities who impose the State's penalties. They are not immune from God's judgment. The words of Romans 13:4 apply to them as well.[10] If the magistrates who have the laws as incentives[11] for justice govern with means that are just and legitimate, they will not be questioned or given over to punishment. Yet, if they rule in such a manner as to subvert justice, or with iniquity, illegality, or tyranny, they shall perish. For God's just judgment is dealt equally to all without favoritism and is not defective.

After his treatment of the State's own accountability to God's sovereign reign of justice, Irenaeus argues that a government established for justice is consistent with God's just nature. He summarizes that earthly rulers have been appointed by God—not by the devil—for the profit of the world's nations. The devil is never at peace and has no desire to see the nations living in peace. The very idea of a human authority that exists for the nurture of peace is contrary to the nature of the devil. Human authority exists so that out of the fear of human rule people will not devour each other as do the fishes. That is, laws exist to suppress excessive injustice among the nations. Therefore, because the suppression of injustice is contrary to the devil's nature, but is in accordance with God's nature, human authorities must be ordained by God. To seal his conclusion, Irenaeus again cites a portion of Romans 13:6: "He is the servant of God."

In *Adv. Haer.* 5.24.3,[12] Irenaeus continues and concludes his argument that human government is ordained by God because its function has continuity with God's nature, rather than the devil's. To begin, he restates the testimony of Paul, in Rom. 13:1, that "the authorities which exist have been established by God." From this he again insists that the devil lied, when he said at Jesus' temptation: " 'All this has been delivered to me, and I give it to whoever I will' " (Luke 4:6). Irenaeus limits the establishment of the State to God because only God is Creator.

31

Irenaeus understands Paul's testimony regarding God's ordination of human authority within the same order as God's creation of humanity. He says that the order of God, which brought humanity into existence, also established kings and placed humanity under their rule. There is continuity between God's activity of creation and God's activity of establishing human rulers.[13] He already made it clear that, as one of the creatures, the devil could not be credited with authority over creation.[14]

Irenaeus also states that God has established these human rulers in a manner that fits those who at any given time are under their rule. There is diversity within the activities of the rulers established by God. He establishes some rulers to provide correction, benefit and preservation of justice for their subjects. He establishes other rulers to provide fear, punishment and rebuke. He establishes still others who conduct themselves toward their subjects with mockery, insolence and pride, for this is what their subjects deserve. Thus, God creates the State and appoints the earthly rulers in such manner that the type of government fits the type of subject.[15] To those due benevolence, he raises up benevolent rulers. To those due harshness, he raises up harsh rulers. To those due insolence, he raises up insolent rulers. For Irenaeus, earthly governments exist to nurture justice, even if that justice comes as punishment through wicked rulers.[16] So he reminds his reader of his earlier statement concerning the deliverance of God's just judgment to all. Irenaeus has developed his view of God's fitting appointment of earthly rulers in order to emphasize the just character of God. God has ordained the governments for justice.

This would not be the case, however, Irenaeus says, if the governments were ordained by the devil—an apostate angel. As such, he can only do what he did at the beginning. He can deceive people and lead them astray in disobedience to God's commands. Also, he may gradually darken their hearts so that they forget the true God and cease to adore him as God. Disobedience and false worship are antithetical to the justice that governments seek to implement. In this light, governments cannot be ordained by the devil.

In the three paragraphs of *Adv. Haer.* 5.24.1-3, Irenaeus sets forth seven principles regarding his view of the State and the Church's relationship to it. First, human government exists through the ordination of God. Second, Christians are obligated to pay taxes to the government ordained by God. Third, human government exists as a concession to humanity's refusal to fear God. Human authorities exist to confront people with the fear of humanity's sword in substitution for humanity's fear of God. Fourth, human government exists as a means to benefit humanity through the structuring of justice. Fifth, the aims of human government to structure peace and justice are consistent with God's own benevolent, just nature and identity as Creator. Sixth, human government conducts itself in diverse ways, both just and unjust. Seventh, although human government exists by God's design as a concession to human rejection of God, in order beneficially to structure justice, it does not supplant God's own sovereign dispensing of universal justice. Whether through the just conduct of the magistrates or God's condemnation of their injustice, God still dispenses just judgment on all.

In this way, to some degree, we are able to gain insight into Irenaeus' understanding of the State and the Church's relationship to it. We are able to see his understanding of the origin, nature, purpose and limitations of government and the Church's civil obligation. Furthermore, we are able to see what biblical texts inform his understanding. Clearly dominant in his thought is Romans 13:1–7. However, with selected texts from this passage he forms a network with other texts from Proverbs and Matthew.

Irenaeus is the first to collect all these texts into a network that argues for God's ordination of earthly governments. Other Christian writers prior to him, nevertheless, do reflect use of some of these texts in a parallel manner and mention the Christian's relation to the authorities.[17] For instance, the *Martyrdom of Polycarp*, after the manner of Romans 13:1–7 and Second Peter 2:13–17, has Polycarp speaking of the Christian's obligation to render honor to the authorities appointed by God. When the proconsul invites him to persuade the crowd in the arena to hear his Christian teaching, he replies, "You, I should deem worthy of an account; for we have been taught to render honor, as is befitting, to rulers and authorities appointed by God so far as it does us no harm; but as for these, I do not consider them worthy that I should make defense to them."[18] Athenagoras, in his *Plea for the Christians*, remarks to the Emperor that he had received his empire from above. He does so on the basis of an inexact citation of Proverbs 21:1, and perhaps a thought of Romans 13:1–2 and John 19:11.[19] In the same vein, Theophilus of Antioch cites Proverbs 24:21–22 and presents language reminiscent of Romans 13:1–7. He affirms that one should honor, revere, obey and pray for the emperor who was appointed by God to judge justly. However, he states, one should worship only God, for God is sovereign over even the Emperor. He writes:

> *Wherefore I will rather honor the king [than your gods], not, indeed, worshipping him, but praying for him. But God, the living and true God, I worship, knowing that the king is made by Him. You will say, then, to me, "Why do you not worship the King?" Because he is not made to be worshipped, but to be reverenced with lawful honor, for he is not a god, but a man appointed by God, not to be worshipped, but to judge justly. For in a kind of way his government is committed to him by God: as He will not have those called kings whom He has appointed under Himself; for "king" is his title, and it is not lawful for another to use it; so neither is it lawful for any to be worshipped but God only. Wherefore, O man, you are wholly in error. Accordingly, honor the king, be subject to him,*

and pray for him with loyal mind; for if you do this, you do the will of God. For the law that is of God, says, "My son, fear thou the Lord and the king, and be not disobedient to them; for suddenly they shall take vengeance on their enemies."[20]

It seems, therefore, that Irenaeus fits into an early tradition that readily confessed God's sovereign ordination of earthly governments and the Christian's obligation of submission from Proverbs 21 and 24, Romans 13 and other New Testament passages.[21] His usage of Proverbs 8:15 for this purpose, however, is entirely unique.[22] So too is his usage of Matthew 17:27 to teach that the authorities spoken of by Paul are human, not spiritual, and to teach that Christians are obligated to pay taxes.[23] The *Epistula Apostolorum* and Melito of Sardis both mention the incident of the payment of the temple tax, but without any development towards civil theory or obligation.[24]

Furthermore, Irenaeus' denial of the devil's authority over the kingdoms and his sensitivity to the potential that acquiescence to the devil's lie may lead to worship of the devil, also fit into an earlier stream of tradition. However, where the earlier stream spoke against the cultural practice of worshipping the Emperor,[25] Irenaeus speaks against the worship of the devil, who ultimately stands behind the falsely conceived Father of the heretics.[26] The immediate pressure of the environment has switched from Emperor-cult to the heretics' theological dualism.

Finally, Irenaeus also shows continuity with earlier thought on God's ordination of the State for the purpose of just judgment. However, the view of the role of the wicked rulers expressed by him seems to make its first explicit appearance with him in *Adv. Haer.* 5.24.2.[27] Wicked rulers, too, bring about a certain justice through their insolent treatment of those deserving insolence. Irenaeus does not discuss certain tensions that his view raises. But this is not his focus. He wishes to assert God's exclusive sovereignty over the world's kingdoms against the devil's claim. His theory of the role of wicked rulers contributes to his argument by removing any idea that if wicked rulers exist, the devil must have established them. The fact of God's exclusive establishment of the State is not challenged by the rule of wicked governors. They also might work justice.

Irenaeus' own discussion of the State and Church must be understood within these traditional concerns for the exclusive sovereignty and deity of the one God. For Irenaeus, God is both Creator and Father of the Lord. Contextually, *Adv. Haer.* 5.24.1–3 fits inside a larger section (5.21–24) treating God's unity. This section argues that there exists only one God, not one of the old covenant and one of the new, because the Lord refused the devil's temptation by using the Mosaic law. Thus:

> *Since this is the case we must not search for another Father besides him or above him, since there is one God who justifies the circumcision by faith and the uncircumcision through faith. Because if there were any other perfect Father above him, the Lord never would have destroyed Satan by means of his words and commandments.*[28]

In addition, the larger section argues that a Christian who has been freed from the devil should be humble and not tempt God by being prideful. The Christian should not be drawn away from the exclusive worship of the one God through a lust for riches and worldly glory fed by the lies of the devil, for the devil is a liar. Again, he writes, citing Romans 12:16, Matthew 4:9 and alluding to Matthew 4:10:

> *Even as the apostle taught, saying, "Do not be concerned with lofty things, but take part with lowly things"; that we should neither be carried away with riches, nor mundane glory, nor present fantasy, but should know that we must worship the Lord God and serve only him, and give no*

heed to him who falsely promised things which are not his, when he said, "all this I will give to you, if falling prostrate, you worship me."[29]

Within this larger context, his argument that the devil is a liar and that God alone ordained the kingdoms supports his concern for the one God who must be worshipped exclusively. The devil cannot be trusted and the Christian must not worship other things or gods on the basis of the devil's words or the teachings of his agents, the heretics. It is significant to our understanding of Irenaeus that in his other treatment of Romans 13:1–6 in *Adv. Haer.* 4.36.6,[30] he employs the passage to argue that there exists one God who owns and governs all things.

It should not surprise Irenaeus' readers that he concerns himself with a theology of government only so far as it contributes to his thesis of the one true God. He writes as a heresiologist and pastor who must protect his community from the tragedy of imagining another god after the manner of the heretics. His controlling concern with the central element of the Church's faith governs the development of his polemical theology. In our day, the question of government has the propensity to create tension, division and to generate debate among God's people. Irenaeus' treatment of the question provides an example of how it ultimately illuminates the foundational element of our faith. Living at the end of the second millennium, we do well to know this.

Endnotes

[1] *Irenee de Lyon, Contre les heresies, Livre 5*, eds. A. Rousseau, L. Doutreleau and C. Mercier, Sources Chretiennes, no. 153 (Paris: Les Editions de Cerf, 1969), pp. 16–194 (hereafter cited as SC 153).

[2] Ibid., pp. 196–306.

[3]Ibid., pp. 260–306.

[4]Ibid., pp. 294–298.

[5]N. Geldenhuys, *Commentary on the Gospel of Luke*, The New International Commentary on the New Testament (Grand Rapids: Eerdmans, 1954), p. 160; S.R. Garrett, *The Demise of the Devil: Magic and the Demonic in Luke's Writings* (Minneapolis: Fortress, 1989) p. 38; G.B. Caird, *Saint Luke*, Westminster Pelican Commentaries (Philadelphia: Westminster, 1963), p. 80. Cf. C.F. Evans, *Saint Luke*, TPI New Testament Commentaries (Philadelphia: Trinity, 1990), p. 259. Evans writes that the devil's claim "is not out of harmony with an increasing dualistic tendency in Judaism . . . and it underlies such passages as John 12:31; 2 Cor. 4:4; Eph. 2:2; Rev. 13:2ff."

[6]Cf. *Adv. Haer.* 1.11.1 (*Irenee de Lyon, Contre les heresies, Livre 1*, eds. A. Rousseau and L. Doutreleau, Sources Chretiennes, no. 264. [Paris: Les Editions du Cerf, 1979], p. 168.) Here *determino* occurs again and translates *diorizo* (Grk.), "to delimit, determine." The verb is applied to the function of the two limits which the Valentinians conceive as separating the highest spiritual Pleroma from: (1) the Aeons derived from the Father, and (2) the Mother, Sophia. *Determino* in *Adv. Haer.* 5.24 is also likely a translation of *diorizo* (cf. the Greek retroversion in SC 153:295). This may indicate that Irenaeus' usage of the verb is informed by *diorizo* in Is. 45:18 (LXX) where it occurs in parallel with other verbs stressing the one, true God's creation of the habitable earth. *Diorizo* occurs with the same force in *Diogn.* 7.2. Apparently, Irenaeus has taken a term from a context of God's sovereignty over earthly rulers on the basis of creation. This is noteworthy, for later in *Adv. Haer.* 5.24.2 (SC 153:302) he states that the same order which creates humans also establishes kings.

[7]SC 153: pp. 298–302.

[8]Cf. the note in *Irenee de Lyon, Contre les heresies, Livre 5*, eds. A. Rousseau, L. Doutreleau and C. Mercier, Sources Chretiennes, no. 152 (Paris: Les Editions du Cerf, 1969), p. 318. Rousseau believes that the Latin translator, with *adstricti*, missed the deliberate image of what was originally in Greek, *paidagogomenoi*. The French translation (SC 153:299) offers "eduques."

[9]See *Adv. Haer.* 4.18.3 (*Irenee de Lyon, Contre les heresies, Livre 4*, eds. A. Rousseau et al., Sources Chretiennes, no. 100 [Paris: Les Editions du Cerf, 1965], 2:598–606; hereafter cited as SC 100:2). Irenaeus mentions the absence of humanity's fear of God in this context and links it to improper neighborly relations and secret sin. Cf. Orbe, *Teologia de San Ireneo*, pp. 519–520; W. Affeldt, *Die Weltliche Gewalt in der Paulus-Exegese: Rom. 13, 1–7 in den Romerbriefkommentaren der lateinischen Kirche bis zum Ende des 13 Jahrhunderts*, Forschungen zur Kirchen—und Dogmengeschichte, no. 22 (Gottingen: Vandenhoeck & Ruprecht, 1969), p. 40.

[10]Wis. 6:1–11 may also be informing Irenaeus' thought at this point as well as previously. Cf. A. Strobel, "Ein katenenfragment mit Irenaeus Adv. Haer. V. 24,2f" *Zeitschrift fur kirchengeschichte* 68 (1957): p. 142; Orbe *Teologia de San Ireneo*, p. 530.

[11]Cf. Orbe, *Teologia de San Ireneo*, pp. 526–527, who favors the original Greek reading as *henausma*, not *henduma*, which the Latin reflects with *indumentum* (SC 153: p. 300). The force of the context supports Orbe's decision, which he translates with "un incentivo."

[12] SC 153: pp. 302–304.

[13]This continuity complements Irenaeus' theme of God's personal, intimate involvement in mundane matters and counters the dualism of the heretics. Cf. *Adv. Haer.* 3.24.2 (SC 211: pp. 476–478).

[14] *Adv. Haer.* 5.22.2 (SC 153: pp. 184–285.

[15]Cf. Orbe, *Teologia de San Ireneo*, pp. 539–540.

[16]Irenaeus leaves undeveloped some implications of this view. Cf. C.J. Cadoux, *The Early Church and the World: A History of the Christian Attitude to Pagan Society and the State Down to the Time of Constantinus* (Edinburgh: T. & T. Clark, 1925), pp. 376–377.

[17]*Biblia Patristica, Index des citations et allusions bibliques dans la litterature patristique*, ed. J. Allenbach et al. (Paris: Editions du Centre national de la Recherche Scientifique, 1975), 1: p. 442.

[18]*Mart. Pol.* 10:2 (A. Lindemann and H. Paulsen, eds. and trans., *Die Apostolischen Vater: Grieschisch-deutsche Parallelausgabe* [Tuibingen: J.C.B. Mohr (Paul Siebeck), 1992], p. 270; translation by M.H. Shepherd, Jr. in *Early Christian Fathers*, ed. ed. C.C. Richardson, The Library of Christian Classics, no. 1 [Philadelphia: Westminster, 1953], p. 153).

[19]Athenag. *Leg* 18.2 (*Athenagoras. Legatio pro Christianis,* ed. M. Marcovich, Patristische Texts und Studien, no. 31 [Berlin: Walter de Gruyter, 1990], p. 56).

[20]Thphl. Ant. *Auto* 1.11 (Migne, *Patrologia Graeca*, 6.1040–1041; trans. by M. Dods, ANF, 2:92).

[21]Cf. *I Clem.* 61; Just. *I Apol.* 17.

[22]Cf. *Biblia Patristica,* p. 206.

[23]Cf. Ibid., p. 268. W.D. Kohler, *Die Rezeption des Mattausevangeliums in der Zeit vor Irenaeus*, Wissenschaftliche Untersuchungen zum Neuen Testament, 2d series, no. 24 (Tubingen: J.C.B. Mohr [Paul Siebeck], 1987), pp. 475–476, 505 and 558.

[24]*Ep. Apos.* 5; Mel. Sard. *Pasc.* 86.

[25]Cf. also Just. *I Apol.* 17.

[26]Cf. *Adv. Haer.* 5.25.2 (SC 153:330–338) where Irenaeus specifically calls the disciples of Marcion and Valentinus the agents of Satan because of their blasphemy against the Creator.

[27]Cf. J. Cadoux, *The Early Church and the World,* pp. 378–380.

[28]*Adv. Haer.* 5.22.1; SC 153: pp. 278–280.

[29]SC 153: pp. 282–284.

[30]SC100.2: pp. 906–908.

Erasmus' Theory of
Christian Government
by Darius Y. Panahpour

*T*o best appreciate what Erasmus had to say about Christian government, let us begin by considering the circumstances that led to his writing of *The Education of a Christian Prince*. This is the most systematic of his political writings over a thirty-year period in which he treated the subject. One consideration to be kept in mind is that Erasmus was writing for a monarchial form of government, though he himself would have preferred an elective over a hereditary monarchy.[1] The differences between effective government in a monarchy and a democracy mean that some of his prescriptions have little bearing upon how we, as Christians, might see our faith more fully reflected in our government. Nevertheless, much of the advice Erasmus gave in the political arena is worthy of consideration and debate today.

Erasmus could address the ethical-spiritual aspect of governing from solid ground as a result of the attention he had devoted to his own Christian growth in his youth and early years as an adult. While his *Adages* were essentially proverbs gathered from both Christian and non-Christian sources concerning various aspects of life, political and otherwise, compiling them helped Erasmus develop his critical abilities to separate gold from dross. After the first edition was published in 1500, he added more sayings throughout his life so that by the time of his death sixty-two editions had come into the public's hands. An even more important work was his *Enchiridion*, or *Handbook of the Christian Soldier*, written in 1501 and reworked for publication in 1503. It had first been written at the urging of a Christian woman whose husband dismissed the need for religious faith. It dealt with the outlook and conduct Christians should exhibit while working for the advancement of Christianity in the world.

Erasmus and Charles V

In 1515 Erasmus became an official counselor of Prince Charles I of Spain. The position came with a salary even though Erasmus was not required to be in residence at the prince's court.[2] Erasmus wrote *The Christian Prince* as an exhortative guide to the sixteen-year-old Charles, who would soon become Emperor Charles V of the Holy Roman Empire, which had holdings from Italy to Spain. Erasmus intended his work to be a practical one directed toward the "needs of his (the prince's) country."[3] As such, it did not attempt to deal explicitly with the relationship between church and state, though several points can be inferred. Furthermore, even though we have no conclusive evidence that Erasmus ever sought a scholar's expertise in the field of politics, insofar as his presence was sought in all educated circles of his day, he had reason to hope that the young prince would heed his advice.

Erasmus saw a parallel between Aristotle's tutoring of the fourteen-year-old Alexander the Great and his own tutoring of the sixteen-year-old Charles.[4] In it, Erasmus tried to undo as much of Charles' "chivalric ideals" and upbringing as possible by stressing the benefits of peace and the horrors of war.[5] Unfortunately, Charles probably never read the book that had been written explicitly for him, and his record as emperor demonstrates that he took no great pains to abide by its guidance.

Erasmus and Machiavelli

The book's relation to Machiavelli's *The Prince* is limited. The two men were contemporaries, Erasmus living from about 1466 to 1536 and Machiavelli from 1469 to 1527. Machiavelli's book had been written before 1513 but went unpublished until 1532, after his death. Erasmus' work was published in 1516, so it is highly unlikely that either work was influenced by the other. Nor did either author ever comment on the other's work.[6] The backdrop for Erasmus' book was the *Pax ecclesiae*, the peace provided by the Roman church, when he wrote his work.[7] For his part, Machiavelli wished for princes to be wise, just and merciful in governing, but he believed the Florence of his day required the tyranny of the Medici family if it were to avoid a worse tyranny under others.[8] This meant that any means of maintaining power was justified and, in fact, recommended. This can be viewed as a theory of government-on-a-slippery-slope, meaning that in order to avoid the most repugnant conditions in society we readily assent to others that we can only hope will not degenerate to the same low level.

While Machiavelli is said to represent the "realist" perspective in Renaissance political thought, Erasmus is credited with advocating a "moralist" approach.[9] "Realism" in political theory means taking a pragmatic approach to governing that tends to discount loyalty to any other particular political ideology and tends to favor the expedient over the principled. "Moralism," by contrast, is an approach to government that is most strongly guided by ethical considerations. What strikes some people as cynicism in "realist" thought will seem to others as merely a fair accounting for human depravity. Yet Erasmus' views on human nature were not at all unrealistic. He warned Charles not to be guided by the uneducated thinking of many of his subjects, of which he must be aware but unaffected: "It is fruitless to attempt advice on the theory of government until you have freed the prince's mind from those most common, and yet most truly false, opinions of the common people."[10] If Erasmus' phraseology sounds elitist to modern ears, let us understand that his purpose was to urge the prince to rule in a godly manner:

> God is swayed by no emotions, yet he rules the universe with supreme judgment. The prince should follow His example in all his actions, cast aside all personal motives, and use only reason and judgment. . . . The prince should be removed as far as possible from the low concerns of the common people and their sordid desires.[11]

Ruling in War and Peace

In dealing with the maintenance of peace and the conduct of war, Erasmus relates the two by saying that the wise prince should strive to his "utmost to preclude any future need for war."[12] To promote peace in his own kingdom, the prince's love for the people he rules should be evident to all, and if it is, their faith and loyalty will be returned and thereby promote the peace.[13] "The best formula," says Erasmus, "is this: let him love, who would be loved, so that he may attach his subjects to him as God has won the peoples of the world to Himself by His goodness."[14] The prince's great respect for his subjects is one of the keys to peace and the prince's own effectiveness in his country. The need for this mutual regard is made clear in Erasmus' sentiment that "no prince really rules unless over free men; no good prince ever requires anything that would not be freely given without compulsion."[15]

As for war itself, Erasmus wrote emphatically against taking it up unless necessary. In fact, he went so far as to write, "In my opinion, Cicero was right in saying that an unjust peace was better than the justest war."[16] Erasmus was aware that some of the most eminent figures in the history of church, such as Augustine and Bernard, had believed in the concept of a "just war." More importantly for Erasmus, however, was the answer to the question, what about the teachings of Christ and his followers? They had never explicitly sanctioned war. Erasmus himself questioned whether any war could rightly be called "just."[17] But in acknowledgement of the depravity of human beings and the pattern of their affairs, he said, "I do not condemn every war, for some are necessary."[18] Before engaging in war, however, the prince should spend a poignant moment considering the painful trials and expense, as well as the grief of the survivors. He even questioned whether a society could incur a greater moral ruin than that brought about by war.[19] When a prince found the last resort of war necessary for whatever reason, Erasmus said the prince should see to it that it ended quickly, avoiding as much suffering, bloodshed and destruction as possible.[20] Many of Erasmus' complaints against war and political machinations were directed against the policies of Pope Julius II, who had been dead for three years by this time.[21] Nearly all of Erasmus' pacifist writings were reiterated and developed at greater length the next year, 1517, in *The Complaint of Peace.*

Treaties

Treaties are a sign that the good faith which should exist between rulers is missing. Too often treaties are made between dishonest parties in bad faith, with the result that lawsuits arise or wars erupt because one side protests that a small clause in the midst of many articles was broken by the other side. In this regard the prince's wisdom must include an understanding of the characters, traits, and customs of the various peoples with whom he must deal. Rather than gaining such knowledge in wandering trips outside of his native land, the prince should seek this type of wisdom from both books and the counsel of those who are already wise by experience in these matters.[22] As for alliances, they should not be close with those who follow another religion or none at all, nor with those who are separated by great distances over land or sea.[23]

Advisers

Though brief, Erasmus devoted an entire chapter to the prince's need to avoid flatterers. In fact, one of the pagan sources he urged the prince to read was Plutarch's *How to Distinguish between a Friend and a Flatterer*. Erasmus cites Diogenes' anecdote: When asked what animal was the most dangerous of all, he said, "If you mean among the wild beasts, I will say the tyrant; if among the tame ones, the flatterer."[24]

The justice demanded of the prince may be thwarted if he listens to "perverted praising" and loses the impersonal judgment he must bring to the people and circumstances in which he governs along with the honest evaluation of his own abilities. [25]

For counselors the prince must choose people who are "sagacious and trustworthy." They should be warned not to be liberal in their assent to the prince's plans, but that it is their duty and that they will be rewarded if they "discharge their office honorably."[26] The same responsibility applies to the prince's friends, who should be made aware that their frank advice is all he need hear.

Administration

In financing the government the prince is to show good stewardship. If he can rule without taxation, so much the better. To increase his revenue, Erasmus recommends that the prince "studiously endeavor to minimize his demands on the people."[27] This means avoiding extravagances that only offend the people, getting rid of unneeded governmental ministries, avoiding wars and seeing to the efficient administration of his kingdom.[28] Interestingly enough, Erasmus does not appear to be a great supporter of unrestricted free enterprise in which, to Erasmus' mind, "too great an inequality of wealth" resulted.[29] Here he concurs completely with Plato, who wanted the citizens neither too rich nor too poor, "for the pauper is of no use and the rich man will not use his ability for public service."[30]

His views are surprisingly modern in that he advocates taxing lightly the goods used by even the poor in society, and taxing more highly those items that are unessential and used almost exclusively by the wealthy; "for example, linen, silks, . . . precious stones, and all the rest of that same category." Erasmus reasons, "by this system only those who can well afford it feel the pinch."[31] Optimistically, he expresses the hope that the wealthy will become less indulgent of their desires and replace them with more admirable habits. If Erasmus could have it entirely his way, he seems to support recreating the ancient office of censor, whose very purpose was to prohibit indecent amounts being spent on buildings, banquets or other amusements. He realized the extreme nature of his view when he wrote:

> *Some one may think it is a severe course that does not allow a person to use or abuse his own possessions in accordance with his own unrestrained whims. Let him reflect that it is much worse for the morals of his subjects to become so depraved through this sort of extravagance that capital punishment is necessary. It is more in keeping for one to be forced into frugality than to be forced into utter ruin by vice.*[32]

Laws

The purpose of laws should be not only to govern behavior by punishing various crimes, but also to work against sin by writing laws in such a way that people are instructed. In other words, crime should be kept under control by appealing to people's reason and desire to see society prosper foremost, rather than through the fear of what will happen if they seek unlawful gain. Furthermore, the laws should offer rewards for good service to the state. Here Erasmus cites an example of the ancients. If a soldier died fighting, his children were provided for by the state.[33] Of course, people should want to do good without the possibility of reward, but doing so would increase the desire in those citizens whose minds were "still but little developed."[34] An award of honor would suffice for citizens with more character while money would satisfy those with less. Thus the laws should affect people by their provisions for honor and disgrace, as well as for profit and loss.[35]

The humanity of the laws should attempt to compensate for the under-protected. This meant a sterner punishment would be proscribed for a crime committed against a poor citizen than for one against a rich person. Likewise, a corrupt official of state or other person of rank would suffer worse punishment for his offense than would an ordinary citizen.[36]

Both the laws and the prince should show a greater inclination to pardon than to punish wrongdoers, in part because this shows harmony with God's own provision. God tolerates much, His anger rising slowly before it demands vengeance. On the human side, good men love God while the wicked harbor the fear of God because of what may befall them. Similarly, the prince should aim to arouse fear in the hearts of criminals, but even with "a hope of leniency, if only they reform."[37]

Like Plato, Erasmus believed those with ability to work should do so, and that idle beggars should be banished from the state. He made provision, however, for those who were enfeebled by old age or illness and who had no family to care for them. People in this group would be given the care they needed in public institutions at the state's expense.

As first guardian of the laws, the prince should reserve his worst punishments for those who administer the laws in a corrupt manner. Because of this possible abuse, Erasmus makes a few final suggestions as to how the laws should be enacted and administered. First, they should be as few and as just as can be managed. They should also be made well-known to the people. Toward this end he holds up the ancient practice of inscribing the laws on tablets to be displayed in public. Also, the language should be clear and devoid of complexities whenever possible. This would make the laws easier to understand and thereby reduce the need for those who carry such exalted titles as "jurisconsult" and "advocate."[38]

Education

For the education of the prince, Erasmus encouraged reading especially helpful books of the Bible such as *Proverbs* and the gospels, and, because he was utilizing the Catholic Bible, the *Book of Wisdom* and *Ecclesiasticus* as well. Of the classical authors, Erasmus recommended certain works by Plutarch, Seneca, Aristotle, Cicero and most of all, Plato.[39] Erasmus' criterion of what books would most benefit the prince, and indeed, anyone, was whether or not they promulgated God's truth. In gleaning wisdom from non-Christian sources, he wrote: "He whom you are reading is a pagan; you who are reading are a Christian. Although he speaks with authority on many subjects, yet he by no means gives an accurate picture of the good prince . . . Measure everything by the Christian standard."[40]

Accordingly, Erasmus recommended reading the historians, Herodotus and Xenophon, with reservations because their writings included a good deal that was not profitable for the prince.[41]

Education was one of "the arts of peace" that the prince should devote himself to obtaining in his youth, and to providing for his people during his reign. As in many areas, his attitude is distinctly modern here: "A prince who is about to assume control of the state must be advised that the main hope of a state lies in the proper education of its youth."[42] He advocated education for girls as well as boys, the goal of which was to "learn the teachings of Christ and that good literature which is beneficial to the state."[43] If this course were followed, the need for laws and punishments would be greatly diminished, "for the people will of their own free will follow the course of right."[44] If Erasmus was optimistic on that note, he showed insight in stressing the importance of instilling a love for the best influences early in life, because nothing was more difficult than obliterating habits that had become second nature.[45] Again, the prince was to lead by his own example, and if the people appeared to be comfortably set in their ways, "then you must bide your time and gradually lead them over to your end."[46]

The Necessity of Leaders Who Possess Excellent Character

Given the lack of confidence and trust in politicians from all levels of government in recent decades, perhaps Erasmus' greatest relevance for today comes in his conception of the qualities of character to be developed in any state's political leaders. Erasmus drew from a long list of classical and medieval sources whenever he sought to illustrate the workings of God's truth in society. In this area, however, he is particularly indebted to Aristotle, Plato and Aquinas for his view that politics is a branch of ethics because both are so directly related to the conduct of human beings.[47] The difference being merely that ethics *per se* dealt with one's private conduct, and politics with that in the public arena.

The prince's teacher must instill good values and the story of Christ as soon as possible. If the teacher recognizes that the prince already possesses a good character, he must pay even more attention to giving proper instruction, for "the better the nature of the soil, the more it is wasted and filled with worthless weeds and shrubs if the farmer does not take care."[48] Later in his youth the prince himself should hold his inexperience and impulsiveness in distrust. Such is the time that he should be most amenable to the advice of older men, though he will of course continue to need them throughout his reign.

Erasmus recognizes that in focusing on the intellectual and moral development of the prince he will encounter protest:

> *But here some one of those frumps at the court, more stupid and worthless than (anyone) you could name, will interrupt with this: 'You are making us a philosopher, not a prince.' 'I am making a prince,' I answer, 'although you prefer a worthless sot like yourself instead of a real prince!' You cannot be a prince, if you are not a philosopher; you will be a tyrant . . . I do not mean by philosopher, one who is learned in the ways of dialectic or physics, but one who casts aside the false pseudorealities and with open mind seeks and follows the truth. To be a philosopher and to be a Christian is synonymous in fact. The only difference is in the nomenclature.*[49]

Erasmus' exhortations to the prince often read like those passages in the New Testament that urge us on to moral excellence. The New Testament writers were, of course, addressing every Christian; Erasmus was emphasizing the greater importance of moral integrity for the prince who, because of his responsibility for the well-being of others, must possess and exercise greater virtue than will many of his subjects.

Indeed, Erasmus sounds like the apostle Paul when he writes:

> *While you are using every means and interest to benefit the state, your life is fraught with care; you rob your youth and genius of their pleasures; you wear yourself down with long hours of toil. Forget that and enjoy yourself in the consciousness of right. . . . Do your private emotions as a man—reproachful anger, love for your wife, hatred of an enemy, shame—urge you to do what is not right . . . ? Let the thought of honor win. Let the concern for the state completely cover your personal ambitions.*[50]

While Erasmus never deviates from his conviction that the only fitting measures of the prince's greatness are his character and how his people are faring under his rule, he does allow for a certain degree of cunning on the part of the prince. In winning the people gradually over to his godly ends, Erasmus suggests the prince do so "either by some subterfuge or by some helpful pretence." He illustrates this with an analogy of wine, which has no effect at first, but soon enough "captivates the whole man and holds him in its power."[51] Nonetheless, the most effective means for the prince to rule his people remains the power of his own example. For better or worse, the people "imitate nothing with more pleasure than what they see their prince do."[52] The prince should take his own inspiration from theology, which includes the "three prime qualities" attributed to God: "The highest power, the greatest wisdom, the greatest goodness. In so far as you can, you should make this trinity yours."[53]

Erasmus agrees with Plato that other than those who are born to it, the only person fit to rule is one who has not run after the office of governing and who has not agreed to it without persuasion. The wicked seek it for their own advancement, which is made worse by the fact that the state is neglected as a result. As for others, "whoever strives after the princely place must of necessity either be a fool or else not realize how fraught with care and trial the kingly office really is."[54] In other words, the princely office is to be shunned rather than sought.

Specific Instructions from Scripture

For practical conduct, Erasmus cites Deuteronomy 17:16–20, in which a king is commanded by God not to exalt himself over the people by acquiring great numbers of horses or wives, or by striving after wealth. And in his own hand the king shall copy the law of God as given to Moses and read in it every day in order to keep and perform its statutes better himself. We can see here the connection between what God himself commands for the prince and what Erasmus upholds in order for the prince to serve as an example to the people. He writes of the Deuteronomy passage: "If a Hebrew king is bidden to learn the law, which gave but the merest outlines of justice, how much more is it fitting for a Christian to follow steadfastly the teachings of the Gospels?"[55] Our American forefathers certainly agreed with this. When political scientists studied over 15,000 writings from the Revolutionary War period to determine where they had gotten their ideas, 34% of their citations came directly from Scripture. This represented a significant plurality over any other one source.[56]

Erasmus took largely the same approach. Though many more of his direct references are attributable to classical sources rather than Scripture, he consistently follows his own rule of measuring all things by the Christian standard. He also exhorts his readers to follow the guidelines given in the gospels and written by the apostles. He mentions specifically Romans 13:1–8, in which Paul tells Christians to obey those set over them, observing that Christians are not lowered by paying taxes or tribute to a pagan ruler.[57]

His interpretation of Matthew 22:17–22, the pericope of Christ and the coin with Caesar's image on it, is significant. He confidently states that Christ's response was essentially this: "You see what you owe to Caesar, whom I do not know; see rather what you owe to God. It is His work I am carrying out, not Caesar's."[58] The need for distinguishing between God and Caesar, between church and state, in the mind of the believer is evident; it is not because one has nothing to do with the other, but rather it is imperative that we live faithfully unto our highest loyalty, the triune God. We honor our other duties, such as that to the state, as Scripture guides and in subordination to our commitment of faith.

On Living under a Faulty Government

This raises the issue of civil disobedience, which Erasmus does not explicitly address. It might seem from the preceding discussion that he would have supported it, but Erasmus was also one who liked to work within the system. For several reasons, the least of which is that he abhorred violence of any kind, he could never compel himself to break with the Catholic church and join the Protestants. [59]

Would Erasmus have advocated rebellion in the event of an oppressive, tyrannical ruler who showed little or no consideration for the welfare of his subjects? Again, I believe the answer has to be no. Even though Erasmus spends a good deal of time bemoaning the evils of a tyrannical prince, he never sanctions violence, but rather channels the indignation at such gross injustice into his argument for the vital necessity of educating future leaders (princes, in his world), instilling Christian teaching and values from the earliest age.

One cannot assume that because Erasmus did not trust anyone who aspired to political power that he would have held a democracy of elected officials in contempt, or that he would have favored term-limitations. On the contrary, Erasmus might well have approved some form of democracy, with its built-in checks and balances. For, since any prince is imperfect,

> It will be better to have a limited monarchy checked and lessened by aristocracy and democracy. Then there is no chance for tyranny to creep in, but just as the elements balance each other, so will the interests of the state hold together under similar control. If a prince has the interests of the state at heart, his power is not checked on this account, . . . but rather helped.[60]

This is Erasmus' answer to the abuse of political power: limit what any one human being can do by the consensus of others who understand their obligation to keep the prince in check in order to best serve the interests of the state. In this he foreshadows the "social contract" theory as developed by later political philosophers such as Hobbes, Locke and Rousseau. He raises the issue of government involvement in the business and economy of its citizens, and he begins the discussion of international law, which was later developed systematically by Hugo Grotius.[61]

Influence of the Education of a Christian Prince

Even though Charles V never made use of Erasmus' *Prince*, others did. It became available to the reading public at the same time it was published for Charles, and over the next twenty years before Erasmus' death it saw eighteen separate editions.[62] In England, John Colet and Thomas More received copies right away; Henry VIII received one the next year, in 1517.[63] Indeed, More and Erasmus shared and reiterated the theme that theoretically it is possible to have a truly good ruler, but the tyrant was always an imminent and real threat.[64] Robert Adams notes that the book was written in England and, presumably for the way in which it treated the subject, he considers it a part of English humanist literature.[65] Also in 1517, Count Friederich II of Bavaria assigned the reading of it or a similar work for three hours a day for the training of his nephew, Prince Philip. In the mid 1500s, Catherine de' Medici ordered a paraphrase made for her sons to study.[66]

Conclusion

In this brief sketch of Erasmus' political views, particularly as they are expressed in *The Education of a Christian Prince*, my purpose has been to highlight the ethical formation and standards necessary for any political leader who would call him or herself a Christian. In addition to the fact that the ethical considerations of Erasmus appear to be the most applicable aspect of his political thought to our own day, this was also the area to which Erasmus himself devoted most of his attention. And even though his book was written over four hundred and seventy-five years ago, clearly, the qualities of character necessary to govern a people biblically have not changed. Nor are the principles of leadership he outlines limited to the political arena. For example, pastors, deacons, elders and teachers are all subject to the same standards of conduct. For just as Erasmus encouraged Christian princes, so all Christian leaders must be involved in the continual evaluation of their own character and performance, and they must remain amenable to the forthright evaluations of other Christians close to them.

This is probably the most applicable of Erasmus' exhortations to the Christian prince, or in our day the Christian leader from any walk of life. The dearth of credible *political* leaders is particularly cliché. The media is especially attuned to the inappropriate conduct of Christian leaders, though the secular world is also capable of honoring the few whose lives are beyond reproach, a fact which the apostle Paul recognized.

If Christians wish to see their faith better reflected in their government, then the starting point offered by Erasmus would be for them to attend to their own souls and conduct in the world. This had been Erasmus' instruction to the prince as both a Christian and a future leader of the people. Equally so, as Erasmus advises the prince's teacher, Christians must inculcate proper values and character in their children. These exhortations make sense from the modern perspective, for not only do they mold us more into God's image, but they also bring into view those with God-given leadership abilities who can be supported by members of the secular society as well.

Endnotes

[1] Léon E. Halkin, *Erasmus: A Critical Biography*, trans. John Tonkin (Cambridge, MA: Blackwell Publishers, 1993), p. 102.

[2] John A. Faulkner, *Erasmus: The Scholar* (New York: Eaton and Mains, 1907), p. 137.

[3] Preserved Smith, *Erasmus: A Study of His Life, Ideals and Place in History* (New York: Frederich Ungar Publishing Co., 1923), p. 198.

[4] Robert P. Adams, *The Better Part of Valor: More, Erasmus, Colet, and Vives, On Humanism, War, and Peace, 1496–1535* (Seattle: Washington University Press, 1962), p. 114. Chapter Seven, "The Genius of the Island—Erasmus' *Christian Prince* (1516)" offers a useful assessment of this often-neglected work, particularly in the contexts of English humanism and European politics at the time.

[5] James D. Tracy, *The Politics of Erasmus: A Pacifist Intellectual and His Political Milieu* (Buffalo: University of Toronto Press, 1978), p. 62.

[6] Halkin, op. cit., p. 315, n. 35.

[7] Adams, op. cit., p. 113.

[8] Faulkner, op. cit., p. 138.

[9] Tracy, op. cit., pre-introduction.

[10] Desiderius Erasmus, *The Education of a Christian Prince*, trans. Lester K. Born (New York: W.W. Norton & Co., Inc., 1936), p. 1. I am heavily indebted to Born for his translation and his insights into Erasmus' political thought.

[11] Ibid., p. 159.

[12] Ibid., p. 205.

[13] Ibid.

[14] Ibid., p. 206.

[15] Lester K. Born, *Introduction to The Education of a Christian Prince*, p. 33.

[16] Smith, op. cit., p. 198.

[17] Erasmus, op. cit., p. 249.

[18] Letter to Christopher von Schydlowitz, August 27, 1528, quoted in part by Smith, pp. 198–9.

[19] Erasmus, op. cit., p. 250.

[20] Born, op. cit., pp. 40–41.

[21] Albert Hyma, *The Life of Desiderius Erasmus* (Assen, The Netherlands: Van Gorcum & Comp. N.V., 1972), p. 91.

[22] Erasmus, op. cit., p. 240.

[23] Ibid., p. 240.

[24] Ibid., p. 193.

[25] Ibid., p. 246.

[26] Ibid., p. 194

[27] Ibid., p. 215.

[28] Ibid.

[29] Ibid., p. 217.

[30] Ibid.

[31] Ibid., p. 218.

[32] Ibid., p. 227.

[33] Ibid., p. 223.

[34] Ibid.

[35] Ibid., p. 224.

[36] Ibid., p. 228.

[37] Ibid., p. 158.

[38] Ibid., p. 234. The modern trend of deriding lawyers is nothing new. Even before Shakespeare's defamation in *King Lear*, Erasmus wrote at this point in the *Prince*: "This profession was once open only to men of the highest standing and carried with it a very high position and very little money. But now the lust for gold which has sapped everything has corrupted this field (as well)."

[39] Born, op. cit., pp. 34, 96. To Erasmus' credit it seems he wrote his work for the most part from memory, needing to look up only a few of his classical references, such was the talent of his mind and the extent of his education.

[40] Erasmus, op. cit., p. 199.

[41] Born, op. cit., p. 34.

[42] Erasmus, op. cit., p. 212.

[43] Ibid., p. 213.

[44] Ibid.

[45] Ibid.

[46] Ibid.

[47] Smith, op. cit., p. 197.

[48] Erasmus, op. cit., p. 145.

[49] Ibid., p. 150.

[50] Ibid., pp. 154–155.

[51] Ibid., p. 213.

[52] Ibid., pp. 156–157.

[53] Ibid., p. 158.

[54] Ibid., p. 160.

[55] Ibid., p. 167.

[56] Donald S. Lutz, *The Origins of American Constitutionalism* (Baton Rouge: Louisiana State University Press, 1988), pp. 140–141.

[57] Erasmus, op. cit., p. 178.

[58] Ibid., p. 179.

[59] Nevertheless, it can be argued that Erasmus was more evangelical than Catholic in spirit, meaning that he frequently expressed his predilection for teaching that was biblical either in itself or in its consistency with other biblical teaching over against that of the Roman church. In this capacity he used the term "evangelical" in his writings from time to time.

[60] Ibid., p. 193.

[61] Born, op. cit., p. 10.

[62] Ibid., p. 28.

[63] Ibid.

[64] Adams, op. cit., p. 112. Many of the ideas Erasmus put forth in his *Prince* would be incorporated by More into his *Utopia*, published seven months after Erasmus' work, though in fact More sent Erasmus a copy of the *Utopia* only two months after Erasmus' work had been published.

[65] Ibid.

[66] Smith, op. cit., p. 201.

The Candle Rekindled: Hugh Latimer on the Temporal Order

by Donald T. Williams

*I*t has become a commonplace observation that the current generation of evangelicals, shocked out of its complacency by the seemingly sudden collapse of the Judaeo-Christian consensus of values which had previously informed public life, has rediscovered the fact that it lives in a hostile secular world to which it must somehow relate. It is no doubt to the good that, no longer content merely to recruit members for a quiescent subculture of populist pietism, we have tried to re-engage the culture and the state on the ultimate questions of what is right and who is Lord. But we can claim no great success for all our efforts. Many factors contribute to that lack of success. One small one may be that, while many leaders do much better, the rank and file seem bent on reinventing the wheel when it comes to relating the church and the individual Christian to the secular order. Yet stalwart heroes of the faith have faced these issues before. One such hero was the great English Reformer, Hugh Latimer.

The Reformation in England can conveniently be divided into phases corresponding to the reigns of the several monarchs who ruled in those days: Henry VIII (r. 1509–1547), Edward VI (1546–1553), "Bloody Mary" (1553–1558), and Elizabeth I (1558–1603). Under Henry, the English Church gained *political* independence from Rome. The king needed a male heir, which his wife, Katherine of Aragon, seemed unable to supply. He wanted to divorce her and marry Anne Boleyn, but to do so he needed a dispensation from the Pope. When it was not forthcoming, Henry took matters into his own hands, declaring himself in the Act of Supremacy of 1534 to be the supreme head of the Church of England. For better or worse, the power of the Holy See was broken, and what Henry had begun for convenience would be pursued by men of conscience in ways the king could not have foreseen.

Though Henry fought for, and won, political freedom from Rome for the English Church, he remained a loyal Catholic in doctrinal matters. This he made clear in 1539 by the publication of the famous "Bloody Articles," one of which defined the denial of the doctrine of transubstantiation as heresy. Thus, though great Reformers like Latimer and Cranmer were already operating during Henry's reign, the reformation of *doctrine* was not able to go forward to any great extent until the accession of Edward VI in 1547, which marks the beginning of the second phase.

During the reign of Edward VI the reformation of the doctrine of the Church in England was carried on with rapid success. Henry's "Bloody Articles" were repealed, reformed scholars were brought in from the continent (including Butzer and Fagius, who were called to Cambridge, and Peter Martyr and Ochino, who came to Oxford), a prayer book was issued in 1549, and by 1552 Forty-Two Articles of Religion, practically identical in content to the Thirty-Nine Articles found in Anglican Prayer-Books today, had been drawn up and ratified. The Reformation suffered a brief though traumatic setback during Mary's reign (1553–1558), but it rapidly re-established and consolidated itself under Elizabeth, bringing the age of Reformation to a close.

The ideas of the Reformation were carried to the people in various ways. Controversial writings abounded. Archbishop Cranmer's genius as a liturgist has perhaps never been surpassed. Tyndale and Coverdale diligently translated the Holy Scriptures. But perhaps nothing captures the imagination quite so vividly as the colorful and learned preaching of the time. Latimer, Hooper, Ridley and Bradford until the Marian persecution, and John Jewel afterwards, are the great names of sixteenth century preaching.

These early Protestant sermons brought the gospel to bear on every aspect of life. Their central theme can be characterized as "zeal for the reform of the Church and society into something more akin to what the reformers take to be God's plan."[1] That theme can be clearly seen in the sermons of Hugh Latimer, who, in the estimation of many, was the greatest preacher of his time. Bishop Stephen Neill notes that:

> While the other Reformers were deeply concerned with individual and personal holiness, Latimer had seen perhaps more clearly than any other man of his day that there is also a necessary holiness of society, and that where that is not in being God is not being glorified. In plain, straightforward English, racy, of the soil, and adorned with vivid illustrations from daily life, he set forth the righteousness of God for England.[2]

Latimer, who preached before both Henry and Edward, had ample opportunity to air his views on the temporal order, and his exhortations concerning "the righteousness of God for England" fell on the ears of those (including the King and his court) who were most practically concerned with the matter. He therefore makes an excellent reference point for our study, and the remainder of this essay is devoted to his views on these matters of state.

Perhaps we can catch a glimpse of Latimer's personality as well as his theological orientation from the following episode. While Latimer was preaching at Cambridge, his bishop decided to pay him a surprise visit. The alert Reformer saw the bishop sneaking into the service, so he promptly changed topics and preached an extemporaneous message on the duties of bishops. The bishop commended the sermon, but requested that Latimer preach the next week a sermon in condemnation of Luther. Latimer's reply was characteristic:

> *I have preached before you to-day no man's doctrine, but only the doctrine of God out of the Scriptures: and if Luther do none other than I have done there needeth no confutation of his doctrine. Otherwise, when I understand that he doth teach against the Scripture, I will be ready with all my heart to confound his doctrine as much as lieth in me.*[3]

Moreover, no one who has ever read them can forget Latimer's last words to Ridley as both were led out to be burned at the stake: "Be of good comfort, Master Ridley, and play the man; we shall this day light such a candle by God's grace in England as I trust shall never be put out."[4]

What then was this feisty reformer's general view of the temporal order? The first principle in importance is the sovereignty of God over his creation. That rule is absolutely basic to all of Latimer's thought. The sovereignty of God is the fountainhead of all human authority, his providence the fountainhead of all human order. Latimer everywhere presupposes these truths, but he also often states them explicitly:

> *The kingdom of God is general throughout the world; heaven and earth are under his dominion. As for the other kings, they are kings indeed, but to God-ward they be but deputies, but officers. He only is the right king; unto him*

only must and shall all creatures in heaven and earth
obey, and kneel before his majesty.[5]

Thus God is sovereign, but He delegates authority to
human sovereigns. The purpose of this delegation is the
providential ordering of creation for the good of God's
creatures. "Yea, forsooth, if the king be well ordered, the
realm is well ordered."[6] A large part of this function consists, in a fallen world, in the forcible restraint of fallen
man's natural tendency to evil and in the judgment,
punishment and eradication of injustice. This negative
side of justice exists ultimately for the sake of a well-or-
dered and prosperous common weal. This point Latimer
makes very strongly:

> *When men may be allowed to do what they will, then it is*
> *a good to have no king at all. Here is a wonderful matter,*
> *that unpreaching prelates should be suffered so long. . . .*
> *Likewise these bribing judges have been suffered of a long*
> *time. . . . To suffer this is as much as to say, "There is no*
> *king in England." It is the duty of a king to have all states*
> *set in order to do their office.*[7]

More specifically, he states: "As the magistrates, their
calling is to see that all things be well, that justice be executed, that the wicked be punished, and the good be
rewarded; also, that the good and godly laws be maintained and executed; and most specially, that the word of
God be taught, that the people be not ignorant in that:
and this is the will of God."[8]

The magistrate is not to usurp the priest's office, but to
see that he performs it; he sees to it that all the estates are
set in order, each to perform its own function. In carrying
out these duties, there is a sense in which the king, with
authority delegated to him by God, stands before the
people in the place of God. Latimer refers to him as
"God's high vicar in earth," and as "God's high minister."[9] However, the king should remember that he rules

by God's permission,[10] which implies God's grace. He carries an awesome weight of responsibility, for, as God's vicar and wielder of the delegated sovereignty of God himself, his law is in a sense God's law, even when it goes beyond the letter of Scripture.[11]

This is not to say that the king is simply a Protestant surrogate for the Pope. He is, as we shall see, by no means infallible. What Latimer emphasizes is the awful weight of the king's responsibility. It matters what he does: he has been given the responsibility for the health of his realm. The person with this terrible weight of responsibility is a man. He is a man who, like all other men, is fallen and in need of redemption. So Latimer dares to say to Henry VIII,

> Here I beseech your grace to pardon me awhile, and to patiently hear me a word or two; yea though it be so that, as concerning your high majesty and regal power whereunto God hath called your grace, there is as great difference between you and me as between God and man: for you be here to me and to all your subjects in God's stead, to defend, aid, and succour us in our right; and so, I should tremble and shake to speak to your grace. But again, as concerning that you be a mortal man, in danger of sin, having in you the corrupt nature of Adam . . . so you have no less need of the merits of Christ's passion for your salvation than I and other of your subjects have, which be all members of the mystical body of Christ. And though you be a higher member, you must not disdain the lesser.[12]

In the same way the king, like all other men, is subject to Holy Scripture and may not ordain laws contrary to it. "In God's behalf I speak: there is neither king, nor emperor, be they ever so in so great estate, but that they are subject to God's word."[13]

It is impossible to overestimate the importance of Latimer's insistence that the king, though the vicar of God, is subservient to Scripture. The entire structure of his thought presupposes the existence of an absolute standard of morals accepted in common by both king and people. It is nonsense to talk about the king restraining evil and promoting good unless he knows what these things are. It is essential that the same God who gives the king his power and authority also set up the boundaries within which he is to use them. Otherwise, Latimer's whole scheme of things would become merely a rationalization for the most oppressive kind of totalitarianism. But in Latimer's mind the commonly accepted moral authority of Scripture acts as a restraint, as a kind of substitute for the checks and balances structured into a modern democracy. This is not a theocracy, for the priest, as we shall see, is strictly forbidden the use of the secular sword. But if experience has taught us some things Latimer had not yet seen about the impotence of publicly professed morality to restrain tyranny apart from a constitutionally institutionalized balance of powers, it may now also be teaching us something of the impotence of constitutional government to preserve human freedom and dignity apart from a common base of shared moral values. He shared the limited vision of his age, as we share the limited vision of ours; perhaps each age also has insights which can benefit the other.

It seems obvious that a system such as Latimer envisioned will work well when the monarch is a wise and devout man who diligently seeks to fulfill his responsibilities under God and in harmony with the Scriptures. It also seems obvious that the weakness in the system is finding a way to ensure that the monarch will be such a man. For, the king being even at best still a fallen human being, there is no guarantee that he will not overstep the boundaries. What happens when that occurs we shall see shortly. In the meantime, Latimer is always ready with advice to help his own sovereign to be the right kind of ruler. Here are some examples of Latimer's fatherly advice to the young King Edward:

First, that he should not trust too much to his own strength and policy; but to walk ordinately with God, and to make him his chief guide. Secondarily, that he live not lasciviously and wantonly; following evil affections, but to live chastely; and when the time shall require, to lead a pure life under the yoke of matrimony. . . . Thirdly, . . . that he should not desire gold and silver too much.[14]

The king owes his subjects the maintenance of order and the restraint of evil, so that they can live their lives in peace to the glory of God. And what of the subjects? What do they owe the king in return for all that he does for them? The question can be answered in one word: obedience. "Subjects may not resist any magistrates, nor ought to do nothing contrary to the king's laws."[15]

We must understand this debt of obedience in light of the whole structure we have been discussing. The king must be obeyed because of who he is: the vicar of God, the chosen channel through which God's providence orders the world. The contribution of the subject then is primarily to live in harmony with the divine decree—to obey his king.

But, as we have seen, the king is also a man. He is God's representative only in an ideal sense. In actuality, he may sin. So the subject must remember that the first principle of the system is the sovereignty of *God*, who alone has a right to absolute obedience. Because the king's authority is derivative from God's, the obedience owed him is therefore in some sense conditional.

I will not make the king a pope; for the pope will have all things that he doth taken for an article of faith. I will not say but that the king and his council may err; the parliament houses, both the high and the low, may err; I pray daily that they may not err. It becometh us, whatsoever they decree, to stand to it, and receive it obediently, as far forth as it is not manifestly wicked, and directly against the word of God.[16]

In other words, just as the same God who ordains the king's authority puts boundaries around that authority by the absolutes of Scripture, that same God, having ordained the subject's obedience, places limits upon that obedience by the same absolutes of Scripture. The subject need not—indeed, he must not—obey a command of his king which is clearly contrary to the Word of him who stands above both of them. But the same principle which forbids the subject to obey also forbids him to rebel. God stands above them both; but the king, though abusing his trust, has still received that trust from God, and is accountable only to him.

> When laws are made against God and his word, then I ought more to obey God than man. Then I may refuse to obey with a good conscience; yet for all that I may not rise up against the magistrates, nor make any uproar; for if I do so, I sin damnably. . . . Our duty is to obey, and commit all the matters to God; not doubting but that God will punish them, when they do contrary to their office and calling. Therefore tarry till God correct them; we may not take upon us to reform them, for it is no part of our duty.[17]

The following passage shows clearly the relationship between the oppressed subject, the unjust king, and God:

> If the king should require of thee an unjust request, yet art thou bound to pay it, and not to resist and rebel against the king. The king, indeed, is in peril of his soul, for asking of an unjust request; and God will in due time reckon with him for it: but thou must obey the king, and not take upon thee to judge him. God is the king's judge, and doubtless will grievously punish him if he do any thing unrighteously. Therefore pray thou for thy king, and pay him his duty, and disobey him not.[18]

If the king's unjust laws merely cause us personal injury, we submit patiently, crying out to God for deliverance;

but if they require us to disobey God's law, then we have the duty of civil disobedience—but still a submissive disobedience. While facing death for his own refusal to obey edicts he considered contrary to Scripture, Latimer wrote these words, which make his position on the proper manner of such disobedience poignantly plain:

> *Though we must obey the princes, yet we are limited how far; that is, so long as they do not command things against the manifest truth. But now they do; therefore we must say with Peter and John, "We must obey God before man." I mean none other resistance, but to offer our lives to the death, rather than to commit any evil against the majesty of God, and his most holy and true word.*[19]

Accordingly, he followed through on them with a dignity and courage that continue to stand out prominently in the bitter history of human martyrdom.

It is very difficult for modern secular men to understand Latimer's point of view. To us it looks very much like a plot to keep the people quiet and submissive while the king gets away with murder. And doubtless it worked out that way in practice too many times. But to understand what Latimer's words must have meant to him and to the people in his congregations, we should have to take the notions of God's justice and mercy as seriously as they did. When Latimer said that the king was in peril of his soul, he was not using idle words; and the affirmation that God was the king's judge carried a weight with him that many of us could not imagine. Neither are we used to waiting patiently and expectantly for God's deliverance. We do not tend to view prayer as a weapon of power. Yet there are those among us who have found God in the Gulag. One wonders if a Solzhenitsyn, say, or a Corrie ten Boom might be better equipped than most of us to comprehend the seriousness with which a man like Latimer could write these words:

When the rulers be hard, and oppress the people, think ever, Cor Regis in manu Domini, *"The king's heart is in the governance of God." Yea, when thou art led to prison, consider that the governor's heart is in the hand of the Lord. Therefore yield obedience: make thy moan unto thy God, and he will help, and can help. Surely I think there is no place in Scripture more pleasant than this, "The heart of the king is in the hand of God," for it maketh us sure, that no man can hurt us without the permission of our heavenly Father.*[20]

So far we have examined the subject's reaction to the dilemma in which he is placed when he lives under an unjust ruler. But what does he do when the system is running smoothly? Is the mere refraining from overt disobedience the only contribution he has to make? Not at all: it is the duty of every faithful citizen to read and study the laws of his realm so he can know what is expected of him.[21] Put that way, obedience can be seen in a positive light as something one *does* that is a positive contribution to the harmony and well-being of the commonwealth. Obedience is as much keeping laws as not breaking them, and in so doing the subject is an active contributor to the peace and prosperity of the realm.

More importantly, the subject has the responsibility to *pray* for his sovereign that he might rule wisely and well. Since God is the author of the system, and since the king's "heart is in the hands of God," prayer is one of the most effective ways of introducing positive content into the system. When I pray for my rulers in this way, says Latimer, "I pray for myself: for I pray for them that they may rule so, that I and all men may live quietly and at rest. And to this end we desire a quiet life, that we may the better serve God, hear his word, and live after it."[22]

Finally, those citizens who are ministers and preachers of the Church have the responsibility to wield the "spiritual sword." By this is meant that, just as the king is subject to Holy Scripture, he ought also to "be obedient;

that is, to hear and follow" sermons that are truly based on Scripture. By this means the Church can advise the king, or even call him to account, though it can do so only by appealing to his conscience, not by force.

> *The king correcteth transgressors with the temporal sword; yea, and the preacher also, if he be an offender. But the preacher cannot correct the king, if he be a transgressor of God's word, with the temporal sword; but he must correct and reprove him with the spiritual sword; fearing no man; setting God only before his eyes, under whom he is a minister, to supplant and root up all vice and mischief by God's word.*[23]

In summary, for Latimer God is the source of all authority and order. The king is God's representative and is therefore sacred, though he can err. Both the king and his subjects are bound by God's word in Scripture. Obedience to the king is mandatory for his subjects except in cases in which the king's command is clearly contrary to Scripture. Even then the subjects may not revolt, but must pray for the king and face death rather than disobey God. At all times the subjects are responsible to pray for the king, to know the laws of the land and obey them, and, if they are clergy, to wield the spiritual sword. The king has the duty to establish the order and restrain evil; and all this is to be done in harmony to the end that men might lead quiet and peaceable lives to the glory of God.

While most evangelical Christians still hold to the basic outline of values and view of the world which Latimer espoused, their views on the nature of government have undergone further developments which require some adjustment. Hugh Latimer could not have imagined a participatory democracy in which citizens have the right and indeed the responsibility to "reform" their rulers and the means to depose them peacefully and lawfully. In such a situation some of Latimer's points simply cease to apply, and others have to be modified: passive resistance is no longer our *only* recourse in the face of injustice; authority now descends, not directly to the magistrate from God, but indirectly from God to him through the people by whose consent he governs. That these are advances is hardly to be debated: few who have enjoyed the rights and freedoms of democracy would be willing to relinquish them.

Yet many who stand in the tradition of the Reformers might argue that the basic moral structure of Latimer's version is still applicable. Unless the system begins with the sovereignty of God, it self-destructs. Unless rights are grounded in God's ordinance for his creation, it is hard to see how they avoid being mere sociological conveniences; unless, that is, we are "endowed" with them by our "Creator," it is hard to see how they can be "inalienable." The magistrate still finds it impossible to govern effectively and avoid social chaos in the absence of a commonly accepted framework of basic moral values to which both he and the people are accountable. With the progressive breakdown of that framework, once provided by the Judaeo-Christian tradition out of which Latimer spoke, people increasingly find themselves faced with the dilemmas of conscience which require—even in a democracy—the kind of civil disobedience that Latimer taught and practiced. From the Tower of London to the jails of Kansas City, from the fires of Smithfield to the nunchucks of overzealous police, may be—spiritually speaking—no distance at all.

We have argued that, as evangelicals re-enter the political arena, they need to reconnect themselves to their own roots, their own mostly forgotten history of engagement with the secular order. This discussion is but a bare beginning in that process. We have not even begun here to survey the tradition, but we have looked briefly at one man who represents it. Even at this stage it might be profitable to ask what that man might have said if he could have seen our struggles today. His observations might not be right, but they would at least give us an older and experienced perspective against that which to measure our own.

He would no doubt be bewildered by the pluralistic landscape we inhabit. Still, his emphasis on the relevance of God's sovereignty for political life—even in an age in which one might have thought this principle could have been taken for granted—might be instructive for us. If even monarchy cannot be healthy apart from a higher Authority who stands above both ruler and ruled, and is recognized by both, how can democracy hope to survive the loss of that same framework? Would not the centrifugal forces of pluralism inexorably drive such a society toward a state in which every person did what was right in his own eyes? With the center unable to hold, would not social order inevitably break down? Do we not find ourselves in an advanced stage of this process even now? Such perceptions indeed play a large role in our motivation for re-entering the political arena.

But what is the solution? Latimer's clear understanding of the different but complementary roles of the state and the church could help us here. Most of us do not really want the church to wield the secular sword, but our opponents almost universally read us as saying we do. Notwithstanding, we sometimes act as if we expect the state to help wield the spiritual sword. Efforts to restore a level playing field so Christian ideas can be heard in the public arena are needed, but will be futile in the long run unless the church becomes more successful at its primary task of making disciples. How many pastors even make an effort to teach their people to apply the biblical world view to the whole spectrum of life? Perhaps instead of berating our nation for departing from values it no longer even remembers ever holding, we should recognize that our real task is to re-evangelize it from scratch. Otherwise, all merely political efforts are useless. The most profound contribution to the political health of our nation we can make, in other words, may not be a *directly* political contribution at all, but a spiritual one: to unsheathe the spiritual sword and relearn its use. We must relearn to preach with power a gospel unaccommodated to secularism and to teach and live by the whole counsel of God. It is primarily by putting its own house in order that the church can be of help in rebuilding the crumbling edifice of the state.

This would not—if we were following Latimer's lead, anyway—be a retreat back into quietism and pietism. His concept of teaching the whole counsel of God included aiming some rather pointed messages at the rulers of society, whether they wanted to hear them or not. It would have involved remembering some foundational truths we seem prone to forget: that our primary concern is with the gospel of Christ and that temporal blessings (including political freedom and justice) are byproducts; that spiritual reform precedes political reform; that you cannot change laws without changing the thinking and values of the people who make, enforce and live under them; that both horses and carts are important and demand attention, but it really does matter which one you put in front.

Latimer might also suggest that our credibility in preaching the gospel may depend in part on how we handled the issue of civil disobedience in the meantime. I doubt, for example, that he would be very sympathetic either with the rescue movement or its critics. To suggest that we should obey laws or court orders which hinder us from saving innocent lives might strike him as tantamount to putting Caesar above God. But tactics such as going limp when arrested or giving false names to authorities to derail the entire justice system might strike him as implying not a protest of particular laws but a disrespect for all law coming from an imperfect authority. From him, both obedience and creating an "uproar" were equally sin. We might profitably ask whether he was right and also whether the manner of our protest might be counter-productive even when the fact of it is justified.

The importance of positive obedience and of prayer as political weapons is hardly controversial. We do not need to discuss those points, but we do need to be reminded of them. Church history in general, and Hugh Latimer in particular, can be a powerful reminder indeed.

Another important principle, which Latimer exemplified, rather than speaking about, was commitment. He stuck to his principles with a consistency that could not be deterred even by the cruelest of deaths. The ardor of that commitment has shown so brightly down through the ages because it was also a commitment to a Person.

> *The more they smothered it, the more it burned*
> *With courage and unconquerable will,*
> *A candle that could never be put out:*
> *It was a blazing soul which only yearned*
> *To sow the seed of light, and then to till*
> *The soil until the fruit shone all about.*
>
> *He saw what only men of faith can see:*
> *"Play the man, and by God's grace we will,"*
> *He said, the promise burning through his doubt,*
> *"Light such a candle as shall never be*
> *Put out!"*
>
> —D.T.W.

The old framework of commonly accepted values rooted in the sovereignty of God is a necessary condition of good government. It has been lost, and must be restored. However, those values cannot be imposed upon people; they must be *won* back to them, and that can only happen as a result of reformation and revival in the church. If Hugh Latimer can help us refocus on the disease rather than the symptoms, he might help us rekindle that old candle once again.

Endnotes

[1] J.W. Blench, *Preaching in England in the Late Fifteenth and Early Sixteenth Centuries* (New York: Barnes & Noble, 1964), p. 263.

[2] Stephen Neill, *Anglicanism*, 3rd ed. (Baltimore: Penguin, 1965), p. 65.

[3] Charles Dargan, *A History of Preaching* (Grand Rapids: Baker, 1954), p. 489.

[4] John Foxe, *Acts and Monuments of These Latter and Perilous Dayes, Touching Matters of the Church*, 8 vols., ed. George Townsend (London: Sedley & Burnside, 1841; repr. New York: AMS Press, 1965), VII, p. 550.

[5] Hugh Latimer, *Works*, 2 vols. ed George Elwes Corrie for the Parker Society (Cambridge: Cambridge University Press, 1844–1845), I, p. 444.

[6] Ibid., I, p. 120.

[7] Ibid., I, p. 193.

[8] Ibid., I, p. 537.

[9] Ibid., I, p. 204.

[10] Ibid., I, p. 355.

[11] Ibid., II, p. 17.

[12] Ibid., II, p. 299.

[13] Ibid., I, p. 250.

[14] Ibid., I, p. 84.

[15] Ibid., I, p. 163.

[16] Ibid., I, p. 148.

[17] Ibid., I, p. 371.

[18] Ibid., I, p. 300.

[19] Ibid., II, p. 260.

[20] Ibid., I, p. 356.

[21] Ibid., I, p. 372.

[22] Ibid., I, p. 391.

[23] Ibid., I, p. 86.

Reformed Establishmentarianism and the Struggle for Toleration: Erastianism in Post-Reformation Europe

by Ronald N. Glass

Latitudinarianism or Establishmentarianism?: The Reformed Dilemma

*E*rastianism was a reaction to the imposition of clerical government by the Reformed Protestants in post-Reformation Europe.[1] Erastianism is, therefore, the theory that "religion is the creature of the State."[2] Walter Hobhouse described the "earnest Erastian" as one who "is sincerely convinced that the strength of the Church is derived from its intimate connexion with the State and its co-extensive-ness with the nation, rather than from its own independent mission."[3] Later, he states: "Erastians value the control of the State as a restraint of spiritual independence and of the extravagances of clericalism."[4] The Erastian magistrate, therefore, both chooses and enforces his own religion upon his subjects. R.I. Wilberforce writes: "By Erastianism I understand that system of opinions and that course of action, which deprive the Church of Christ of independent existence and resolve it into a function of the civil government."[5] Or again, Erastianism "is the absorption of the Church by the civil government—the resolution of Christ's Kingdom into a function of the State. In Erastianism the institutions of the old, swallow up those of the new creation; and nature triumphs over grace."[6]

More recently, William M. Lamont has written that "Erastianism is now understood as the claim of secular power to control belief; it carries with it pejorative connotations of a cynical indifference to moral questions."[7] As J. Llewelyn Davies points out, W.E. Gladstone surely went much too far when he described the "Erastian idea" to be that "it does not matter what god we worship, or how we worship him, provided we derive both belief and worship from the civil ruler, or hold them subject to his orders."[8] Figgis, Hobhouse and others suggest that a more accurate term might be "Byzantism." The epithet "Erastianism" has often been applied in polemical situations without sufficient concern for ideological or historical accuracy.[9]

Opposition to clerical authority in civil affairs is not in itself a new development. Throughout the history of the Western Church, kings had asserted their supremacy over ecclesiastical institutions and officials, realizing that wherever the state acknowledged papal supremacy, it necessarily limited its own power. Nonetheless, the pervasive influence of the Roman Church reigned in any tendencies toward caesaropapism, and the Holy Roman Empire persisted as a theocratic institution—one society with two roles, "sacerdotium" (priestly) and "imperium" (royal), these two functions being carried out by different officials.[10]

The greatest burden of this struggle, however, fell upon the German emperors, who generally regarded the popes less as adversaries than as allies. Other European princes resented papal jurisdiction, and thus the question of supremacy was never far away. Who was to be regarded as the ultimate authority in the state, the spiritual or the temporal powers? The controversy surrounding this question generated a significant body of medieval literature, including the classic statement of the Roman Church's position on the relationship of church to state by Thomas Aquinas, who believed that through the state earthly aims were obtained, but since eternal happiness superseded them, the state had to be subordinated to the church. God had ordained the protection of Christendom by the two swords of the church and the state, but both of those, in turn were given by God to the pope, who then handed the temporal sword to the civil rulers.

As might be expected, the civil authorities did not concede the point, and they had their defenders, including Dante Alighieri, who in his *De Monarchia*, insisted that the temporal monarchy was essential for the well-being of the world, and that, in fact, it was through the jurisdiction of the emperors ordained by Christ that Rome had become such a great empire. The pope and emperor were both necessary guides in life, the one concerned with eternal matters, the other with temporal happiness.[11]

Marsilius of Padua dealt with the matter of excommunication in a way that anticipated Erastus. In his *Defensor Pacis*, published in 1324 as a defense of the imperial rights of Louis IX, he declared the complete independence and authority of the state, and repudiated all political claims by voluntary ecclesiastical organizations. All human actions, including those of the priests, were to be subject to civil law. Those who enjoyed the privileges of belonging to the state were not to exempt themselves from the laws of the state.

Coercive power was the prerogative neither of the pope nor of the bishops and clergy, but of the state alone, which had a right to seize church property and appoint ecclesiastical officers. The pope's authority was restricted to spiritual matters. The proto-Reformer, John Wycliffe, also showed strong caesaropapist leanings. For him, reform could only come through the authority of the king, since only the sovereign head of state could force the clergy to do what they would not otherwise voluntarily do.[12]

Hence, during these centuries, the concept of a dynamic harmony between church and state was being replaced by one of distinctiveness, at times even opposition. The culprit in this change of attitude was the growing domination of ecclesiastical power over the civil magistracy. This ecclesiastical power, however, was always the Roman Church. Prior to the Reformation, therefore, the controversy *inter imperium et sacerdotium* (between the political power and the priesthood) witnessed the defense, on the one hand, of this Romanist subjection of civil authority to ecclesiastical domination and, on the other, the insistence by those who opposed Roman tyranny that the religious hierarchy be properly subject to the civil powers. With the advent of the Reformation, however, this situation began to shift, as in some places the ecclesiastical powers exercising dominion over civil affairs turned out to be Protestant. This new Protestant ecclesiastical domination of civil affairs gave rise to a new Protestant opposition to clerical tyranny. This opposition eventually came to be known as Erastianism.[13]

Civil Government and the Reformed Churches

The immediate impetus for the development of Erastianism came not so much from Lutheranism as from the Reformed (Calvinist) wing of Protestantism. The seeds of Erastianism were planted by Luther, but the crisis that forced them to blossom was precipitated by the appearance of Calvinistic theology and political theory. In fact, Erastianism was inevitable once Calvin crossed swords with Luther over the relationship between civil and ecclesiastical power. Ideally, the state should be governed by a Christian magistrate who subjected himself to the judgment of God's Word.[14]

The office of magistrate, in fact, was established by divine providence and according to holy ordinance, and was invested by Him with a great dignity. Civil rulers are nothing less than vicars of God.[15] In fact, Calvin went so far as to assert that "no one ought to doubt that civil authority is a calling, not only holy and lawful before God, but also the most sacred and by far most honorable of all callings in the whole life of mortal men."[16] Calvin described the ideal government as something of an aristocracy, seasoned with democratic elements.[17] Only a Reformed state church was sufficient to maintain a pure orthodoxy. This promotion of Christianity by the state in the name of biblical stewardship on the part of the civil authorities led naturally to the establishmentarianism of so much of sixteenth and seventeenth-century Reformed theology, and it was precisely this establishmentarianism that Erastianism opposed.

As might be anticipated, considerable tension developed between the growing Protestant theological diversity and Reformed establishmentarianism. Who, asked the magistrates, would hold a pluralistic nation together against external enemies? On the other hand, the clerical authorities were even more concerned. Who would maintain orthodoxy in a pluralistic environment? Certainly not every error could be tolerated! But then if the Christian Church was powerless to act decisively in the cause of truth, who would defend the faith? The answer, as it developed, was the same for both sides in the conflict, namely, the Christian magistrate. The battle lines were therefore drawn: Protestant toleration against Reformed establishmentarianism. Just as the latter seemed to be on the verge of gaining the upper hand in Germany, it collided head-on with a vigorous new source of opposition, namely, Thomas Erastus and his sympathizers.

Heidleberg vs. Geneva: The Development of Erastianism in Germany

Erastianism surfaced after the first generation of Reformers passed from the scene. Its appearance in Heidelberg surrounded the life and thought of the German physician and lay theologian, Thomas Erastus. Erastus was born Thomas Luber (or Lieber or Liebler) in Baden, Switzerland, on September 7, 1524.[18] He entered the University of Basle in 1542, and upon so doing, took the Greek equivalent of his family name, "Erastus." Associating himself with the philosophical faculty there, he studied the classics, mathematics and theology. In 1544, due to an epidemic of the plague, he left Basle and went to Italy where, by means of a wealthy and generous patron, he was able to spend nine years—three at Bologna and six at Padua—studying philosophy and medicine. Upon receiving the doctorate degree, he was appointed court physician in Henneberg, a town in southern Germany, where he quickly gained the reputation of being an outstanding practitioner of enlightened medical science.

Almost simultaneously, Erastus received offers from two German princes, the Duke of Saxony, whose court was at Dresden, and Otto Henry, the Elector of the Rhenish Palatinate. The latter invited him to serve as professor of medicine at the University of Heidelberg. He accepted, and in May, 1558, Erastus joined the newly organized faculty of medicine as professor of therapeutics. Later that same year, having distinguished himself in the arduous administrative task of organizing the program of academic studies, he was elected to the rectorship of the University to serve the following year. While at Heidelberg, Erastus earned the Doctor of Philosophy degree, and at the same time, became actively engaged in the intellectual life of the university community, furthering the cause

not only of medicine, but of science and culture generally, and the church specifically. He was elected to the
Church Council of the Palatinate, a position he held until
he voluntarily resigned in 1564. That immediately placed
him in the midst of the confessional debates which were
common in Heidelberg, a city that, even at that early
date, was a refuge for a variety of eccentric theological
views.[19]

At the time of Erastus's arrival in Heidelberg, the Elector
was a "tolerant Lutheran,"[20] and the city was divided into
two theological camps, the Lutheran and the Swiss. The
Lutherans, in turn, were divided between the strict party
and the more moderate Philippists (those who followed
Melanchthon), while the Swiss were split between the
Calvinists and the Zwinglians.

Throughout his life, Erastus was a Zwinglian; in fact, he
was the leading Zwinglian layman in Heidelberg. As such,
he incurred the hostility of the Lutheran faculty, especially when, in 1559, he opposed Hesshus, the dean of the
theological faculty, over a dispute centering on whether
or not to confer a degree upon Etienne Sylvius, a
Zwinglian student who refused to attack the Zwinglian
doctrine of the sacraments as he did the Roman dogma.
That same year, the tolerant Otto Henry died, only to be
succeeded as elector by the rigorously devout Frederick III
(the Pious, elector from 1559-1576). Frederick had a
strong pro-Calvinist and anti-Lutheran bias, and quickly
appointed a number of Calvinist theologians as his ecclesiastical advisers. In 1560, colloquies were held between the Reformed theologians of the Palatinate and the
Lutherans of Saxony (Wittenberg). Erastus was asked by
the Elector to defend the Reformed (Zwinglian) view of
the Lord's Supper. In spite of the fact that he was a lay
theologian, he performed admirably, and in so doing not
only helped to turn the tide in favor of Reformed theology in the Palatinate, but also won the approval of Kaspar
Olevianus (1536–1587), who, as one of Frederick's ad-

visers, had been appointed director of the College of Wisdom at Heidelberg.[21]

The Excommunication Controversy

The Reformed faith was formally introduced in Heidelberg in August, 1560, and both Romanism and Lutheranism were banned by official edict. It was only a matter of time before the triumphant Reformed party, with its refugees from France and the Netherlands, attempted to institute the "discipline" that distinguished Geneva. This discipline involved a hierarchy of ecclesiastical synods, all independent of the state, governing the conduct of church discipline and the imposition of excommunication. Of particular importance for the Erastian controversy, Olevianus advocated, probably with excessive zeal, the employment of ecclesiastical censures—what Erastus called "febris excommunicatoria" ("excommunication fever") and deemed to be unwise. At this point, Erastus became a crusader against ruling elders and for the laity. After all, he reasoned, here was a small minority of Protestants, surrounded by their Roman Catholic antagonists, expelling members from their own number! Moreover, how could they censure them for not being good Calvinists when they were not Calvinists in the first place? These people needed conversion, not excommunication. Such discipline, said Erastus, was no better than the abuses of the Spanish Inquisition![22]

On June 10, 1568, the controversy over church discipline broke open in Heidelberg. It involved an attempt to reverse the laxity in the churches of the Palatinate by imposing more rigorous requirements for admitting celebrants to the Lord's Table. George Withers, of Bury St. Edmonds, later to become Archdeacon of Colchester, was a religious refugee from England, having fled during the Vestiarian Controversy.[23] During his exile, he took a doctorate degree from Heidelberg, offering a thesis on ecclesiastical ceremonies, an issue to which Erastus referred as "a dispute concerning indifferent things." The theological faculty was in no mood to offend Archbishop Parker and the whole Anglican establishment, however, and they consequently rejected Withers's disputation on the subject. They suggested, nonetheless, that he treat the matter of excommunication, which he subsequently did.[24]

Following the Calvinist model of Geneva (where he had visited prior to arriving at Heidelberg), Withers defended his thesis in support of the authority of ministers, in conjunction with the presbytery, to carry out church discipline, including excommunication, if necessary, upon all offenders, including princes. The discipline of excommunication, according to Withers, was an act *jure divino* (by divine authority), a part of the church's "power of the keys" (Mt. 16:19; 18:18; Jn. 20:23), and had nothing to do with the civil magistrate. In Articles 81–85, the Heidelberg Catechism had affirmed this right with regard to those who were impenitent or hypocrites.[25]

It did not, however, give supreme authority to the ministers, since it was the prince who was given the right of pronouncing and enforcing the sentence of excommunication, the main force of which was banishment from the sacrament of the Lord's Table. Erastus hoped that Withers' defense would merely be an acceptable forum for the young man to exercise his theological talents in the pursuit of "public honors," and not an attempt to decide the controversy. But his hopes were in vain, and the name-calling started immediately.

On the first day of Withers' defense, Erastus was absent, but he did attend the following day when a private debate *in collegiam sapientiae* (in the council of wisdom) took place, pitting Olevianus and the Calvinists, including Ursinus, Zanchius, and Tremellius, on the side of Withers and against Erastus and his supporters.[26] The debate centered on two theses:

I. In connection with the sincere preaching of the word, and the lawful administration of the sacraments, the office of government or discipline in the church must be maintained.

II. This office I thus state: That the ministers in connection with the elders should both have and exercise the power of convicting, reproving, excommunicating, and of executing any thing else that pertains to ecclesiastical discipline, upon any that offend, not even excepting Princes themselves.[27]

The Erastian party argued that the office of discipline could be maintained only where the Word and sacraments were rightly administered, and because discipline had not been maintained in many churches, then force of logic required the Calvinists to say that the Word and sacraments were not rightly administered either. But to say such a thing was absurd, they said. Ursinus replied that there was no such connection; even where discipline was imperfectly administered, it was still the church's duty. Moreover, in the Helvetic churches, the Word and sacrament were rightly administered, so discipline was clearly appropriate.[28] Another objection was then raised by Erastus and his associates, namely, that the doctrine of excommunication was not established by God's Word; there was no mention either of eldership or excommunication in Matthew 18. Besides, eldership had to do with the Jewish civil council (Sanhedrin), who had no right of temporal punishment.[29] Moreover, to be regarded as a heathen and a publican was not to be excommunicated, but merely to be regarded as such according to the individual judgment of church members. No, answered the Calvinists, for to be regarded in this way by one was really to be regarded so by all. Hence, to be accounted as a publican does indeed mean to be excommunicated.

According to the Erastians, the wicked could conceivably be regarded as publicans and heathens without the infliction of excommunication. Not so, said Withers' supporters, and those "who at this day oppose the exercise of discipline on the part of the church, endeavor to evade the source of the examples recorded by the Apostle Paul in two ways."[30] First, they denied that he spoke about excommunication in First Corinthians 5, and second, while perhaps admitting that he had excommunication in mind, they would nonetheless say that such discipline presently had no force, since the church had Christian magistrates. Once again, Olevianus and his allies rejected both claims, declaring that the presence or absence of Christian magistrates had nothing to do with the church's responsibility to excommunicate wicked persons. But, said the anti-Calvinist party, ministers cannot exclude anyone from the kingdom of God! True enough, was the reply, but that is not what Paul did in urging excommunication by the Corinthian Church. Excommunication is a matter of declaring "the rejection of those whom God declares in his word that he has rejected."[31]

But if excommunication was indeed what Paul was advocating, responded the Erastians, he would have said so expressly. The Calvinists answered simply that Paul did not need to be any clearer, since the Corinthians understood perfectly what he meant. This reply, however, was met with the objection that a brother was not to be excommunicated, and therefore the example of Paul was not to be followed, especially in his excluding Hymeneus and Alexander (1 Timothy 1:20), since he acted without the consent of the church. Olevianus and the Calvinists responded by agreeing that no one can act alone and apart from the church to excommunicate another, but, they said, Paul's example was different, since he had special apostolic authority. "What was lawful for the Apostle to do by apostolic authority, that is also lawful for the ministers of the church to do by ordinary power and authority."[32]

During the time of the disputation surrounding Withers' thesis, Erastus was preoccupied, tending to German soldiers who had returned from France with diseases contracted there.[33] But by August, he had produced what he called a *commentarium* against the suggested discipline, put together hastily and without regard to an orderly arrangement (it was written, according to his own words "confusedly and immethodically"). In it, he insisted that the church did not have the right, much less the obligation, to exercise this kind of discipline. The control of human behavior was the prerogative of the secular state alone. The Genevan model with its consistories, he said, could only serve to undermine the state in its administration of justice.

Erastus submitted his work to his colleagues—among them some of his opponents—for their evaluation. Apparently he was not gratified by the results. One unnamed colleague stalled and would not finish reading it; another man, whom he thought to be "the best Friend I had in the world," would not even read it at all. The "very men I had so fondly conceived to have been my best Friends, turn'd suddenly my Enemies, and would not so much as speak to me," he wrote sadly. He was also told that since divines did not meddle in other professions, so those of such professions should stay out of divinity! In order to facilitate its dissemination, therefore, he abridged and organized his manuscript into one hundred theses. His ideas were beginning to gain some credence, especially among certain of the German students, so that the theological establishment was finally forced to reckon with the work. In spite of his pleading for gracious dialogue, however, Erastus found himself with new enemies. Refutations began to appear, and after a month of hostility, he reduced the one hundred theses to seventy-five and organized them more logically.[34]

Originally, Erastus apparently had no intention of widely circulating these theses, but manuscript copies found their way beyond the German borders. Support for his position was forthcoming from Zurich, but from Geneva there was only opposition. There, Theodore Beza secured a copy, and in reply wrote his *Tractatus pius et moderatus de Vera Excommunicatione et Christiano Presbyterio* (An Honest and Restrained Treatment of True Excommunication and Christian Eldership).[35] In the interest of peace, however, Beza did not publish the work, though he did send it to the Elector of the Palatinate. Overwhelmed by the controversy, the Elector attempted to cut off any further discussion of the matter, but was unsuccessful in doing so. In the meantime, moreover, he married the widow of a Belgian nobleman, strengthening his ties to the Calvinists (1569).[36] Frederick responded by requesting a judgment on Erastus's theses from both Zanchius and Ursinus. Ursinus provided just such an evaluation in his *Judicium de Disciplina Ecclesiastica et Excommunicatione* (A Judgment on Church Discipline and Excommunication). He insisted that all the Reformed churches and divines, both those practicing excommunication and those not practicing it, agreed that it was the church's business and not the state's. But being reluctant to become involved in the controversy, he qualified his support of the disciplinarian view with reservations in favor of the civil powers. He had no desire to affirm the authority of any oligarchy apart from the church or the civil government, but neither could he accept an individual's desire to receive the sacrament as sufficient proof of his repentance.[37] As for Zanchius, his position resembled Beza's.

By Christmas, 1569, Erastus completed a much longer work entitled *Thesium (quae de excommunicatione positae fuerant) Confirmatio (A Confirmation of the Theses [which were posed on Excommunication])*, which was a defense of the convictions stated in the seventy-five theses. He insisted that not everyone should be admitted to partake of the sacrament; admission should be according to the procedure observed in Heidelberg requiring the suspension of profane and scandalous persons from the observance, and in the event that they continued in their offensive behavior, their excommunication. He also listed seven sorts of persons who were not to be regarded as members of the church: idolaters, apostates, ignorant persons (not knowing true doctrine), heretics and sectaries (those who do not accept sound doctrine), those wanting to receive the sacrament in other than the correct manner, those who defend their own wickedness and those who refuse to confess and repent of their sins.[38] Five of the six books comprising the *Thesium Confirmatio* were directed at Beza (whose refutation Erastus had secured), and the sixth towards Ursinus, Zanchius, and Peter Boquin (dean of the theological faculty at the University, and the moderator of the June 11 *collegium*).

The debate dragged on for two years before the Calvinists, led by Olevianus, finally gained the upper hand in an electoral edict (the so-called Edict of July) issued on July 13, 1570, the effect of which was to place all the administration of discipline, with the single exception of excommunication, under ecclesiastical jurisdiction. A body of lay elders was to guard against those citizens who deviated from the faith, and to them was assigned the ultimate weapon of exclusion from the sacrament.[39] During this time, however, Erastus let it be known that he believed that the church had no independence apart from the state in these disciplinary matters. In short, this debate precipitated controversy between the two major Reformed parties, the Calvinists and the Zwinglians, with the Erastians holding a position very near that practiced in Zurich, Berne, and others of the German-Swiss churches.[40]

Erastus was once again elected Rector in 1572, but just two years later, was himself excommunicated by the Heidelberg consistory, and in the following year (1575) was even accused of anti-Trinitarian (Unitarian) views, charges, however, that were cleared by a theological commission in 1576. But a radical change in the situation at Heidelberg occurred on October 26 of that year when Frederick III was succeeded by Ludwig VI, who immediately reintroduced Lutheranism into the Palatinate. The Lutherans forced the abandonment of the Heidelberg Catechism and dismissed the Reformed theologians both from the court and the church. By July, 1579, the Elector, who himself was a signatory to the Formula of Concord, demanded that the University faculty adopt it as well or resign. Erastus and his party chose to resign, and in 1580, he went to Basle where his brother-in-law was a professor of theology. Early the following year, he was inducted into the *collegium medicorum* (the college of physicians) there, and that summer began to lecture on ethics. In January of 1581, he was made professor of ethics, and by the end of the year was elected to the governing council of the University. Erastus died on December 31, 1583. Although his abilities and achievements were inferior to many of the second generation Reformers, his epitaph in St. Martin's Church, Basle, reads in part: "Acutus Philosophus, Elegans Medicus, Sincerus Theologus, Heidelbergensis Academiae Columen, Basiliensis Lumen."[41]

The Erastian Dispute: What Was at Stake?

When the Reformed theologians began advocating that the presbyters were fit to judge who was or was not worthy to participate in the Lord's Supper, Erastus was puzzled and alarmed, "since scarcely the thirtieth part of the people did understand or approve the Reformed Religion; all the rest were our violent enemies."[42] At one time, he had regarded excommunication to be the right of the church alone. But believing that it was time to induce people into the church, and not to throw them out, he came to the conviction that the Reformed churches, in promoting such discipline, were risking schism. The presbyters, he said, had not proven themselves to be of sufficient judgment or authority to discharge the responsibility of excommunication in a worthy manner. The church was threatened with significant loss, but his own counsel of caution had gone unheeded.

That caution had arisen from Erastus's doctrine of the church. His was essentially a dualistic concept, and on a number of points it differed from that of most Calvinists.

> The "internal and spiritual society of Christ" which in-
> cludes only the true members of Christ is sharply con-
> trasted to the 'external and visible church' composed of
> both the true and false members. As far as discipline and
> excommunication are concerned, his main interest lies in
> the external and visible church which is marked by such
> visible signs as the profession of the same faith, the confes-
> sion of the same doctrine and participation in the same
> sacraments.[43]

Excommunication, in Erastus's opinion, had less to do
with faith and doctrine than with fellowship since, to
him, it was primarily a denial of participation in the
Lord's Table. Hence, jurisdiction over it should be assigned to the magistrates, who were the guardians of the
visible, external church, and not to the pastors, who were
overseers of the internal life of the church.[44] The pastoral
office, he insisted, was persuasive only, and had no power
of the keys, thus resembling the office of the professor as
it related to the university students. A pastor could rebuke
a magistrate in a sermon, but pastors could not subject
that magistrate to judicial review, which Erastus regarded
as an assumption of governmental authority.

When Jesus, in Matthew 18:17, instructed the disciples
how to take the final step of discipline, the offender
having refused to heed the offended party or that party
together with witnesses, He told the leadership to "tell it
to the church" (dic ecclesiae). Erastus agreed with the Calvinists that the church, mentioned in this passage, was actually the Jewish Sanhedrin (Synedrium, or the magistrate
of the people and religion).[45] To the Calvinists, the Sanhedrin was an ecclesiastical council; to Erastus, it was a
civil council. To treat the erring brother as "a heathen and
a publican" did not mean to excommunicate him, but
rather meant that he thenceforth became liable to action
against him in the state courts. If he did not act like a
Christian, then he should be treated merely as a citizen.[46]
Moreover, with regard to the Apostle Paul's charge to the

Corinthians that they deliver the sinning member to Satan for the destruction of the flesh (1 Cor. 5:5), Erastus did not interpret this as meaning that he be excommunicated and suffer the anguish of sorrow for his sin until the day he was assured that the Apostle, by virtue of his unique authority, had forgiven him. Rather, it was a prayer that he might be removed from the world, that is, that he be supernaturally killed, as happened with Ananias and Sapphira. Erastus's point in all of this was simply that "when the Church has Christian magistrates, both jurisdictions [civil and ecclesiastical] properly belong to the magistracy."[47] He further justified this view of Scripture by pointing out that the authority and power of the Old Testament kings had been transferred to Christian magistrates.[48] There could not be "two authentic Governments in the same people."

On the face of the matter, therefore, the primary point of contention between Erastus and the majority of the Calvinists, represented by Beza, was excommunication. Yes, agreed Erastus, there were times when it was warranted. Even more, however, he was concerned about the "disciplinary tyranny" of the Calvinist system. He believed that the manner of excommunication had been left open by Christ to the church's discretion, and that the church should find the least troublesome way of handling it.[49] His opinion was reinforced by what he considered the lack of unanimity among ancient scholars, medieval schoolmen and more recent writers. The church that was most wisely ordered, therefore, was the one that most nearly paralleled the "constitution of the Jewish Church."

Erastus conjectured, however, that the Heidelberg Calvinists were intent upon stirring up disorder.[50] In general, he held that censures issued by the church were not the proper method for preventing crimes. Was it lawful, for example, for ecclesiastical officers to exclude professing Christians who were guilty of immorality from taking the sacrament? Beza said it was, but Erastus, going back to

Old Testament precedents, to the Apocrypha, and to the practice of ejection from the Jewish synagogues, denied it.[51] It was not permissible to bar those who had sinned, but who had nevertheless professed the faith and were desiring to participate (in his estimation a sufficient proof of their repentance) from the Table.

Thus, Erastus reasoned, the sacraments were means of grace—what he called "incitements or invitements to Piety"[52]—and should not be made instruments of punishment.[53] "Does Scripture warrant such actions or give any examples of excommunication?" he repeatedly asked. Looking back to the Law of Moses and to Jewish history, he could not find excommunication used as a penalty for moral offenses. Specifically, the Law made provision for unclean Israelites to eat the Passover, and neglect of the feast was punishable by death. Moreover, guilty sinners were to bring their sacrifices. Neither were the ceremonially unclean (such as lepers) condemned or barred from proper ritual observances connected with their afflictions. Excommunication could not be defended by those passages declaring that God does not will the sacrifices of the wicked, since God's concern in them had to do with the sinfulness of the heart, not the ceremony itself. And when it came to the New Testament, Erastus saw that even the Lord Jesus did not deny the Last Supper to Judas Iscariot, nor did the apostles practice excommunication. Paul, for example, said that in partaking of the Lord's Table, every man should examine himself—not another—and that those who ate unworthily were subject to the Lord's—not man's—punishment. Thus, excommunication was not commanded by God, but was a human invention common to the Roman tyranny and to Calvinism alike.

As far as Erastus was concerned, the only reason for which a person could be justly barred from the ordinances of the church was theological (what he called "infidelity").[54] He who was excommunicated was barred from professing the faith and approving of the doctrine as well as from the sacrament. Erastus emphatically denied the Roman Catholic bifurcation of excommunication into lesser (a denial of the sacraments) and greater (anathema).[55] To reject the church's doctrine, then, would prohibit a member from partaking of communion; but that was not the case in the event of other offenses such as immorality. The church had the right to decide who were members and who were not, and thereby to determine who could and who could not participate in its privileges; but it could not withhold those privileges as a means of inflicting punishment for the cause of moral misconduct.[56] If any person desired to partake of the sacrament, was orthodox in his doctrinal beliefs, and although having sinned, had declared himself penitent, that was sufficient proof of his repentance, since human judgment could only be external.

Furthermore, Erastus disagreed that excommunication was necessary in order to separate good men from evil. Those who were evil, he argued, could not defile those who were good merely by participating in the Lord's Supper. After all, godly Israelites were not corrupted by frequenting the Temple where wicked men were also present. Furthermore, the presence of Judas at the Last Supper defiled neither Christ nor His disciples.[57]

While disavowing any desire to weaken church discipline, Erastus was bothered by the question of who, in a Christian state, had the authority to exclude believers from the sacrament. Who, in other words, was the ultimate disciplinary authority? Punishment, he concluded, should come from the secular magistrates, providing they were Christians. Looking back to Deuteronomy 4, Erastus declared that "the power of refraining unclean and criminal persons was in the magistrate, whose duty it was not only to punish these men according to the Law of God, but likewise to constitute all the external religion [in other words, to enforce the observance of religion]."[58] This was the responsibility of Moses and Joshua, not Aaron and Eleazer. Likewise, David organized the priestly office, Solomon consecrated the Temple, and both Jehoshaphat and Hezekiah led spiritual reforms. Thus, "wheresoever the magistrate is pious and Christian, there is not read in any person, who under another name of life should govern or punish."[59] But while they had the right to punish, magistrates did not have the right to excommunicate; that was reserved to the church.

Hence, in Erastus's opinion, all men were subject to two governments: the invisible, which had God as its Head, and the visible, over which the magistrate (understood to be Christian) ruled. Thus, as Macleod points out, Erastian polemics agreed that the Lord Jesus was Head and King of the church as His mystical body, but not as supreme Governor of the visible church.[60] No state could tolerate two or more independent coercive authorities, said Erastus, and he condemned the notion of an *imperium in imperio*, one independent government within another, or that which Moncrieff defines as "a power within the State not subject to the authority of the State."[61] Whereas the Roman Church vested this authority in the pope, Erastus granted it to Christian magistrates.

Thus, the church had no right to exercise any power of repression independent of the state. To assign temporal power to the church, said Erastus, was to rob Caesar of what rightly belongs to him. The very idea of trying and excommunicating princes before an ecclesiastical tribunal was to sanction the illegitimate appropriation of power. The Christian magistrate should not be set in opposition to the church. Conversely, Erastus denied that religious interests and institutions should be subordinated to the state.[62] The church could properly warn and censure transgressors, and on questions of faith, the magistrate would, as a matter of course, consult with the theologians who would teach him what the Word of God had to say on the matter,[63] "but punitive action belongs to the magistrate alone."[64] In other words, two co-extensive authorities were incompatible. In a Christian state, where all profess true religion, all coercive power, with the exception of excommunication, therefore belongs to the magistrate. The church's role is one of worship, teaching and exhortation. Church tribunals would be appropriate *only* where the magistrate is unorthodox, or not a Christian at all, and even then, their role should be limited to withdrawal of "private commerce" or to public rebuke, but should not include excommunication. None but God can judge the heart.[65]

That Erastus was concerned here with the "Christian state" is a fact of central importance. Figgis observes that, "Erastus was concerned solely with the question as to the proper method and authority for enforcing ecclesiastical discipline in a State which was uniform in its religion. He was not concerned either with the question as to the right to proclaim truth, or as to the coercive religious authority of a State which allowed more than one or persecuted the true faith."[66] It is true that Erastus's paradigm included only Christian elements, but more than Figgis appears to realize, Erastus was concerned about the question of pluralism. Within the Christian state there could still be ecclesiastical tyranny—oppression by the religious majority or by the state religious establishment. At the time Erastus was embroiled in this controversy, he was clearly contending that his minority view be allowed to coexist with the doctrine of the Calvinist majority. In reality, his vigorous rejection of excommunication was a plea for religious toleration.

Erastus was not impressed by those who argued that from post-apostolic times excommunication had been practiced, even by holy men of God. He suggested that the godly scholars of his own age were only then refuting the Catholic errors, such as the doctrines of *limbus patrum*, purgatory, the intercession of the saints, priestly celibacy and prayers for the dead. Excommunication, like these errors, was a matter that needed to be studied, and would eventually be condemned.[67] From his own reading of history, Erastus suggested that it was introduced into the church about the time of Novatus and Victor of Rome (ca. A.D. 200) to bridle and punish the vices of heretics. The difficulty was that when the magistrates became Christians, the bishops retained the power of excommunication, partly because it was viewed as a divine institution, and partly because the princes feared them. They had persuaded many that Christ was the author of this institution, and they were strengthened by the view that there was grace (spiritual safety) in the sacraments. Men therefore came to fear excommunication.[68] According to Erastus, the error was failure to recognize that, given a godly magistrate (a condition that did not exist in New Testament times), the office of ruling elder, which had been a temporary substitute for a godly magistracy, had ceased, and with it, so had excommunication.[69] The pernicious effects of this practice, as Erastus saw it, included that trust in the sacraments which, by extension, subjected most of the populace of Europe to the papacy.[70]

Thus, Erastus was a committed Zwinglian who opposed the theocratic disciplinary authority espoused by Calvinism as implemented in Geneva. Specifically, he concentrated on the issue of excommunication, attempting to defend his views from Scripture and reason. In so doing, he did not concern himself with the broader question of the supremacy of the civil authorities over the whole spectrum of the church's spiritual life. He did not believe that the church should be governed by the civil magistrates. The fundamental problem he and his followers faced was that of religious intolerance by the Reformed majority towards the Protestant minority. Their fear was that the result of a Calvinistic establishmentarianism might be an ecclesiastical tyranny, exemplified in an unfettered system of excommunication, a tyranny as bad or worse than that of Romanism. Even so, this broader authority of the state over the church was the focus of the position that eventually took Erastus's name, and that primarily because he was the first Protestant to advocate the subordination of church to state in any significant way.[71] To his credit, Erastus affirmed that the civil magistrate was to guide any decisions he might make concerning the church by the Word of God, and in this he differed from some of those who followed him who held that civil law, regardless of whether or not it conforms to the Scriptures, is the proper rule for administering church affairs.[72]

Erastus and Erastianism

An important question naturally arises at this point, namely, that concerning the extent to which Thomas Erastus was what was later to be called "Erastian." Did he actually believe and teach the doctrine that eventually bore his name? Did he hold that religion is the creature of the state? Some preliminary answers have been suggested above, but the questions bear additional thought. J.N. Figgis suggests that Erastus did not advocate the supremacy of the state over the church as did fully developed Erastianism, but that some of his convictions approximated it in significant ways.[73]

Erastus's objective was not directly to support the state as exercising power over the church, but to oppose the Presbyterian position on excommunication, which he saw as the harbinger of a new ecclesiastical tyranny. His primary concern, therefore, was the cause of religious toleration among the Protestant minority in Heidelberg in the face of the increasingly bold intolerance of the Reformed majority, which really was the Protestant state church at that time. His views with regard to the function of magistrates merely supported that objective.

As he saw it, Presbyterianism, like Romanism, virtually amounted to a state, wielding both civil and ecclesiastical power. That was simply too much power to be vested in one institution. To judge men's motives in prohibiting them from partaking of the Lord's Table was to encroach upon the prerogatives of divine justice. The right of excommunication would confer undue power upon ecclesiastical oligarchies, power that lay properly only within the magistrate's domain. The role of pastors was to persuade and to shepherd their flocks. Theirs was a heavenly authority, but it was not secular or coercive. They had to do with men's consciences, not with their bodies or property. As a matter of fact, in his own day, Erastus was not often charged, even by Beza, with giving too much power to the magistrates.

> *The main object then of Erastus was not to magnify the State, nor to enslave the Church, but to secure the liberty of the subject. . . . What Erastus disliked was not only the attempt to steal from the prince his power, but also the arrogant assumption of ability to do God's office and read the thoughts of his heart.*[74]

Erastus recognized that excommunication had been abused by Romanism, for in claiming external authority and infallibility over kings and princes, the popes had arrogated to themselves the power of deposition. After all, a king who had been excommunicated could not be allowed to govern a Catholic people. Erastus simply feared that this kind of thinking was developing among the Calvinists, and as Figgis remarks, "a glance at the writings of Knox will convince us that his fears were not unreasonable."[75] His concern, therefore, was to check the establishment of a Reformed ecclesiastical tyranny, with power vested in an elite oligarchy of theologians.

Was Erastus an Erastian? Undoubtedly less so than some who later bore that title—Whitgift, Selden, or Hobbes, for example. Yet his views were certainly tinged with caesaropapist hues. In the Christian state, he said, only the magistrate could enforce piety and morality. All coercive authority belonged to the state. And yet, once his convictions were torn from their original context in the struggle for toleration in Heidelberg and generalized, they led with little resistance directly to full-blown Erastianism. Hence, "Erastus paved the way for a theory more imposing, more systematic, and more antagonistic to reason than his own."[76]

The *Explicatio* and Beza's Response

Erastus' views found a receptive environment in Zurich, where Johann Heinrich Bullinger (1504–1575), Zwingli's successor and chief pastor of the city, together with Rudolf Gualther, saw the potential for a conflict damaging to all concerned, and therefore attempted to prevent a public controversy on the subject.[77] Due to their efforts, both sides refrained from publishing their works. Consequently, things remained quiet until after the death of Erastus, following which his widow remarried and moved to England. There, in 1589, John Whitgift (1530–1604), Archbishop of Canterbury, sponsored the publication both of the theses and the *Confirmatio under the title, Explicatio gravissimae quaestionis, etc.* (An Explanation of the Most Serious Question, etc., 1568.[78] This publication was undoubtedly edited by Erastus' widow's husband, G. Castelvetro, and was published by John Wolf. Attached to it were letters of recommendation from Bullinger and Gualther. Whitgift did this as an Anglican polemic against the Puritans, Thomas Cartwright (1535–1603)[79] and Walter Travers (1548–1635), both of whom sought to establish and practice Presbyterian discipline. He apparently bought the manuscript from Erastus' widow and then had it published in London under the names of a fictitious place and printer.[80]

When Beza, by this time seventy years of age, learned of this publication, he was tempted to write a new treatise. Hindered both by advancing age and other pressing circumstances, however, he immediately (1590) published his original response to Erastus' theses, his *Tractatus pius et moderatus*. In a lengthy preface to this treatise, he explained his understanding of the controversy and promised a full answer to the *Confirmatio*, a project he failed to complete. His convictions were nonetheless clear. Beza believed that to follow Erastus meant to deny the church its proper spiritual authority. As he saw it, Erastus' position was a system of "anarchy." Excommunication amounted to a great deal more than it did for Erastus; it was indeed a matter of faith and doctrine. What was at stake was sin, not merely civil injury. Thus, it concerned the ministry more than it did the magistracy. Beza also found ample biblical warrant for the practice, both in the Old and in the New Testaments. For example, in the *dic ecclesiae* clause of Matthew 18:17, he identified the *ecclesia* with the *presbyterium*.[81]

Fundamentally, therefore, Beza disagreed with Erastus' concept of the church. His understanding of the church as the *spirituale Christi regnum* (spiritual reign of Christ) and its government is distributed in a threefold way: (1) it is under Christ the King, who is in heaven (and it is therefore a monarchy); (2) it is governed by a presbyterial assembly (and is therefore, in a way, an aristocracy); and (3) it is subject to the "universal multitude of the faithful," the congregation (and therefore also bears the marks of a democracy). As such, the church is protected by Christian magistrates. Hence, if the civil authorities interfere with the spiritual affairs of Christ's kingdom, it ceases thereby to be a monarchy, and becomes a two-headed monster. Beza also disagreed with Erastus over the Old Testament kings. In post-Mosaic Israel, there was an established order, with the levitical priesthood in charge of doctrine and worship, with priestly judges ruling in matters of ecclesiastical law, and with civil tribunals dealing with worldly affairs. In many cases—those involving murder, for example—both civil and ecclesiastical jurisdictions were involved. The proper order here was for the ecclesiastical council to judge *de jure* according to God's Word, while the civil tribunal would judge *de facto* according to the civil code.[82]

Beza understood Christ to be the autocrat over his church, with the presbytery as the earthly tribunal maintaining his cause in it. Presbyterial jurisdiction, he replied to Erastus, was not tyrannical, but divine, and that included their jurisdiction over excommunication. To further underscore this, Beza reminded Erastus of the power of the keys (Mt. 16:19; 18:18; Jn. 20:23). The decision of the presbytery on earth, including that to excommunicate, would be ratified by the Lord in heaven.[83] The presbytery, however, was responsible both to the pastors, to whom the Word of God had been committed, and to the congregation, thereby preventing it from becoming a tyrannical oligarchy.

Erastus objected to this kind of thinking, characteristic as it was of the Calvinists. It held the presbytery to be of two sorts: the teaching pastors-doctors, and the ruling lay elders. He believed that this scheme really amounted to a church that had both a presbytery and a civil magistracy.[84] Beza replied by pointing to the administration of ancient Israel where, at critical times, the king would submit to the high priest.

In all of this, then, Beza insisted that excommunication was the domain of the presbytery and not of the magistracy. Even so, he insisted, the two jurisdictions must be distinguished, not separated. Both have an obligation to work together on behalf of the purity of the church's doctrine, worship and discipline. Those whom the church excommunicates the state must therefore expel.[85]

By the end of the sixteenth century, therefore, the shape of Erastian doctrine was becoming well-defined. It was an attempt on the part of a Reformed minority to resist the potential danger of a new ecclesiastical tyranny at the hands of a Calvinistic majority. Christian magistrates were petitioned to inhibit the institution of a rigid Presbyterian establishment and to preserve religious pluralism among the Protestants. As an important corollary, the Erastian appeal for toleration contained the seeds of a more thoroughgoing latitudinarianism. Moreover, as W.M. Hetherington has insightfully observed, the disadvantage of Erastianism

> in the most mitigated view that can be taken, was, that it reproduced what may be termed a civil Popedom, by com-

bining civil and ecclesiastical jurisdiction, and giving both into the possession of one irresponsible power,—thereby destroying both civil and religious liberty, and subjecting men to an absolute and irremediable despotism. In another point of view, the Erastian theory assumes a still darker and formidable aspect. It necessarily denies the mediatorial Sovereignty of the Lord Jesus Christ over His Church,—takes the power of the keys from His office-bearers and gives them to the civil magistrate,—destroys liberty of conscience, by making spiritual matters subject to the same coercive power as temporal affairs naturally and properly are; and thus involves both State and Church in reciprocal and mutually destructive sin,—the State, in usurping a power which God has not given; and the Church, in yielding what she is not at liberty to yield—the sacred crown rights of the divine Redeemer, her only Head and King.[86]

The Erastianism of Erastus was of the first sort, a union of civil and ecclesiastical jurisdiction. That which was to arise in England, however, eventually came to epitomize the second—a virtual abdication of ecclesiastical authority by the church in favor of the state, a danger that always lurked where the magistrate was not genuinely Christian and the church was either not strong enough or not vigilant enough to look out for its own interests.

Endnotes

[1]The term "Erastianism" itself has been afflicted by a "notorious fluidity." James Hastings, ed. *Encyclopedia of Religion and Ethics* (Edinburgh: T. & T. Clark, 1912), s. v. "Erastianism," by John Young Evans. The term itself was not popularly employed until the 1640s in England, when it was first used by the Scottish Commissioners in the Westminster Assembly. But what did it mean? J.N. Figgis suggests that "Perhaps the theory is expressed in the barest and therefore most complete form by

Selden in his 'Table Talk' in the words 'Whether is the Church or the Scripture the judge of Religion? "In truth, neither, but the State." ' Such a view is clear enough. It places all the truth at the mercy of the civil power and utterly denies any rights of conscience to either individual or Church. It places the claims of expediency above those of reason. It makes political convenience the sole test of belief." J.N. Figgis, "Erastus and Erastianism," *Journal of Theological Studies* 2 (1901): p. 82.

[2] Ibid., p. 83.

[3] Walter Hobhouse, *The Church and the World in Idea and History* (London: MacMillan, 1910), p. 295.

[4] Ibid., p. 329.

[5] Robert Isaac Wilberforce, *A Sketch of the History of Erastianism* (London: J. Murray, 1851), p. 2.

[6] Ibid., p. 71.

[7] William M. Lamont, *Marginal Prynne, 1600–1669* (London: Routledge & Kegan Paul, 1963), p. 155.

[8] J. Llewelyn Davies, "Erastianism," *The Nineteenth Century* 45 (1899), p. 1014.

[9] For a critical overview and evaluation of Erastian doctrine, see William Cunningham, *Historical Theology* (1862: reprint, London: The Banner of Truth Trust, 1960), 1:396–402.

[10] The terms "Byzantism" and "caesaropapism" are equivalents, designating the view which later came to be called "Erastianism," namely, that doctrine which assigned priority over the church to the state.

[11] Figgis observes that Dante saw in Henry of Luxembourg the possibility of realizing a Christian world-monarchy, the advent of the ideal universal empire according to the doctrine of Augustine's *Civitas Dei*, with the pope and the emperor functioning as dual rulers, but each with limits; and "in so far as Dante sets the temporal above the spiritual Lord and asserts the right of the State to be, uncontrolled by ecclesiastical expediency, his work is a prophecy—a prophecy of the modern State, and of that doctrine of the Divine Right of kings, which formed for long its theoretical justification against clerical pretensions." John Neville Figgis, *From Gerson to Grotius*, 1 (Cambridge: At the University Press, 1907, p. 28.

[12]Weldon Samuel Crowley, *Erastianism in England, 1640–1662* (Ph.D. diss., University of Iowa, 1966), p. 1.

[13]What the Reformers did do, of course, was to abandon the Romanist notion of ecclesiastical hierarchy, entailing as it did church government by a priestly class. They affirmed the divine origins and lawful rights of civil government, this not only in opposition to the Roman abuses of civil authority, but also to the contention of some Anabaptists that all such authorities were unlawful and that Christians were not bound to acknowledge them. The Reformers also generally viewed church and state as distinct, neither being wholly subject to the sovereignty of the other. But a vacuum had been left in the Protestant churches by the elimination of the ecclesiastical and jurisdictional administrative structures of Roman Catholicism. Where canon law and coercive ecclesiastical power no longer held sway, temporal powers began to assert their authority. Where there were no more bishops, there were nonetheless princes. On the whole, the Reformers were not what were to become typical Erastians; they had no intention of subjecting religion to the whim of politics. Even so, they assigned to the civil authorities the power of imposing punishment for religious offenses, but this was primarily for the purpose of expediting reforms. They held that all coercive power was required, and the state was morally obligated to use it in punishing heretics, since dissent from orthodoxy was a serious crime.

[14]John Calvin, *Institutes of the Christian Religion*, IV. xi. 4, trans. Ford Lewis Battles, ed. John T. McNeill, Library of Christian Classics, vol. 21 (Philadelphia: Westminster Press, 1960), 2:1216.

[15]Thus, "they should watch with all care, earnestness, and diligence, to represent in themselves to men some image of divine providence, protection, goodness, benevolence, and justice." Ibid., IV. xx. 6, 2:1491.

[16]Ibid., IV. xx. 4, 2:1490.

[17]Calvin had no room for pluralism in his thinking. In the enlightened state, there was no alternative but for the magistrates both to profess the Christian faith themselves, and to promote it among their subjects.

[18]On the life of Erastus, see Auguste Bonnard, *Thomas Eraste et la Discipline Ecclesiastique* (Lausanne: George Bridal & Cie., 1894), and Ruth con Wesel-Roth, *Thomas Erastus: Ein Beitrag zur*

Geschichte der Reformierten Kirche und zur Lehre von der Staatsouver (Baden: M. Schauenburg, 1954). No full-scale treatment of Erastus' life exists in English, however. Among the best sources are J.N. Figgis, "Erastus and Erastianism," *Journal of Theological Studies* 2 (1901): pp. 66–101, and Hastings, "Erastianism." Figgis's article also appears as a chapter in his *The Divine Right of Kings*, 2nd ed. (Cambridge: at the University Press, 1914), pp. 293–342. There is also a useful life of Erastus appended to Thomas Erastus, *The Nullity of Church Censures, or a Dispute Wherein Is Proved by the Holy Scriptures and Sound Reason that Excommunication, and Church-Senates or Members, Exercising the Same are not of Divine Institution; but a Meere Humane Invention* (London: Printed for G.L., 1659). The same life is also included in a nineteenth-century edition of this same work, entitled *The Theses of Erastus Touching Excommunication*, trans. Robert Lee (Edinburgh: Myles Macphail; London: Simpkin and Marshall, and G. Bell, 1844).

[19] Figgis remarks that Erastus "appears to have had one great quality of a leader, the power of attracting loyalty" ("Erastus and Erastianism," p. 68).

[20] Ibid., p. 69.

[21] Olevianus wrote to Calvin praising Erastus and declaring that "few theologians were his equals in learning and wisdom." Ibid.

[22] Figgis, "Erastus and Erastianism," op. cit., p. 71.

[23] The Vestiarian Controversy was a dispute over clerical dress begun under Edward VI and continuing during the reign of Elizabeth I. The refusal of thirty-seven London clergymen to comply with Archbishop Parker's orders by wearing academic gowns and linen surplices caused considerable disruption, and was one of the foundational elements of Puritanism. Withers had come to Heidelberg in search of support for the Puritan position. He appears not to have been an irenic soul, however, and Robert Kingdon calls him a "a wild English visitor." Robert McCune Kingdon, *Geneva and the Consolidation of the French Protestant Movement, 1564–1572; a Contribution to the History of Congregationalism, Presbyterianism, and Calvinist Resistance Theory* (Madison: The University of Wisconsin Press, 1967), p. 123.

[24] Erastus writes: "Now our divines would not admit of this man to his Doctorship, for fear of giving distaste to the English clergy . . . ; but it seems they thought the peace and tranquility

of our own Church, a trifle not worth regarding." "To the Pious Reader, and Such as is Studious Truth," preface to Thomas Erastus, *A Treatise of Excommunication* (about 1568; English translation, London: printed for L. Curtis, 1682), n.p.

[25] Zacharias Ursinus, *The Commentary of Dr. Zacharias Ursinus, on the Heidelberg Catechism*, trans. G.W. Williard, 4th American ed. (Cincinnati: Elm Street Publishing Company, 1888), pp. 424–463. The "power of the keys" was necessary to prevent the sacrament from being profaned, to preserve the purity of doctrine and worship, for the safety of the church, for the salvation of sinners, and for the prevention of scandals (444–445).

[26] Ibid., pp. 453–463, which is the record of Ursinus's refutation delivered at the June 11 meeting.

[27] Ibid., p. 453.

[28] Ibid., pp. 453–454.

[29] Ibid., p. 457.

[30] Ibid., p. 458.

[31] Ibid., p. 461.

[32] Ibid., p. 463.

[33] Erastus, "To the Pious Reader," preface to *A Treatise of Excommunication*, n.p.

[34] Among the extant English translations of the Seventy-Five Theses are the following: the forementioned *The Nullity of Church Censures* (1659); *A Treatise of Excommunication* (1682); and the previously cited *The Theses of Erastus Touching Excommunication* (1844).

[35] Theodore Beza, *Tractatus pius et moderatus de Vera Excommunicatione et Christiano Presbyterio* (Geneve: Apud Ionnem le Preux, 1590).

[36] Figgis, "Erastus and Erastianism," op. cit., p. 74.

[37] Ibid., p. 75, n. 1.

[38] George Gillespie, *Aaron's Rod Blossoming* (London: Printed by E.G. for Richard Whitaker, 1644; reprint, Harrisonburg, VA: Sprinkle Publications, 1985), pp. 76–77.

[39] Crowley, op. cit., p. 4.

[40] Tadataka Maruyama, *The Ecclesiology of Theodore Beza: The Reform of the True Church* (Geneve: Librairie Droz, 1978), p. 109.

[41]"A keen philosopher, a choice physician, a sound theologian; Pillar of the Heidelburg Academy, the Light of Basle." Erastus also wrote scientific and medical treatises in which he attacked such superstitions as astrology and alchemy, and justified the reality of witchcraft. He was a pioneer in testing medications for treating previously incurable diseases, and also wrote on comets. As regards Erastus personally, he seems to have been mild-mannered, so eager to learn that he was willing to be publicly corrected, as is apparent from the prefaces to his works. Nonetheless, he did not blindly accept just anyone's authority, preferring instead to follow the dictates of his own reason.

[42]Thomas Erastus, "To the Reader that is pious and desirous of the Truth," preface to *The Nullity of Church Censures*, n.p.

[43]Maruyama, op. cit., p. 114.

[44]Ibid.

[45]Erastus, *The Nullity of Church Censures*, pp. xli, 37. "But there are solid arguments to prove that Christ in this place by the word Church will not have us to understand the multitude, and common meetings of the Jews, but the Jewish Magistracy or Senate" (xlviii, 49).

[46]Ibid., xlv, 45, and lii, 58; see also Figgis, "Erastus and Erastianism," p. 84. Figgis notes that the same argument was employed by Musculus in his *Loci Communes* and *De Magistratibus*.

[47]Maruyama, op. cit., p. 115. Erastus himself declared: "The sum is that, in a Christian commonwealth, there is one magistrate, to whom God has committed the external government of all things which belong either to civic life or to godly and Christian life; that the right and authority to rule and to judge has not been granted to ministers or to any other persons. This must be understood to be said of a commonwealth in which the magistrates and the subjects profess the same religion, and that the true one. In this, I say, there ought not to be two distinct jurisdictions. . . . As in the case of secular matters the magistrate is not free to transgress the bounds and limits of equity, justice, and honesty, so in ordering sacred matters, or such as relate to divine worship, he is still less free to depart in any particular from the prescription of God's Word, which he ought to follow as a rule in all things, and nowhere to diverge a

hair's breadth from it." Quoted in Davies, "Erastianism," p. 1016.

[48]Ibid., p. 117. "Erastus, we see, had in view a commonwealth in which the ruler and the subjects professed the same religion, and that the true one," Davies, "Erastianism," p. 1016.

[49]Erastus, "To the Reader," op. cit., n.p.

[50]Maruyama, op. cit., p. 109.

[51]Erastus, *The Nullity of Church Censures*, op. cit., pp. ix–xxv, 4–26.

[52]Ibid., p. 19.

[53]Erastus "saw that the attempt to judge whether a man desirous of communicating was sincere or not in repentance involved an impossible claim to a knowledge of motive, and was therefore in this respect an encroachment on the divine justice, no less than it was in another a usurpation of human." Figgis, "Erastus and Erastianism," p. 87.

[54]Erastus, *The Nullity of Church Censures*, pp. iv, 2. He writes, ". . . no man ought to be excommunicated, or ought to be esteemed for an excommunicated person, as the Holy Scriptures witnesseth, except he that is convicted of heresy." Ibid. Appendix 92; (English updated).

[55]Ibid., pp. vii, 3–4.

[56]*Cyclopedia of Biblical, Theological, and Ecclesiastical Literature*, 1891 ed., s.v. "Erastus."

[57]Erastus, *The Nullity of Church Censures*, op. cit., pp. lxxvii–lxviii, 80–81.

[58]Ibid., pp. lxxiii, 87 (English updated).

[59]Ibid., pp. lxxiv, 88–89 (English updated).

[60]Macleod, *Scottish Theology*, p. 36.

[61]Moncrieff, *The Free Church Principle*, p. 176. Erastus was adamantly opposed to the double jurisdiction, in which civil magistrates were obligated to punish the same immoral acts the church was already punishing. Crowley, *Erastianism in England, 1640–1662*, p. 7.

[62]*New Encyclopedia Britannica*, 15th ed., s.v. "Erastus, Thomas."

[63]Erastus, *The Nullity of Church Censures*, pp. lxxiv, 89; ". . . for doctrine, the magistrate ought ever to consult them that are most acquainted therewith" (English updated).

[64] Hastings, "Erastianism."

[65] Erastus, *The Nullity of Church Censures*, pp. lxxv, 89–90.

[66] Figgis, "Erastus and Erastianism," p. 66.

[67] Ibid., pp. lxix, 81–82.

[68] Ibid., pp. lxx, 82–84.

[69] Ibid., pp. lxxi, 84.

[70] Ibid., pp. lxii, 84–87.

[71] See Cunningham, *Historical Theology*, 2:570–572.

[72] Samuel Rutherford specifically charges Erastus with teaching that the civil magistrate is allowed to minister the Word and the sacraments. Figgis, however, argues that there is no certain evidence that Erastus would allow this. Figgis, "Erastus and Erastianism," p. 81, n. 2; but see p. 91.

[73] Figgis, "Erastus and Erastianism," op. cit., p. 83.

[74] Ibid., p. 94.

[75] Ibid., p. 95.

[76] Ibid., p. 96.

[77] Cunningham points out, however, that their agreement with Erastus centered on the issue of excommunication, and did not include his notions concerning the powers of the civil magistrate in general. Moreover, in his preface to the *Tractatus* (where he included letters from these two Swiss churchmen), Beza showed through their writings that they did not even concur with each other at every point on the excommunication question. Cunningham, *Historical Theology*, 2:574–575.

[78] The full Latin title is as follows: *Explicatio gravissmae quaestionis, utrum Excommunicatio, quaetenus Religionem intelligentes et amplexantes, a Sacramentorum usu propter admissum facinus arcet; mandato nitatur Divino, an Excogitate sit ab hominibus.* Evidently no English translation of this work has ever been made. The general arrangement of the book and much of the argumentation, however, can be discerned from some of the English polemical works, especially George Gillespie's *Aaron's Rod Blossoming*, and Samuel Rutherford's *The Divine Right of Church Government*.

[79] Cartwright, as Lady Margaret Professor of Divinity at Cambridge, lectured in 1570 advocating the abolition of the episcopacy and a return to the pastor-deacon offices of the New

Testament. He lost his chair as a result, and subsequently moved to Geneva.

[80]Daniel Neal, *The History of the Puritans; or Protestant Nonconformists from the Reformation in 1517, to the Revolution in 1688*, red. ed. (London: Thomas Tegg and Son, 1837), 1:378, n. 2. The publisher was listed as Baiocius Sultaceterus and the place as Pesclavii. Ostensibly, publication was due to both a death-bed wish of Erastus and the publisher's love of the truth. Beza argued that Erastus would have wished no such thing, and that Whitgift was at the bottom of it all. More than likely, Castelvetro's motivation was pecuniary. Figgis, "Erastus and Erastianism," p. 77. Crowley notes that the *Stationer's Register* contains an entry for June 20, 1589, listing the publisher as John Wolf and attesting to the approval of the Archbishop of Canterbury. He also points out that John Selden declared that he had seen the printer's presentation copy in Whitgift's library. Crowley, *Erastianism in England, 1640–1662*, p. 17, n. 25.

[81]Maruyama, op. cit., pp. 115–116.

[82]Ibid., p. 119.

[83]Ibid., p. 120.

[84]Ibid., p. 121.

[85]Ibid., p. 122.

[86]William Maxwell Hetherington, *History of the Westminster Assembly of Divines*, 5th ed., ed. Robert Williamson (Edinburgh: James Gemmell, 1890), pp. 134–135.

The Theocratic Impulse in American Protestantism: The Persistence of the Puritan Tradition

by James Alan Patterson

*F*or Americans steeped in the hallowed principles of church-state separation and accustomed to the cultural realities of an ever deepening pluralism, the term "theocracy" sounds hopelessly antiquated or remote. Indeed, the notion of a "theocratic impulse" understandably evokes frightening historical memories: imperial Rome's legislation against non-Christian religions in the late fourth century; a worldly and corrupt Caesaropapism in the medieval Byzantine Empire; the grisly legacy of the Crusades and the Inquisition for Western Europe in the Middle Ages; or Reformation Geneva's fiery execution of Michael Servetus for his unorthodox views on the Trinity.[1] These grim chapters of Christian history, often the result of a promiscuous union of political and ecclesiastical power, readily explain why many believers today are quick to repudiate the theocratic tradition.

Yet the theocratic solution to the thorny problems of church and state continues to hold a stubborn appeal, even in a nation that is constitutionally committed to religious freedom and a non-establishment *modus operandi*. As political scientist Glenn Tinder contends, some Christians veer toward theocracy because they perceive it as a legitimate application of their distinctive worldview to all of life:

> *Many Christians have sought the unity (although rarely the total fusion) of Church and state. They have envisioned a unified Christian order of life, implicitly denying the antithesis of community and society. It is natural for this to happen. If you feel deeply in touch with the truth—as any Christian must—you naturally and properly want it everywhere known and fully lived; you envision it in an order of life.*[2]

This analysis clearly suggests that deep-rooted convictions about Christian faith and mission have helped to shape the theocratic impulse.

In fact, theocracy represents a very troublesome but also inescapable issue for Christians precisely because it involves ultimate theological issues concerning the kingdom of God. Thus the facile dismissals of theocracy as (1) political rule by the clergy (hierocracy); (2) the stern application of biblical law to civil society (bibliocracy); or (3) "the church and saints exercising definitive power in the political order," manifest two shortcomings.[3] First, they fail to account for the complexity and the resiliency of the theocratic impulse in American Protestantism. Second, and more seriously, they obscure the unmistakable link between theocracy and the biblical affirmation of God's sovereignty. Allen Verhey points to that relationship and its inherent political dimension:

God reigns and will reign. That theocratic vision is non-negotiable for the church, as are her Scriptures. That theocratic vision may not be reduced to its political implications, but neither may it be emptied of them. God's reign is not merely political, but it is nevertheless surely political.[4]

If Verhey is correct, then all Christians are theocrats, at least in the broadest sense of the word. Nonetheless, American Protestants certainly have not produced a unified theocratic front. Rather, the search for a Christian "order of life" has taken diverse paths and also has provoked much controversy over how the theocratic vision is achieved, and whether it is even desirable. From colonial Puritans to modern day Reconstructionists, the theocratic pattern for Christian engagement with politics has survived many twists and turns.

Puritan New England: The Quest for a Christian Commonwealth

For the past century and a half, historians have vigorously debated the nature of church-state relations in early New England. Despite these efforts, no scholarly consensus exists on even the most basic questions. For example, did the Puritan experiments eventually contribute to the rise of democracy in America, or were they the last vestiges of a territorial, state church system that had prevailed for so long among both Roman Catholic and Protestant powers in the Old World? And if the latter, were they therefore theocratic in the same sense?[5]

Although the Puritan colonies in New England probably were not classical theocracies, ministers and political leaders alike put theocratic spins on their "errand into the wilderness."[6] They never fully realized their lofty goals and ideals, but they articulated and defended a theocratic ideology that profoundly inspired their pursuit of coherent political, social, and ecclesiastical structures. In short, an undeniable theocratic impulse undergirded the

Puritan attempt to fashion a Christian commonwealth in the New World.

The Puritan concept of theocracy functioned on several levels. First, and most generally, the Puritan theocrats embraced traditional Reformed assumptions about God as "the source, sustainer, and judge of all that exists."[7] That the doctrine of God's sovereign rule permeated Puritan thought finds ample support in sermons, literature and formal treatises on government. Urian Oakes, a Puritan pastor and educator, spoke for most of his fellow New Englanders when he delivered "The Sovereign Efficacy of Divine Providence" as an election day sermon in 1677. In his exposition of Ecclesiastes 9:11, he sought to capture the significance of God's reign for human agents in both church and state:

> We see here something of the Power, and Greatness, and Glory of God appearing in his Efficiency, whereby He works all in all. As He is himself Independent, so all Things have an absolute Dependence on Him. He giveth Success, or causeth Disappointment, as He pleaseth . . . In Him we live and move, and have our Being. The Counsels of the ablest Statesmen, how rational soever, shall not prosper without Him: Ministers, how sufficient soever, pious, learned, industrious, zealous, shall convert no man, edify no man, comfort & establish no man, without Him.[8]

Oakes' purpose was not to denigrate human instrumentality but, in typical Puritan style, to exalt the majesty of God.

In a more explicit work of political philosophy, John Davenport drew the natural conclusion that divine sovereignty established God as the ground or source of all human authority. Thus the New Haven founder upheld theocracy as "the best form of government in a Christian commonwealth" because it acknowledged God as "our governor" and gave Christ "his due preeminence."[9] At the same time, Davenport paid his respects to the more mundane issues of political theory; but he gave priority to these transcendent allegiances as the absolutely vital foundation for legitimate government.

From the theological premise of God's supreme reign, the Puritans deduced a much less elevated role for temporal authorities. In fact, their theology, along with their experiences under authoritarian monarchies in England, engendered a healthy skepticism toward all rulers and governments. Even John Cotton, one of the most vocal advocates of theocracy in colonial Massachusetts, insisted that "all power that is on earth be limited, Church-power or other."[10] While the idea of governmental boundaries appeared purely theoretical in some theocratic contexts, it would eventually wield a huge influence in American constitutional history.[11]

For the Puritans, a firm declaration of God's sovereignty was necessary but not sufficient for genuine theocracy. After all, as H. Richard Niebuhr pointed out, the highly suspected ventures of Roger Williams in Rhode Island and of William Penn in Pennsylvania were theocratic in this broad sense.[12] Thus, to a much greater degree than these alternative models, the Puritan theocratic impulse employed the language of covenant to elucidate a special, corporate relationship with the sovereign God. Indeed, Perry Miller carefully traced this covenantal thread through the entire Puritan theological enterprise, viewing it as "the theoretical foundation both for metaphysics and for the state and the church in New England."[13]

It was in this second defining element of theocracy that Puritan leaders most often compared their calling with that of Old Testament Israel. In his stirring "sermon" aboard the *Arbella* in 1630, John Winthrop nearly assumed a Mosaic role as he exhorted his compatriots to ponder soberly the conditional nature of their covenant with Jehovah. The Massachusetts Governor then beckoned his audience to carry out their divine "Commission" with an acute sense of common purpose: "we must be knitt together in this worke as one man." Further, the challenge of the virgin territory to which they were sailing demanded that they fully accept their covenant obligations: "for wee must Consider that wee shall be as a City vpon a Hill, the eies of all people are vppon us." Winthrop reinforced the parallels to ancient Israel by finishing with a charge from Deuteronomy 30:19–20 to "choose life."[14]

Winthrop's oratory reveals that the Puritan concept of covenant was closely joined to a sense of mission or destiny. Miller sharply contrasted this aspect of Puritanism with the less consciously avowed ideals of the Pilgrim colony in Plymouth: "The Bay Company was not a battered remnant of suffering Separatists thrown upon a rocky shore; it was an organized task force of Christians, executing a flank attack on the corruptions of Christendom."[15] In other words, their covenant-inspired mission required a commitment to cultural transformation. Their "errand" was not a desperate escape from a rotting civilization but rather an aggressive undertaking to achieve societal as well as ecclesiastical reform. It is not surprising to find that this cultural mandate was usually accompanied by a firm millennial hope that their efforts composed a prelude to the impending reign of Christ on earth.[16]

The third feature of the Puritan theocratic impulse was the expectation of a cooperative, even cozy relationship between church and state, where both conformed "to the pattern of the divine covenant."[17] Puritan clergy like John Cotton and John Davenport reasoned that, in a Christian commonwealth, the two orders should be coordinated but not completely melded together. In response to an inquiry from an English Puritan concerning church-state matters in Massachusetts, Cotton clearly indicated how this delicate balance could be attained. He placed the primary burden for protecting ecclesiastical prerogatives squarely upon secular authority: "It is better that the commonwealth be fashioned to the setting forth of God's house, which is his church: than to accommodate the church frame to the civill state." He also counseled against democracy, affirming instead that theocracy was the divinely ordained pattern "in the commonwealth, as well as in the church."[18] He did not seem to anticipate the problems that this might cause in keeping church and state distinct.

Both Cotton and Davenport, however, dismissed the notion that ordained ministers should officially hold governmental positions. As Edmund Morgan remarked, "of all the governments in the Western world at the time, that of early Massachusetts gave the clergy least authority."[19] Nevertheless, the Puritan theocratic ideal called for the ranks of political leadership to be filled by the elect. Davenport's *Discourse* specifically excluded unbelievers from "the power of civil administration" because he was convinced that church members were "fitter to judge and determine according to God than other men." At the same time, he conceded that the denial of civil liberties to non-communicants would "have the commonwealth swallowed up [by] the church." Davenport resolved the apparent tension in his political theory by drawing a sharp distinction between "free burgesses" and "free inhabitants"; the right to rule did not necessarily accompany the right to reside in a community or state. Thus he assigned "the public trust and power" for the management of civil government solely to church members.[20] The Puritan theocrats may have shunned hierocracy, but they still entrusted the body politic to the safe control of the pious laity. As Jerald Brauer summarized it, the Christian magistrate "was to be the instrument of the fullest possible exemplification of the will of God in church and state."[21]

The fourth and, in historical retrospect, the most unsavory mark of the Puritan theocratic impulse was the potent measure of coercion that was necessary to establish and maintain a Christian commonwealth. The prospect of force, in fact, was embedded in the ideal of a fraternal church-state alliance where both orders labored together

121

for the common welfare. Inevitably Puritan leaders were compelled to deal with those who refused to conform to a tight system that featured an ecclesiastical monopoly, mandatory church attendance, and tax subsidies for the churches.[22] Covenant theology pushed the Puritans toward a theory of voluntary consent of the governed; but in practice, they enjoined civil sanctions against idolatry, blasphemy, heresy, desecration of the Sabbath, and other forms of religious misconduct.[23]

The civil government's exercise of coercion in religious matters tended to underline the Puritan commitment to intolerance as a theocratic virtue. Nathaniel Ward, a Puritan pastor who spent twelve years in early Massachusetts, boldly announced in a pamphlet penned in 1645 that religious dissenters were unwelcome in New England:

> I dare take upon me, to be the Herauld of New-England so farre, as to proclaime to the world, in the name of our Colony, that all Familists, Antinomians, Anabaptists, and other Enthusiasts, shall have free Liberty to keep away from us, and such as will come to be gone as fast as they can, the sooner the better.
>
> Secondly, I dare averre, that God doth no where in his word tolerate Christian States, to give Tolerations to such adversaries of his Truth, if they have power in their hands to suppresse them.

He also feared a slippery slope, using a musical analogy to argue that religious toleration would lead to moral pluralism: "That State that will give Liberty of Conscience in matters of religion, must give Liberty of Conscience and Conversation in their Moral Lawes, or else the Fiddle will be out of tune, and some of the strings cracke."[24] It was but a short step from the defense of intolerance to the "rituals of exclusion" that were employed against nonconformists in Massachusetts throughout the seventeenth century.[25]

By commissioning government to help police against religious crimes, the Puritan colonies in New England strengthened the hand of secular authority in ways that seemingly clashed with the principle of God's sovereign rule. Roger Williams, a Separatist who left Massachusetts Bay under duress in 1636, later questioned whether the judicial artillery that was turned upon "heretics" betrayed a lack of trust in the sovereignty of God. The founder of Providence much preferred spiritual weapons "to break down those mighty and strong Holds and Castles, which men have fortified themselves withall against [God]." For Williams, the theocratic reign of Christ absolutely precluded the flexing of the state's coercive muscle in areas pertaining to the first table of the Law. He called for a different approach:

> Is not Christ Jesus the truly and onely King of Israel? And is not his sword, his two-edged sword, and his mighty weapons, spiritual (2 Cor. 10.) entering into the very Heart, and Spirit, and Conscience, and thoughts of the Heart?[26]

Williams, himself a victim of Puritan civil restraints, thus stood squarely against theocratic coercion and for church-state separation in colonial New England. His unsettling challenge cast doubt on some cherished assumptions and ultimately weakened the theocratic impulse, even among some Puritans.

Puritanism's problematic response to religious dissent was not the only factor that contributed to the ebbing of theocracy during the eighteenth century.[27] Other causes of decline include (1) a more direct political control of the American colonies by England; (2) the gradual realization that, as Franklin Littell expressed it, "a church which stresses membership confirmed by live faith and fortified by internal discipline cannot include the whole population in its regimen"; (3) the somewhat antitheocratic character of the First Great Awakening with its greater emphasis on individual conversion than on cultural transformation; (4) the related low level of interest in civil affairs by Puritan leaders like Jonathan Edwards, for whom the "millennial theocracy" supplanted more traditional modes; and (5) the reality of a new disestablishment pattern that was embodied in the United States Constitution and the Bill of Rights, and which rendered some versions of theocracy obsolete.[28]

Although the Puritan theocratic impulse definitely retreated, it somehow endured this onslaught and persisted into the nineteenth and twentieth centuries, albeit in significantly modified guises. Protestant theocrats reaffirmed the reign of God as a foundational theological proposition. They also continued to utilize the Puritan framework of covenant, ambitiously projecting it on a larger scale and adorning it with the rhetoric of national purpose or destiny. In light of historical realities, the Puritan views on church-state relationships and coercion required the most reworking; yet even these elements of the theocratic vision did not entirely disappear. The durability of theocratic themes in the American experience allows David Chidester to postulate a deep "substratum of America's collective memory which is occupied by the Puritan theocracy."[29] In what follows, three short case studies will illustrate the persistent manifestations of the theocratic impulse in American Protestantism.

Lyman Beecher, Walter Rauschenbusch, and Gary North: The Continuing Pursuit of the Christian Commonwealth

In the context of the Second Great Awakening, Lyman Beecher emerged as one of the most vocal representatives of the theocratic tradition. Nurtured at Yale under the guiding hand of Timothy Dwight, Beecher became one of the leading evangelical personalities in antebellum America as he artfully juggled the roles of pastor, revivalist, seminary president, and social reformer. Like many of the New England Congregationalists of his day, he deeply appreciated his Puritan heritage, even as he recognized that new religious and political conditions demanded a creative reinterpretation of older ideals. Beecher clung tenaciously to the Puritan dream of a Christian commonwealth but, as Jerald Brauer aptly commented, he "transformed its mode of operation and found a more effective way of bringing it into reality."[30]

Like his forebears, Beecher perceived the world in terms of God's "providential government." As a New Divinity theologian, he ascribed a greater role to human agency than more traditional Calvinists; yet his concept of divine sovereignty was well within the bounds of Reformed orthodoxy. His theology clearly magnified the glory of God and declared a transcendent governance of the world "in accordance with a purpose or plan known and approved of by him from the beginning."[31]

Beecher also presumed that the same sovereign God who covenanted with the founders of New England in like manner entered into a special relationship with the American nation. For instance, Beecher enthusiastically praised the U.S. Constitution as a Christian document that was in full conformity with biblical law:

> There is no position more susceptible of proof than that, as the moon borrows from the sun her light, so our constitution borrows from the Bible, its elements, proportions, and power. It was God that gave these elementary principles to our forefathers, as the "pillar of fire by night, and the cloud by day," for their guidance. All the liberty the world ever knew is but a dim star to the noon-day sun which is poured on man by these oracles of Heaven.[32]

Further, he substantially broadened the Puritan "errand" with the assertion that the nineteenth-century revivals "seem to declare the purpose of God to employ this nation in the glorious work of renovating the earth." For Beecher, the duties of the national covenant pointed directly to "our high providential destiny."[33]

125

At the same time that Beecher consciously appropriated these elements of the Puritan theocratic legacy, he also acknowledged that altered church-state relationships had effectively displaced the earlier patterns of coercion. When Connecticut dismantled its "standing order" in 1818, the Litchfield pastor candidly revealed how the initial trauma jolted Congregationalism out of its spiritual complacency:

> It was a time of great depression and suffering. . . . The injury done to the cause of Christ, as we then supposed, was irreparable. For several days I suffered what no tongue can tell for the best thing that ever happened to the State of Connecticut. It cut the churches loose from dependence on state support. It threw them wholly on their own resources and on God. . . . This created that moral coercion which makes men work. Before we had been standing on what our fathers had done, but now we were obliged to develop all our energy.[34]

Beecher and other Protestant theocrats proved equal to the task, confronting those new challenges with an aggressive optimism.

Since the Christian commonwealth could no longer be constructed through the power of civil law, Beecher pressed for a new theocratic strategy based on the ministries of the voluntary societies which made up the "Benevolent Empire." He welcomed these associations as "providential substitutes for those legal provisions of our Fathers, which are now inapplicable by change of circumstances. In these the nation must enroll itself spontaneously, and the spirit of the Puritans be revived, for the preservation of their institutions."[35]

In short, the institutions spawned by revivalism provided Beecher and his colleagues with a whole new arsenal for advancing the theocratic cause. These weapons were much more suited to their era than the political and legal sanctions used by their Puritan predecessors.

Beecher envisioned that a Christian society would be incarnated in America through the promotion of moral reform, religious literature, Sunday schools, Christian colleges, temperance and the Sabbath. Some of these crusades, of course, followed political trajectories, so Beecher never completely relinquished the Puritan model of the Christian magistrate. He fully expected that those in government would assist these righteous causes:

> Our civil rulers owe to God and their country now, the same illustrious piety, the same estimation of the doctrines of God's Word, the same attendance upon the ordinances of the Gospel and co-operation for their support, and the same strict and pure morality, which rendered the civil Fathers of our land so illustrious in their character, and so benign in the power of their example upon their own and upon other generations.[36]

Thus Beecher maintained a pronounced continuity with the Puritan theocrats, even as he unintentionally stirred fresh concerns about coercion.[37]

In the late nineteenth and early twentieth centuries, Walter Rauschenbusch further refined the theocratic impulse. The famed social gospeler attempted to rescue the ideal of a Christian commonwealth from the seismic forces of change that threatened to engulf it. As a pastor in the Hell's Kitchen section of New York City, he confronted the harsh realities of an industrialized, urban America that was far removed in time and character from Puritan Boston or, for that matter, even from Beecher's Boston.[38] While Rauschenbusch was not as obviously indebted to the Puritans as Beecher, he nonetheless shared the inclination to reformulate theocratic themes in light of different historical circumstances.

Rauschenbusch most explicitly discussed theocracy in *The Righteousness of the Kingdom*, a manuscript written early in his career but not published until many years after his death.[39] In that work, he considered theocracy primarily in reference to the kingdom of God, which functioned as his organizing theological principle.[40] Rauschenbusch began his exegesis of the kingdom by first examining its roots in ancient Israel, noting that "the idea of the covenant and the theocracy" dominated the religious life of the Jews.[41] For Rauschenbusch, these Old Testament conceptions strongly implied some expectation of a kingdom of God on earth. He then found significant continuity between Israel's prophetic hope and the "messianic theocracy" of Jesus:

> *If Jesus had brushed aside the idea of the reign of God on earth, he would have brushed aside the entire Old Testament and the entire past of Israel. And if any of the professed followers of Christ teach a Christianity in which that same idea is not the core and center, then they may protest their belief in the Old Testament, in its inspiration, its inviolability by criticism, and its divine contents, but they belie their own words. In theory they call it holy and wise, in practice they call it foolish and impracticable.*[42]

Thus his desire to understand the reign of God in biblical terms and to place it at the center of his theology predisposed him to embrace the theocratic impulse in its broadest sense.

In addition, his theology of the kingdom caused Rauschenbusch to criticize those who were satisfied with the conversion of individuals. He readily accepted the theocratic task of social transformation, urging that "we must christianize societies, organizations, nations, for they too have a life of their own which may be made better or worse." This process, Rauschenbusch continued, needed to encompass national laws, social customs and corporate institutions: "Every step toward such reconstruction, as well as every individual conversion, is an extension of the reign of God, for God reigns when his will is done."[43] Here was a renewal of the already familiar quest for the Christian commonwealth; Rauschenbusch simply redefined it in terms compatible with the social gospel. In later books, he spelled out more specifically what the Christianization of society actually entailed, giving particular emphasis to economic programs with a decidedly socialist cast.[44]

As Rauschenbusch further developed his theology of the kingdom, he inevitably faced questions about the degree to which the reign of God could be realized in human history. This issue, in turn, raised more pragmatic considerations about strategies for attaining social reconstruction. In this vein, the social gospel's foremost advocate found it necessary to address other matters of theocratic relevance like church-state relationships and coercion. His solutions, while certainly different from those of the Puritans and Beecher, still revealed some theocratic continuities.

In *The Righteousness of the Kingdom*, Rauschenbusch spoke against established churches and warned Christians against the use of force, constraint, or "carnal means" for selfish purposes. At the same time, he intimated that the church had a duty to "influence legislation for the abolition of wrong" and to express itself "in regard to injustice or sin."[45] The social reformer also sketched out a basically separationist view of church and state:

> *The church must be independent of the state, neither oppressed by its commands nor bribed by its support. And it must as a body abstain from all attempts to control the machinery of government or to fill its offices. On the other hand, it is free to influence the ethical conceptions of the people and to stimulate the people to righteous actions.*[46]

In short, the early Rauschenbusch stressed the prophetic and moral responsibilities of the church vis-a-vis the state.

As Robert Handy demonstrates, Rauschenbusch modified some of his thinking on church and state in later years; even though he was a Baptist, he began to sense some limitations in strict separationism.[47] By 1907, when he published *Christianity and the Social Crisis*, he set forth a vision of church-state cooperation that colonial Puritans or the theocrats of the Second Great Awakening likely would have applauded:

> *When the State supports morality by legal constraint, it cooperates with the voluntary moral power of the Church. . . . When the Church implants religious impulses toward righteousness and trains the moral convictions of the people, it cooperates with the State by creating the most delicate and valuable elements of social welfare and progress. . . . The machinery of Church and State must be kept separate, but the output of each must mingle with the other to make social life increasingly wholesome and normal. Church and State are alike but partial organizations of humanity for special ends. Together they serve what is greater than either: humanity. Their common aim is to transform humanity into the kingdom of God.*[48]

Here Rauschenbusch conceived of government in highly positive terms, viewing it as an almost redemptive agent in the Christianization of American society, thus investing it with a sacred calling.

But Rauschenbusch's "liberal version of theocracy," as Martin Marty labels it, failed to solve the problem of coercion, or even to soften its consequences.[49] Older theocratic models sought sanctions primarily against religious and moral nonconformity; the social gospel endeavored to apply the force of law more against economic and political sins, without entirely abandoning some of the earlier moral agendas (e.g., temperance). Rauschenbusch may have appeared more "politically correct" than John Cotton or Lyman Beecher, but his theocratic pursuit of a righteous commonwealth was no less ambitious or intense.

In the late twentieth century, the prospects for a Christian commonwealth have dimmed considerably. Features of Rauschenbusch's theocratic model survived for several decades in agencies like the Federal (later renamed National) Council of Churches. But after the civil rights and peace activism of the 1960s, mainline Protestantism fell on hard times and its hopes for social reconstruction lagged noticeably. Meanwhile, conservative Protestants lamented a series of cultural and legal setbacks that seemed to confirm their worst fears about the secularization of American society. Beginning in the late 1970s, they counterpunched and the New Christian Right was born; in this setting the theocratic impulse was rejuvenated once again.[50]

Among those who have tried to nudge evangelicals to a more aggressive cultural and political stance, Gary North stands as one of the most controversial and uncompromising promoters of theocracy. This prolific Christian Reconstructionist represents a movement that is set apart from the rest of evangelicalism by its "commitment to defining and carrying out an approach to building society that is *self-consciously defined as exclusively Christian*, and dependent specifically on the work of Christians."[51] He earned a Ph.D. in economic history from the University of California, Riverside, and now heads the Institute for Christian Economics in Tyler, Texas.[52]

In contrast to Beecher, who admitted that a complete restoration of the Puritan theocratic model was not feasible, and to Rauschenbusch, who did not even refer explicitly to it, North draws heavily on what the Puritans established in their colony at Massachusetts Bay. In *Political Polytheism*, a bulky jeremiad against pluralism, North proudly defends the Puritan "errand" against what he regards as unfair treatment in contemporary evangelical historiography. He warmly portrays the Puritan venture as "probably the most self-conscious experiment in building a comprehensive Christian civil order in the midst of a wilderness that any group has come close to achieving in history."[53] In addition, his interpretation of seventeenth-century New England elevates John Winthrop as a theocratic hero and impatiently dismisses Roger Williams as a pluralistic villain.[54]

Like the Puritans, North grounds theocracy in God's absolute sovereignty and in covenant theology. First, several statements in an early section of *Political Polytheism* indicate his lofty concept of God's rule:

> *God is the absolutely sovereign Master of all that comes to pass in history. Nothing takes place outside His sovereign decree. . . . God creates and sustains all things in history. . . . Nothing lies outside the sovereign providence of God.*[55]

Second, North quickly affirms that God's reign is largely structured through covenant law. This brings him to the heart of the "pro-nomian" or theonomic position: God's law is "an integrated, unbreakable whole, an explicitly *covenantal* system of biblically revealed law."[56]

North also echoes the Puritans in his delineation of the theocratic import of covenantalism. For instance, he asserts that God's rule mandates a civil covenant based on "the continuing judicial validity of Old Testament civil law."[57] The colonial Puritans, North maintains, accepted this legal standard and thus entered into a covenant relationship with God that was similar to ancient Israel's. This civil covenant gradually weakened and was finally broken with the ratification of the U.S. Constitution. Whereas Beecher found providential congruity between Scripture and the Constitution, North classifies the latter as a "humanist covenant" because of its failure to declare the Bible as "the law of the land."[58] He also proposes that "the Masonic revolution of 1787–88" could be overthrown with two constitutional changes: (1) modify the Preamble to identify "the people" as "the lawful delegated agents of the Trinitarian God of the Bible"; and (2) revise Article VI, Clause 3 to include "a Trinitarian religious Test" as a qualification for public office.[59]

North's advocacy of a civil or national covenant also involves the notion of the state as a district covenant institution. In a theocratic theory of civil government, which has some affinity with that of Rauschenbusch,

North proclaims his hope in "the progressive sanctification of the State."[60] For North, as well as for Rauschenbusch, the state plays a major role in the construction of a Christian commonwealth. In fact, a Christian government functions as a servant of the advancing kingdom of God.

It is not surprising, therefore, that eschatology shapes North's approach to theocratic strategy. As an optimistic postmillennialist, he envisions the advent of genuine theocracy as largely the transforming work of the Holy Spirit:

> *Theonomic postmillennialists argue that long-term cultural faithfulness to God's covenant law can only be sustained by the continuing work of God's Holy Spirit in the hearts of men. Large numbers of people will have to be brought to eternally saving faith in order to sustain a worldwide holy commonwealth. . . . We are calling for a bottom-up transformation of society. We are calling, in short, for* democratic theocracy—*the social, cultural, and (last of all) political product of a majority of eternally saved people.*[61]

In a subsequent elaboration of this majoritarian principle, North forcefully repudiates the imposition of theocracy by a bureaucratic elite. He instead anticipates "the shrinking of the centralized power of civil government" in the divinely ordained theocratic republic.[62]

North apparently thinks that his proposals for a "bottom-up" Christian commonwealth and a scaled-down state will allay fears of theocratic coercion. But there appears to be an unresolved tension when North contends that civil government simultaneously "must be restrained by God's law and enforce God's law."[63] It is North's discussion of the second part of this formula that stirs up memories of some disturbing aspects of the Puritan theocratic ideal. While it is true, as North notes, that all governments are inherently coercive, he raises the stakes considerably by assigning to the state the task of applying covenant sanctions. This solemn responsibility requires "a Christian civil hierarchy, Christian civil laws, Christian civil sanctions, and Christian civil conquest in history."[64] It also necessitates "exclusive control over the franchise" by Christians: "Those who refuse to submit publicly to the eternal sanctions of God by submitting to His Church's public marks of the covenant—baptism and holy communion—must be denied citizenship, just as they were in ancient Israel."[65] Thus "covenant breakers" would not fare any better in North's theocratic republic than they did in colonial Massachusetts. What is not clear, however, is how a reduced and decentralized civil government will have the resources to keep non-Christians in line, especially since North projects that enacting "the whole law-order of God . . . will probably take several centuries."[66]

Ultimately North's Christian commonwealth founders on the assumption that biblical law can be interpreted, applied and enforced almost automatically by finite, fallen creatures. He fails to see that resistance to theocracy is not a rejection of God's rule nearly as much as it is a deep skepticism about human authorities who *claim* to rule in God's name or in accordance with the divine will. The history of theocratic experiments in New England and elsewhere reinforce all too well Bruce Barron's incisive criticism that "dominion theology presumes an all-encompassing Christian competence that does not exist."[67]

Conclusion

The theocratic impulse continues to attract American evangelicals today. First, it obviously has shown such a resiliency over time that some now embrace it nostalgically as part of America's cultural heritage. Second, the notion of a holy commonwealth appears to do justice to God's sovereignty, a central tenet of biblical theology. Third, the pursuit of theocracy encourages Christian participation in the political arena. Finally, the theocratic vision appeals to many as a vehicle for affirming moral absolutes in a relativistic and pluralistic society. Thus frustrated Christians have eyed the theocratic impulse as a tempting strategy for the culture wars of the 1990s.

Nevertheless, the theocratic model is not a viable solution to the complicated problems of relating Christian faith to the political order. First, as Brooks Alexander points out in his analysis of Augustine's political theory, "the function of the Church is not to baptize the State into the Kingdom of God."[68] Most American theocrats have been guilty of attempting to do just that. In the process, they have justified the use of the secular sword of the state as a weapon in what are essentially spiritual battles.

Second, the theocratic impulse often confuses the politics of morality and the politics of justice. Although he was not writing specifically on theocracy, political scientist Stephen Monsma's comments are pertinent:

> *The difficulty of a government pursuing morality apart from justice is made apparent by the basic fact that no one can be forced to be good, to be moral, since morality is a matter of the inner self, the heart, and governments can deal only with outward actions. . . . Justice is a matter of overt acts, and that is what government can and should control.*[69]

The pursuit of a politics of morality helps to explain the negative reactions to the theocratic impulse, both in the past and today.

Finally, and perhaps most seriously, theocratic politics is a "politics of glory." As such, it makes glib and unrealistic assumptions about Christian political leaders, implying that somehow they can transcend the burdensome limits of sin and culture. In 1940, Reinhold Niebuhr warned against seeking redemption through politics:

It ought to be particularly significant for those who hold a Christian faith and who look at the world in terms of Christian insights that political issues are continually confused by all sorts of simple illusions, all of which contain the basic illusion that it is possible for some group of men or nations, either by virtue of a superior intelligence or by virtue of a superior economic organization, to overcome the sinfulness of the human heart and achieve some vantage point of perfection from which they can look down upon the evil world.[70]

If Niebuhr is correct, theocracy administered by human agents in God's name is impossible in this present age. But the theocratic impulse remains a dangerous illusion because it anticipates that coercive power and "dominion" exercised by mere mortals will help usher in the kingdom of God. It thus creates unrealistic expectations for Christian political activity in a fallen world.

Endnotes

[1]On theocracy's bad track record, see Gary Scott Smith, "The Principled Pluralist Response to National Confessionalism" in *God and Politics: Four Views on the Reformation of Government*, ed., Gary Scott Smith (Phillipsburg, NJ: Presbyterian and Reformed Publishing Company, 1989), pp. 216–217.

[2]Glenn Tinder, *The Political Meaning of Christianity: The Prophetic Stance* (San Francisco: Harper, 1991), p. 61.

[3]For a challenge to hierocracy, bibliocracy and other standard definitions of theocracy, see Allen Verhey, "In Defense of Theocracy," *Reformed Review* 34 (1981): 100. On the limitations of the third definition, see Jerald C. Brauer, "The Rule of the Saints in American Politics," *Church History* 27 (1958): 241.

[4]Verhey, p. 100.

[5]For reviews of the relevant literature, see Sydney E. Ahlstrom, "The Puritan Ethic and the Spirit of Democracy," in *Calvinism and the Political Order*, ed. George L. Hunt (Philadelphia:

136

Westminster Press, 1965), pp. 89–95, and Allen Carden, "God's Church and A Godly Government: A Historiography of Church-State Relations in Puritan New England," *Fides et Historia* 19 (February 1987): 56–63. On European backgrounds, see Eugene P. Heideman, "Theocracy in the Reformation," *Reformed Review* 34 (1981): 81–88.

[6]Samuel Danforth supplied the "errand" image in an election day sermon in 1670. See Perry Miller, *Errand into the Wilderness* (New York: Harper & Row, 1964), p. 1.

[7]Brauer, 242. See also Ahlstrom, 101–103, and H. Richard Neibuhr, *The Kingdom of God in America* (New York: Harper & Row, 1937), pp. 45–87.

[8]Urian Oakes, "The Sovereign Efficacy of Divine Providence," in *The Puritans: A Sourcebook of Their Writings*, rev. ed., eds. Perry Miller and Thomas H. Johnson (New York: Harper & Row, 1963), 1:362–363.

[9]John Davenport, "A Discourse about Civil Government" in *Church and State in American History*, ed. John F. Wilson (Boston: D.C. Heath and Company, 1965), p. 7. In line with traditional scholarship, Wilson attributed this writing to John Cotton. For a discussion of Davenport as the probable author, see Avihu Zakai, "Theocracy in New England: The Nature and Meaning of the Holy Experiment in the Wilderness," *Journal of Religious History* 14 (1986): 137.

[10]John Cotton, "Limitation of Government," in *The Puritans*, 1:213.

[11]For an insightful discussion of this, see Neibhur, *The Kingdom of God in America*, pp. 75–87.

[12]Ibid., pp. 45ff.

[13]Miller, p. 89. For additional background on covenant theology, see Allen Carden, *Puritan Christianity in America: Religion and Life in Seventeenth-Century Massachusetts* (Grand Rapids: Baker Book House, 1990), pp. 71–78.

[14]John Winthrop, "A Modell of Christian Charity," in *The Puritans*, 1:195–99.

[15]Miller, op. cit., p. 11.

[16]On the Calvinistic model of Christ as "the transformer of culture," see H. Richard Niebuhr, *Christ and Culture* (New York: Harper & Brothers, 1951), pp. 190–229. For a discussion of the

relevance of millennialism for the Puritan theocracy, see Zakai, pp. 133–34 and 144.

[17]David Chidester, *Patterns of Power: Religion and Politics in American Culture* (Englewood Cliffs, NJ: Prentice Hall, 1988), p. 27.

[18]John Cotton, "Copy of a Letter from Mr. Cotton to Lord Say and Seal in the Year 1636," in *The Puritans*, 1:209–10. See Davenport, "A Discourse about Civil Government," in *Church and State in American History*, pp. 4–5, for his advice on preserving harmony between church and state.

[19]Edmund S. Morgan, *The Puritan Dilemma: The Story of John Winthrop* (Boston: Little, Brown and Company, 1958), p. 96.

[20]Davenport, op. cit., pp. 6–7. See also Cotton, "Copy of a Letter from Mr. Cotton to Lord Say and Seal in the Year 1636," in *The Puritans*, 1:210–11.

[21]Brauer, op. cit., p. 248.

[22]Miller, op. cit., p. 144.

[23]Chidester, op. cit., p. 32. On the theory of consent, see Miller, pp. 147–148.

[24]Nathaniel Ward, "The Simple Cobler of Aggawam," in *The Puritans*, 1:227 and 230.

[25]Chidester, op. cit., pp. 35–46.

[26]Roger Williams, *The Complete Writings* (New York: Russell & Russell, 1963), 3:357 and 7:265.

[27]Samuel T. Logan, Jr., makes the case that, even in the seventeenth century, theocrats like Cotton and Ward had only a limited influence on the civil code in Massachusetts Bay. See "New England Puritans and the State," in *Theonomy: A Reformed Critique*, eds. William S. Barker and W. Robert Godfrey (Grand Rapids: Academic Books, Zondervan Publishing House, 1990), pp. 353–84.

[28]See respectively Chidester, 46; Franklin H. Littell, *From State Church to Pluralism: A Protestant Interpretation of Religion in American History* (New York: MacMillan Company, 1971), p. 8; Douglas F. Kelly, *The Emergence of Liberty in the Modern World: The Influence of Calvin on Five Governments from the 16th through 18th Centuries* (Phillipsburg, NJ: Presbyterian and Reformed Publishing Company, 1992), pp. 127–29; Gerhard T. Alexis,

"Jonathan Edwards and the Theocratic Ideal, " *Church History* 35 (1966): 328–43 and Kelly, 133–35.

[29]Chidester, op. cit., p. 46.

[30]Brauer, 251. For other insightful analyses of theocratic revision, see Fred J. Hood, "Revolution and Religious Liberty: The Conservation of the Theocratic Concept in Virginia," *Church History* 40 (1971): 170–81; James Fulton Maclear, " 'The True American Union' of Church and State: The Reconstruction of the Theocratic Tradition," *Church History* 28 (1959): 41–62; and Elwyn A. Smith, "The Voluntary Establishment of Religion," in *The Religion of the Republic*, ed. Elwyn A. Smith (Philadelphia: Fortress Press, 1971), pp. 154–82.

[31]See his "Faith Once Delivered," in Barbara M. Cross, ed. *The Autobiography of Lyman Beecher* (Cambridge: Belknap Press of Harvard University Press, 1961), 1:413.

[32]Beecher, "The Republican Elements of the Old Testament," in *Works* (Boston: John P. Jewett & Company, 1852), 1:189–90.

[33]Beecher, "The Memory of Our Fathers," A Sermon Delivered at Plymouth, December 22, 1827, 2nd ed. (Boston: T.R. Marvin, 1828) pp. 15 and 17. The millennial aspects of the new "errand" are discussed in Maclear,"The Republic and the Millennium," in *The Religion and the Republic*, pp. 183–216.

[34]*The Autobiography of Lyman Beecher*, 1:252–53 and 336. The emphasis is Beecher's.

[35]Beecher, "The Memory of the Fathers," p. 23. The theocratic implications of these agencies are discussed in John R. Bodo, *The Protestant Clergy and Public Issues, 1812–1848* (Princeton: Princeton University Press, 1954), pp. 13–22.

[36]Beecher, "The Memory of the Fathers," p. 25.

[37]For example, see the alarms sounded by Richard M. Johnson, William Ellery Channing and Calvin Colton in *Church and State in American History*, pp. 100–110.

[38]On Rauschenbusch's New York pastorate, see Paul M. Minus, *Walter Rauschenbusch: American Reformer*, (New York: MacMillan, 1988), pp. 49–70.

[39]On the rediscovery of the manuscript, see the editor's introduction in Walter Rauschenbusch, *The Righteousness of the Kingdom*, ed. Max L. Stackhouse (Nashville: Abingdon Press, 1968), pp. 14-20.

[40]Ibid., pp. 79–116.

[41]Ibid., p. 79.

[42]Ibid., pp. 81–82.

[43]Ibid., pp. 102 and 104.

[44]See especially Rauschenbusch, *Christianizing the Social Order* (New York: MacMillan, 1912). For the overall historical context in which the theme of Christianization developed, see Robert T. Handy, *A Christian America: Protestant Hopes and Historical Realities*, 2nd ed. (New York: Oxford University Press, 1984).

[45]For his discussion of force, see Rauschenbusch, *The Righteousness of the Kingdom*, pp. 88–95.

[46]Ibid., p. 168.

[47]Handy, *Undermined Establishment: Church-State Relations in America, 1880–1920* (Princeton: Princeton University Press, 1991), pp. 109–112.

[48]Rauschenbusch, *Christianity and the Social Crisis* (New York: MacMillan, 1907), p. 380.

[49]Martin E. Marty, "The Protestant Principle: Between Theocracy and Propheticism," in *Cities of God: Faith, Politics and Pluralism in Judaism, Christianity and Islam*, eds. Nigel Biggar, et. al. (Westport, CT: Greenwood Press, 1986), p. 110.

[50]For a handy survey of more recent trends in American Protestantism, see Erling Jorstad, *Holding Fast/Pressing On: Religion in America in the 1980s* (New York: Praeger Publishers, 1990). For a negative assessment of theocratic renewal in a particular denomination, see Joseph Samuel Isgett, Jr., "Religious Liberty and the Theocratic Vision: Southern Baptists and Church-State Relations, 1960–1981" (Ph.D. diss., Southern Baptist Theological Seminary, 1989).

[51]Bruce Barron, *Heaven on Earth? The Social and Political Agendas of Dominion Theology* (Grand Rapids: Zondervan Publishing House, 1992), p. 14. The emphasis is Barron's.

[52]Gary North, *Political Polytheism: The Myth of Pluralism* (Tyler, TX: Institute for Christian Economics, 1989), p. 773.

[53]Ibid., p. 261. Cf. Mark A. Noll, et. al., *The Search for Christian America* (Westchester, IL: Crossway Books, 1983), pp. 28–47.

[54]North, op. cit., pp. 538–39.

[55]Ibid., pp. 36–37.

[56] Ibid., p. 59.

[57] Ibid., p. 631.

[58] Ibid., pp. 410–11.

[59] Ibid., p. 653.

[60] Ibid., pp. 207–09.

[61] Ibid., pp. 156–57. For more on the implications of his eschatology, see North, *Millennialism and Social Theory* (Tyler, TX: Institute for Christian Economics, 1990).

[62] North, Political Polytheism, p. 585.

[63] Ibid., p. 102.

[64] Ibid., p. 640. On the coercive nature of government, see ibid., pp. 101–02.

[65] Ibid., p. 87. See ibid., p. 599, for North's insistence on infant baptism, "infant communion or very young child communion," and weekly communion.

[66] Ibid., p. 647.

[67] Barron, op. cit., p. 166.

[68] Brooks Alexander, "Burden of Conflict: Church and State in a Fallen World," *SCP Journal* 17 (1993): 53.

[69] Stephen V. Monsma, *Pursuing Justice in a Sinful World* (Grand Rapids: Wm. B. Eerdmans Publishing Co., 1984), p. 47.

[70] Reinhold Niebuhr, *Christianity and Power Politics* (New York: Charles Scribner's Sons, 1940), pp. 133–34.

God, Caesar and
Charles Spurgeon
By William G. Travis

*T*herefore laying the axe at the root of the system, we demand the abolition of every union between church and state, and the disallowance on the part of Caesar with things which belong to God."[1] Charles Spurgeon penned these words in 1868 when addressing the issue of the disestablishment of the Irish Anglican Church. While his comments related specifically to that issue, they nicely raise for us the matter at hand: to what extent did Spurgeon get involved in God and Caesar issues?

Charles Haddon Spurgeon (1834–1892) was pastor for 38 years of the then-largest independent Protestant congregation in the world. His London congregation, the New Park Street Baptist Chapel (where Spurgeon began ministering in 1854), grew from small beginnings to over 6,000 members. Located in Southwark, an area south of the Thames River noted for warehouses, Spurgeon's basic constituency was lower middle class.

Spurgeon was the first major preacher in modern times to have a worldwide audience. By the end of his career, more than 2,200 of his sermons had been published. Typically, a sermon preached from notes on Sunday morning was taken down stenographically by one of his assistants, edited by Spurgeon as he went over the copy on Monday, sent to the publisher, printed, mailed and at booksellers by Friday. The effect was a blanketing not only of Britain (where some of his sermons were read the following Sunday by pastors to their congregations) but of the world. All told, perhaps as many as 100,000,000 copies of his sermons were sold during his lifetime.

Spurgeon is probably most noted as a preacher; a very recent biography is subtitled "Prince of Preachers."[2] When considering the enormous output of sermons and the extensive influence of Spurgeon on preaching both in his own era and since, it hardly seems worth challenging the received picture of Spurgeon. However, studies done in recent years have rounded out this central understanding of Spurgeon by emphasizing the various social enterprises, either conducted through Spurgeon's Metropolitan Tabernacle or encouraged and supported by Spurgeon apart from the Tabernacle. Orphanages, an almshouse, colportage and various organizations working with the poor were attached to the Tabernacle. Beyond that, Spurgeon often encouraged others who engaged in social works, especially those who aimed at helping the poor.[3]

Spurgeon was also drawn into larger public issues. Given his reputation and willingness to speak frankly on a variety of matters, it was probably inevitable that he would speak out on matters of public interest. A Gladstone Liberal in politics, he commented on education, disestablishment, war and Irish home rule among other matters. This chapter surveys the public interest side of Spurgeon in an attempt to delineate one more of the many facets of the prince of preachers.[4]

That Spurgeon got involved politically meant he disagreed with those who considered the political arena as off limits for the Christian. Of such an approach, he said, "a more un-Christianlike sentiment, a more selfish statement, never degraded spiritual minds." This is not the same as saying that a Christian ought to get embroiled in every facet of politics, particularly the seamier side.

Rather, the Christian "should be prompted by religious principles, not the party whip." Spurgeon felt strongly enough about the need for the Christian to operate in the political sphere that he published in 1870 an eleven-point list of queries, the logical answer to each demonstrated the necessity for Christian involvement. By the end of that decade he wrote, "We have long ago ceased to draw a boundary for our religion; we believe it should enter into everything and affect all our relationships. If we could not pray over politics we should doubt their rightness."[5]

Spurgeon responded to criticisms of his political involvement with sharp words and with humor. In an editorial in *The Sword and the Trowel* in 1873 he addressed those in the secular press who questioned his "meddling" in political matters by pointing out the dilemma his participation created: "Cease to be a man, and you will be a *pious dissenter;* but speak out and show the slightest independence of mind, and you will be an odious *political dissenter.*" Though some cost had to be paid, Spurgeon risked being branded a political dissenter. A few years later in response to a letter writer who felt Spurgeon should not be in the "defiled arena" of politics, he said that "I can assure you that I vote as devoutly as I pray." After wishing his correspondent well, he stated, "[i]n things divine we are probably at one; and you shall abstain from voting *as unto the Lord* and I will vote *as unto the Lord* and we will both give him thanks."[6]

The Education Bill of 1870 was a turning point in British education history. Before that time there had been no provision for a general, public-funded education system. This meant that most education was in private hands. It also meant that the poor would not have much access to education, and therefore not have much possibility of rising out of their poverty. In light of this, early in the nineteenth century the creation of "ragged schools," so called because of the ragged clothing worn by the children, sought to reach the poorest of all. While statistics are incomplete for knowing the number of Londoners who lived in poverty, an estimate of one-third of the inhabitants from the 1850s to the 1870s seems a reasonable figure. Among the poor were several classes of people, as shown in Henry Mayhew's extensive four-volume study, *London Labour and the London Poor*. Beyond the working poor were the destitute who had to receive charity in order to survive. The worse-off among them were packed into slum areas called "rookeries." There, in crowded housing and filthy streets, with disease endemic, the poorest of the poor tried to manage.[7]

Spurgeon involved himself in education. Formed in 1844, the Ragged School Union acted as a clearing house and information agency for the large number of schools that had sprung up, many of them operating on a shoestring. The Metropolitan Tabernacle supported the Ragged School movement with funds, by Spurgeon's appeals, and by supporting members and former members who were doing ragged school work, as well as by running its own ragged school. Additionally, a day school for up to 400 children of the working poor (there was a small charge to pupils), was run by the Metropolitan Tabernacle in its complex of buildings, right down to the year of the passage of the Education Act. While Spurgeon was only indirectly involved in its operation, he was the chief mover behind its creation. Other educational enterprises included the schools attached to the two orphanages that Spurgeon inspired and helped run and the Pastor's College.[8]

Early on, Spurgeon agreed with most Dissenters of his time that a public education act was not good for Britain. It contradicted the principle of voluntarism, for one thing, and had the potential of including Established Church teachings in its curriculum, for another. But in 1868, in a series of comments made in *Sword and Trowel*, he changed his position. Since the nation insists "that every child shall be taught to read and write," "the great question of the hour seems to be a national system of education." Spurgeon argued that the public schools could be secular. By this he did not have in view "secular" in a twentieth-century sense; he meant that no specific doctrine should be taught in the state-sponsored schools, and that religious training left be in the hands of the home and the churches. He hoped for continued state aid to the already in-place Church and Dissenter schools, for free-of-charge state schools where none existed, and for compelling all children to attend one or the other.[9]

Two issues surfaced in the debates leading up to passage of the Education Act, and Spurgeon addressed both. One was the contention by some radicals, including some clergy, that Bible reading be taken out of the secular schools. Spurgeon strongly opposed this position, advocating instead a "nondenominational" use of the Bible in the state schools. He threatened to "counsel Christians to refuse to send their children to the schools if the Bible be excluded." He even attended a debate at Exeter Hall on the question and commended the people in attendance when only twenty votes out of a much larger number were registered for the opposing position. The other issue centered around clause twenty-five in the Act, permitting school boards (The term often applied to the schools created by the act was "board schools.") to pay the fees of school children at either the board or voluntary schools. Fearful that this meant the subsidizing of schools run by Anglicans, by far the larger number of the voluntary schools, Spurgeon and other Dissenters worked to have the clause repealed. They did not succeed.[10]

Once the Act was passed, Spurgeon worked to convince his fellow Dissenters to accept the newly created system. He advocated electing appropriate candidates in the London school board election, contended that no clergyman should be elected to that body, and hoped that at least one working man would gain election to the board. Throughout the 1870s, Spurgeon continued his efforts on behalf of the new system, attempting to convince other Nonconformists that it was the right way to go.[11]

The defining characteristic of Spurgeon as a figure in public affairs was his espousal of the Liberal party. The nineteenth century Liberal party in England, heir of the eighteenth century Whigs, was for Spurgeon the only possible choice for a Dissenter. The Conservatives (the Tories) were much too close to the established Church. They represented the wealthy few, and Spurgeon deemed the House of Lords (where the bishops sat) a house of Conservative outlook. When the Irish Disestablishment Bill was being delayed by Lords in 1869, Spurgeon excoriated the "tyrannical action," and pleaded for removal of the bishops from the House. Those bishops, he said, "are always the friends of everything oppressive."[12]

On two occasions, 1880 and 1886, Spurgeon got directly involved in the general elections. In 1880, the national election pitted Prime Minister Disraeli's Tories against Gladstone and the Liberals. Gladstone was head of the Liberal party through much of Spurgeon's London ministry, and while he was an Anglican, he was evangelical in his beliefs, and much appreciated by Spurgeon. Already against the Tory party on grounds of principle, Spurgeon's antipathies were further exacerbated by Disraeli's foreign policy in places like Afghanistan, the Balkans and South Africa. Because national elections in Britain are fought out at the local level, Spurgeon concentrated his efforts in the local boroughs of Lambeth and Southwark. To that end, he circulated leaflets in both places, urging voters to get to the polls. He laid out his reasons for support of the Liberals: "Every man must this day exercise his franchise without fail. . . . Let those who rejoice in war vote for the Tories; but we hope they will not find a majority in Southwark. . . . In the name of Peace, Justice, Reform, and Progress, muster your forces."[13] The Liberals and Gladstone won, and so did the two Liberal representatives whom Spurgeon endorsed.

Through Gladstone's rule over the next six years, Spurgeon supported him on virtually every issue. Nevertheless, in the election of 1886, he split with him over Home Rule for Ireland. The Irish question had been a vexation in British politics for centuries, and still is. The Home Rule issue was but one more point at which contention about Ireland surfaced. Like a number of other Nonconformists, and some Churchmen as well, Spurgeon's fear was for the Protestant minority in Ireland, and especially for the Protestants in Ulster. Bolstered by his strong anti-Catholic sentiments, and fearful of Catholic backlash after generations of suppression, Spurgeon broke with Gladstone over the latter's proposal to give at least partial Home Rule to Ireland. *The Times* of London quoted Spurgeon as saying that he could not see "what our Ulster brethren have done that they should be cast off."[14] Spurgeon's opinion, however, did not prevail.

It is almost impossible to gauge Spurgeon's influence on the electorate. What can be said with assurance is that many listened to him, and no doubt agreed with his politics. How often his influence was directly translated into the polling booth cannot be known. What we do know is that a number of contemporary commenters believed that he exercised notable influence among the voters of the district where the congregation was located and perhaps also in the district where he lived. A writer in the *Weekly Dispatch*, not a friend of Spurgeon's, summed up what others thought of the political actions of Spurgeon's followers: "[t]heir human sympathies . . . have been warmed by the flame which burns in the bosom of the devout and fearless Great Heart of the Metropolitan Tabernacle."[15]

When it came to foreign affairs, Spurgeon generally favored Liberal causes. But the context of foreign policy in his era was imperialism. One of its accompanying modes was war. Spurgeon was an opponent of war as a national policy and had major questions about imperialism. One of the matters in imperialism that bothered him was the treatment of native populations. In 1880, he fulminated against the opium trade as an act of British imperialism: responsibility for the opium trade "is clearly shown to sit with the British government of India and consequently with England and the British Crown." Four years earlier he questioned the wisdom of sending missionaries to the Chinese at the same time the opium trade was in force: "Was ever inconsistency more glaring?" he asked.[16]

Where Spurgeon stood on the race issue, a historically important element in imperialism, is not clear. He does seem to have risen a little above the prevailing opinion of his time. He viewed the black race as (younger) brothers, and considered them worthy of receiving the gospel, calling for an end of the curse of Ham. Yet, even with this implied white superiority, he was adamantly against slavery, to the point of condemning American Christians for their compliance in that system. He lost American friends and American financial support because of his strong stand. By the latter 1880s, Spurgeon's views on race had moderated in a more positive direction: "we ought never to be moved by the supposed superiority of a race." All persons should be sought for the gospel, "[t]hey are men; that is enough."[17]

By the mid-1880s, the European scramble for Africa was at its zenith. Even the Gladstone government did not escape Spurgeon's wrath on this matter. General Gordon, leader of the British forces at Khartoum in the Sudan, was killed when that city fell in 1885. Spurgeon, like others, lamented the loss, but added a perspective that few others had: "[t]he evil lay in our first interference, and the sooner we quit the place the better, if honourable engagements permit. Peace is our duty." Of course Spurgeon believed that European civilization, affected as it was by the presence of Christianity, was superior to other civilizations. Those other civilizations needed Gospel light, not European and British imperialism. The imperial presence was as much a hindrance to the Gospel as a help. He even contended that the gospel would likely have made greater headway in a place like India if India had not been dominated by the British. He went so far as to say, "I had rather go to preach to the greatest savages that live, than I would go to preach in the place that is under British rule." Twenty years later he decried the fact that England would "bully Russia, invade Afghanistan, pour out our wrath upon the Zulus, and stand sword in hand against Burmah." Such actions do not mesh with gospel activity.[18]

Spurgeon and others constituted the famed Victorian conscience in foreign affairs. However shortsighted this was in the rough and tumble of everyday international politics, these Victorians argued for a higher road than some of the British governments took in international affairs. Spurgeon complained in 1880 that Disraeli's policies were for self and pride, not peace and righteousness, and gave a ringing indictment of those policies: "[t]ime was when high principle ruled British hearts, and all parties in the state paid homage to liberty, to justice, and even to humanity; but now we are another people, ruled by other lords. Can there be too much speaking against this? . . . We think not."[19]

Spurgeon was also strong in his opposition to war as an instrument of national policy. This does not mean he was a pacifist; it means that war was for him only a last resort. Too often it was turned to much quicker than ought to be the case. For example, Spurgeon condemned both France and Prussia when war broke out between them in 1870. He looked askance at General Gordon, a Bible-toting military man, not in regard to the man's integrity, but because it seemed so incongruous for a believer to figure so prominently in war activities.[20]

If the gospel came in, war should go out: "All soul-saving work is a blow at the war spirit. Make a man a Christian, and he becomes a lover of his race; instruct him, and he becomes ashamed of blows and battles; sanctify him, and he sweetens into an embodiment of love."[21]

In a long editorial in 1878, Spurgeon detailed his opposition to war. On occasion the world goes mad: "England, at set seasons, runs wild with war lunacy, foams at the mouth, bellows out, 'Rule Brittania,' shows her teeth, and in general shows herself like a mad creature." Why do we not learn from the past in these matters; why do we repeat the blunders of our ancestors? Because a "mysterious argument, founded upon the protection of certain mythical 'British interests,' is set up as an excuse," and off we go into war. What causes these periodical outbreaks of passion? "The immediate causes may differ, but the abiding reason is the same—man is fallen . . . Civilized man is the same creature as the savage; he is washed and clothed, but intrinsically he is the same being." What can be done about this? Spread the spirit of love and gentleness, which is the spirit of Christ. Tell the truth about war, "the sum of all villanies" that "brings out the demon in man." At times, war as "the last resort of an oppressed people" may be heroic, but "war wantonly undertaken, for self-interest, ambition, or wounded pride is evil, only evil, and that continually."[22]

Given Spurgeon's nonconformity, his advocating the separation of church and state comes as no surprise. As a nonconformist, he resented the power of the Anglican Church and the inferior place in society of dissenting denominations. Though Dissenters were gradually having impediments removed during the nineteenth century, it still was galling that burial in Church graveyards, the legalizing of weddings and the power of ecclesiastical courts in disputes over wills gave the Establishment unfair social power. Especially upsetting was the fact that all citizens in their paying of taxes ("rates" in the British terminology) were helping the Anglican establishment.

As was true of many activist Dissenters, Spurgeon belonged to the Liberation Society, an organization founded in 1844 to agitate for reform. Spurgeon arrived at New Park Street Church the year the Liberation Society commenced its more active campaign for disestablishment. Always a sought-after speaker for Liberation Society meetings, Spurgeon railed against the various restrictions, and even as the restrictions began to fall only seemed to wish all the more for the end of Establishment: "We can never rest till Episcopacy is disestablished and perfect religious equality is found everywhere . . . all men must stand equal before the law whatever their creed may be; and until this is the case our demands will not cease."[23]

The Reform Bill of 1867 expanded the electorate in Britain, and gave a boost to the hope of the Liberation Society to accomplish its aim of disestablishment. The first order was to seek disestablishment in Ireland, as a prelude to disestablishment throughout the realm. Spurgeon was now entering the most influential years of his career, and he moved into the fray. In a *Sword and Trowel* editorial in March, 1868, he urged Dissenters to send to the Parliament in that year's elections those who would aim to "disendow the Irish Church, and abolish church rates at once, . . . Truth and righteousness demand of Christian electors that they should bestir themselves." In May, Spurgeon addressed the Liberation Society, calling the disestablishment fight a "Waterloo," and urging ministers to arm their congregations with the right principles so that they vote the right way. He also began issuing through his publishers, Passmore and Alabaster, a series of "Tracts for the Times" (in conscious mimicry of the earlier Tractarian movement) which not only sought disestablishment, but also attacked the Church of England for its alleged Catholicism.[24]

Parliamentary elections in the fall of 1868 gave the Liberals a majority of over 100 seats. The following March the bill to disestablish the Church of Ireland was brought up in the House of Commons. Though the bill passed Commons without much difficulty, a stalemate threatened in Lords. Gladstone, a friend of Spurgeon but an Anglican with High Church sympathies, was caught in the middle. But, in July, 1869, the bill passed into law.

What was anticipated as the beginning of the move toward English disestablishment turned out to be the high point. By 1873 the motion in Commons to disestablish the Church of England received fewer votes than it had in 1869. Gladstone in his years as Prime Minister never saw fit to bring the issue up, and of course the Disraeli governments were not interested in the idea. Though Spurgeon continued his belief in voluntarism as the right principle for church-state relations, he became more philosophical about the issue in later years, writing in 1884: "I sometimes think it is a *providential* arrangement that the State Church should be permitted to exist," because it keeps Nonconformists in the Liberal party—and for Spurgeon nothing could be more incongruous than a Nonconformist Tory. In April, 1891, he resigned his membership in the Liberation Society.[25]

Charles Spurgeon was first and foremost a preacher, and secondarily a pastor interested in social outreach. His involvement in public affairs grew out of these two primary facets of his life. Meredith has captured it well:

> *Spurgeon was careful to keep that rare balance between the spiritual and the temporal. While always willing and ready to speak out on the political issues of his day 'for the guidance of the people,' he never let political concerns alone become his end. Politics were important to him, but only because he believed every area of life should be used for the ultimate glory of God and, in that sense, the political sphere was always subservient to the spiritual.[26]*

Charles Spurgeon was a spokesman for God who did not flinch from addressing Caesar when the occasion demanded it, and who was quite willing to tell Caesar to stay out of God's domain: "Caesar had better mind his own things, and let the things of God alone." No doubt some of Spurgeon's contemporaries wished he had let the things of Caesar alone. But he did not, and that fact provides us with one more facet of this unusual man, a prince of preachers with a highly developed social conscience.[27]

Endnotes

[1] *The Sword and the Trowel* (hereafter *Sword and Trowel*) 4 (May 1868): 227. Spurgeon founded the magazine in 1865 and remained its editor and a major contributor until his death.

[2] Lewis A. Drummond, *Spurgeon: Prince of Preachers* (Grand Rapids: Kregel Publications, 1992). Still the best source for Spurgeon's career is the four-volume *Autobiography* compiled by Spurgeon's wife Susannah and his secretary, Joseph Harrald, published in 1897–1900. The Banner of Truth has issued a two-volume condensation of the original four volumes: Iain Murray, ed., *C.H. Spurgeon: The Early Years, 1834–1859* (London, 1962) and *C.H. Spurgeon: Autobiography: The Full Years, 1860–1892* (Edinburgh, 1973). Over 20 biographies have been written on Spurgeon, most of them quite laudatory, including recent ones like Ernest W. Bacon, *Spurgeon: Heir of the Puritans* (Grand Rapids: Eerdmans, 1968) and Arnold Dallimore, *Spurgeon* (Chicago: Moody Press, 1984). While the Drummond volume has much to commend it, a major critical biography of Spurgeon remains to be written.

[3] An exposition of Spurgeon's social outreach is my " 'To Them I Must Keep': The Social Ministries of Charles Haddon Spurgeon," in Norris Magnuson, ed., *Proclaim the Good News* (Chicago: Harvest, 1986): 223–244. Beginning in 1855 and running continuously to 1917, Spurgeon's sermons were published weekly. The sermons were also published in book form, each volume an annual set, 62 volumes in all; the entire series has been republished by Pilgrim Publications of Pasadena, Texas. The 100,000,000 figure in the previous paragraph is in Charles Ray, *A Marvelous Ministry: The Story of C.H. Spurgeon's Sermons, 1855–1905* (London: Passmore and Alabaster, 1905), p. 8. A fine analysis of Spurgeon's social philosophy is David Nelson Duke, "Charles Haddon Spurgeon: Social Concern Exceeding an Individualistic Self-Help Ideology," *Baptist History and Heritage* 12 (October 1987): 47–56.

[4] The major secondary sources for this part of Spurgeon's career are Albert R. Meredith, "The Social and Political Views of Charles Haddon Spurgeon, 1834–1892" (Unpublished Ph.D. dissertation, Michigan State University, 1973), and Patricia Stallings Kruppa, *Charles Haddon Spurgeon: A Preacher's Progress* (New York: Garland, 1982). I am indebted to both these works for

their insights on Spurgeon's political views. In addition, I have relied heavily on Spurgeon's writings in *Sword and Trowel* for primary materials.

[5] The quotations are from C.H. Spurgeon, "The Present Crisis," *Metropolitan Tabernacle Pulpit* 25 (1879): 390–91; Meredith, "Social and Political Views," p. 58; and *Sword and Trowel* 15 (May 1879): 245. The eleven-point list is in ibid 6 (July 1860): 330–331.

[6] C.H. Spurgeon, "A Political Disaster," *Sword and Trowel* 9 (March 1873): 107; the letter quoted is in Kruppa, *Spurgeon*, p. 291. Apparently Spurgeon's brief article on political Dissent was prompted by those who had attacked him publicly and privately for his having "expressed our belief that Caesar had better mind his own things, and let the things of God alone"; Spurgeon, "Political Dissenter," p. 106. Spurgeon was not alone as a politically active Dissenter; for the fuller picture of Dissent and politics after 1870, see D.W. Bebbington, *The Nonconformist Conscience: Chapel and Politics, 1870–1914* (London: George Allen and Unwin, 1982). I am using Dissenter and Nonconformist as synonymous terms in this paper.

[7] A summary account of ragged schools is in Kathleen Heasman, *Evangelicals in Action: An Appraisal of Their Social Work in the Victorian Era* (London: Geoffrey Bles, 1962), pp. 69–87. The Mayhew volumes were influential for the study of London in the 1850s and following. A thorough description of one of the most notorious rookeries is Edward Leach, "The Poor of St. Giles," *Sword and Trowel* 7 (October 1871): 415–28.

[8] These enterprises are described in *C.H. Spurgeon, The Metropolitan Tabernacle: Its History and Work* (London: Passmore and Alabaster, 1876).

[9] C.H. Spurgeon, "Can Nothing Be Done for the Young?" *Sword and Trowel* 4 (April 1868): 147; Ibid., 4 (March 1868): 139, 140. Spurgeon went on to propose in his April article that the week-day school teacher could not be expected to instruct in the faith and suggested one or two evening meetings in the churches where such instruction could be given ("with the liberty of clapping their hands and cheering every now and then"), including participation by the children: "We have never developed the capabilities of youth as we should have done. We have been afraid of encouraging too much, and have discouraged. We have

been dubious of the depth and sincerity of children's graces," pp. 149, 150.

[10]*Sword and Trowel* 6 (June 1870): 285; Kruppa, *Spurgeon*, pp. 327–28.

[11]Ibid., pp. 328–30.

[12]*Sword and Trowel* 5 (August 1869): 381.

[13]Cited in Meredith, "Social and Political Views," pp. 65–66. For a full exposition of Gladstone's career, in a work sensitive to the religious dimensions in his life, see David W. Bebbington, *William Ewart Gladstone: Faith and Politics in Victorian Britain* (Grand Rapids: Eerdmans, 1993).

[14]Cited in Bebbington, *Nonconformist Conscience*, p. 90. Spurgeon did not actively campaign for the Conservatives in the election, but he did endorse only those Liberal candidates who opposed the Irish policy of Gladstone.

[15]The quotation in the following paragraph is from Ibid., p. 67.

[16]*Sword and Trowel* 16 (January 1880): 38; *Sword and Trowel* 12 (September 1876): 433.

[17]C.H. Spurgeon, "The Cry of the Heathen," *New Park Street Pulpit* 4 (1858): 197; C.H. Spurgeon, "One Lost Sheep," *Metropolitan Tabernacle Pulpit* 35 (1889): 252.

[18]*Sword and Trowel* 21 (March 1885): 147; C.H. Spurgeon, "Independence of Christianity," *New Park Street Pulpit* 3 (1857): 335; *Sword and Trowel* 15 (1879): 338. Quite in contrast to the oft-repeated accusation that in the nineteenth century the gospel followed the flag, Spurgeon wishes in his 1857 sermon that missionaries had gone to India without the British presence, for he asserts that "the help of the government would have been far worse than its opposition. I do regret that the [East India] Company sometimes discourages missionary enterprise; but I believe that, had they encouraged it, it would have been far worse still, for their encouragement would have been the greatest hindrance we could receive." "Independence of Christianity," p. 334.

[19]*Sword and Trowel* 16 (January 1880): 41.

[20]*Sword and Trowel* 6 (August 1870): 352–53; Meredith, "Social and Political Views," p. 94.

[21]*Sword and Trowel* 6 (September 1870): 433; C.H. Spurgeon, "Periodical War Madness," Ibid. 14 (April 1878): 149. Spurgeon's

views on war are well explored in David Nelson Duke, "Asking the Right Questions about War: A Lesson from C.H. Spurgeon's *Evangelical Quarterly* 61 (January 1989): 71–80.

[22]Spurgeon, "Periodical War Madness," *Sword and Trowel* 14 (April 1878): 145–49.

[23]*Sword and Trowel* 12 (June 1876): 285–86.

[24]*Sword and Trowel* 4 (March 1868): 140; Kruppa, *Spurgeon*, pp. 301–302, 311–14.

[25]Ibid., p. 320.

[26]Meredith, "Social and Political Views," pp. 99–100.

[27]Spurgeon, "Political Dissenter," p. 106.

Groen Van Prinsterer: Political Paradigm from the Past
by David W. Hall

Following the 1992 elections, numerous evangelicals turned to Scripture, to other Christians and to the history of the church for possible direction. In such searches, many Christians discovered that their spiritual fathers were the likes of Francis Schaeffer, Carl Henry and others. They, in turn, had spiritual fathers of their own, both on occasion, acknowledging their indebtedness to Abraham Kuyper, an earlier evangelical.

Abraham Kuyper, the Dutch statesman (prime minister in 1900) who combined principles and politics par excellence, thought that no aspects of life (even politics), "should remain untouched by the Christian. There is no important question of life in which the believer should refrain from seeking an answer from the Lord."[1] For Kuyper, and later Schaeffer, "the believer has a divine mandate to be the servant of Christ in every aspect of life . . . The Christian must seek to integrate scriptural norms with the realities of public life. The result must be the articulation of Christian political principles applied in a concrete national situation."[2] Kuyper saw the major political options in his own day as a choice between the "Liberty Tree" or the "Cross," and protested "Christ, not Voltaire, is the Lord Messiah over the nations."[3] Kuyper's counsel to evangelicals in his own day was as perceptive as it is for ours: "The question is not if the candidate's heart is favorable to Christianity, but if he has Christ as his starting-point *even for politics*, and will speak out for his name."[4] In that light, Kuyper criticized his own theological family: "the Evangelical Awakening as a spiritual movement was naively unaware of the titanic struggle between belief and unbelieving secularity, [and was] unhistoric in its ignorance of its own ties with the Christian past and lacking in theological substance."[5] Further, when it is noted that Kuyper exhorted, "As for us and our children, we will no longer kneel before the idol of the French Revolution; for the God of our fathers will again be our God,"[6] the spiritual genetic code, linking the likes of Kuyper and Schaeffer is all the clearer. Yet, this spiritual gene pool extends back at least one more generation from Kuyper. Much of Kuyper's thought was shaped by a previous generation's evangelical leader, William Groen Van Prinsterer (1801–1876), the subject of our examination.

In this discussion, I shall draw heavily upon his primary work, *Lectures on Unbelief and Revolution* (1847). Heretofore, except for a few aphorisms, no English translation of Groen Van Prinsterer's work has been available until very recently, despite the fact that at least 12 Dutch editions have been published.[7] This great gap led Henry Donald Morton to remark that an American Calvinist (or any evangelical for that matter), "deprived of access to the writings of Groen Van Prinsterer is like any American deprived of access to the thought of John Adams or Abraham Lincoln, like any Englishman unable to read Lord Acton or Edmund Burke!"[8] To help remedy this, Harry Van Dyke undertook an English translation of *Unbelief and Revolution* in 1974. In 1989 the first major English translation was completed.[9]

This essay will concentrate not on the full scope of Groen Van Prinsterer's thought, but on the narrower question of Christian political principles, seeking to distill his major tenets for use in our own day. This discussion will highlight and extract the following political notions from Groen Van Prinsterer's seminal and largely-unknown work in order to guide modern Christians in their efforts to pursue righteousness and morality in social policy. From this discussion, the following political principles emerge:

1) Political programs are inescapably value-laden, or based on ultimate philosophical principles.

2) Antithetical and irreconcilable ideologies are at war.

3) The dangers of rights-ism must be analyzed and exposed.

4) The limiting of pure democracy is necessary to honor the sovereignty of God.

5) The fruit of systemic unbelief is seen in our modern western governments.

6) Theology is necessary both for a correct ethic and a correct politic.

7) An analysis of systemic unbelief is a starting point for evangelical political involvement.

Biography of the Grandfather of Evangelical Political Action

Born in Voorburg on August 21, 1801, Groen (whose Christian name given at baptism, Guillaume, was reserved only for official use) was the oldest child of a physician. His father was a progressive and descendant from a line of preachers, while his mother was an aristocratic heiress from a prestigious banking family in Rotterdam. Such parentage afforded Groen many benefits and privileges. It also acquainted him with the tradition of the bourgeois. Receiving an excellent education in the classics, Groen was also catechized at his father's behest, making a formal profession of faith at age 17.[10]

At age 16 he entered college at Leyden, studying law and the classics. After six years of study he submitted and defended *two* doctoral dissertations on the same day, one on the Justinian Code, and the second on Plato. Following his academic work at Leyden, he practiced law in The Hague and continued his historical studies. In 1827 he became engaged to Elisabeth van der Hoop, a pious young lady who would later introduce Groen to J. H. Merle d'Aubigne, whose reformational preaching led in large measure to Groen's conversion. Groen and Elisabeth were married in the spring of 1828. She was a god-send in many ways, even assisting Groen and others in establishing nursery schools and other diaconal ministries near The Hague by 1832.[11]

In late 1827, Groen began to work in a series of government clerical appointments and gained access to the House of Orange family archives. During these years his reading of Burke, Haller, and Lamennais wrought a lasting influence on his thought. He also underwent a gradual but forceful conversion, likely around 1831 – 1832. D'Aubigne had become the court preacher in 1828, and through his regular Bible exposition, Groen came to understand the Lordship of Christ, not only over the individual soul but over politics and society as well. Although the specifics of his conversion can only be inferred, by early 1832 Groen is writing of his hope "that by God's grace that purely intellectual conviction may soon be personally applied to myself and genuinely appropriated."[12] Shortly thereafter, this thirst for righteousness seems to have been satisfied. The consistent witness to this conversion continued uninterrupted from 1833 to his death in 1876. The role of d'Aubigne in both expounding the scriptures and in impressing this new disciple, with the applicability of reformation thought to current issues, is undisputed. So close were the families, that d'Aubigne named his own son Willem, after Groen's Christian name.[13]

While what would become *Lectures on Unbelief and Revolution* was begun as early as 1831, Groen's first post-conversion writing was his *Essay on the Means by Which Truth is Known and Confirmed* (Leyden, 1834). During the balance of the 1830s, Groen devoted himself to archival research from the papers of the House of Orange, and accordingly has been dubbed the "father of modern Dutch historical research."[14] By the early 1840s, Groen had begun an overtly Calvinistic interpretation of Dutch history, *A Handbook of the History of the Fatherland* (completed in 1846). Groen was also an active churchman, supporting the Reveil, as well as an advocate for freedom in education.

By the late 1840s, Groen had established a reputation as an insightful social analyst. He gathered a group of about twenty influential thinkers to audit the series of lectures that formed his *magnum opus*. During 1847, these lectures were given and later published with little revision by Luchtmans in Leyden. Carrying a wide influence (particularly on Kuyper and the next generation), Groen's *Lectures* have gone through five revisions (and twelve separate editions, with theologian J.H. Bavinck writing the Preface to the 1904 edition). Finally, an English version was released in 1989, for the first time delivering Groen van Prinsterer directly to English speaking readers.

Groen served in the Second Chamber of government from 1849–1865, only voluntarily interrupting his service from 1857–1861 in order to complete a second series (five volumes) of *Archives*. From 1850–1855 he was Editor-in-chief of the daily *De Nederlander*, while serving in Parliament. Throughout the 1850s and 1860s, Groen was a vocal, if not always effective, advocate for anti-revolutionary principles in Dutch politics, repeatedly pleading for an educational system based on competitiveness, with Christian schools being allowed to compete on equal footing with secular schools. His death on May 19, 1876 occurred three years prior to the establishment of the first organized political party of the Netherlands, fittingly named for Groen van Prinsterer's thought, the Anti-revolutionary Party.

Among his other writings[15] were: *Oration on the Reasons for Making Known the Nation's History* (Brussells, 1829); *The Measures Against the Seceders Tested Against Constitutional Law* (Leyden, 1837), a defense of ecclesiastical separatists; *Documents Relative to the Refusal of a Privately Endowed School in The Hague* (The Hague, 1844); *Constitutional Revision and National Concord* (1849); *Selected Writings* (1859), various short essays from periodicals and journals. In addition, various unpublished treatises and essays (e.g. *Essay on the History and Consequences of the Growing Unity of Civilised Nations*) still await translation.

Political Principles from our Paradigm

(1) Political programs are inescapably value-laden, or based on ultimate philosophical principles. In other words, ultimate ideas have practical consequence.

Groen, unlike many evangelicals today, did not divide theology from politics. He realized that in politics, as in other endeavors, there was no true neutrality. The practical programs and policies that are adopted invariably have philosophical and ethical roots. If one begins with an agnostic or man-centered approach, that notion will infiltrate not only the ideas and macro-goals, but also the individual political implementations. There is an unavoidable connection between ultimate principles and their outworking in policy. Christians involved in politics need to recognize this inseparability, and analyze accordingly.

Groen Van Prinsterer noted as he began his lectures that he was doing so in a period of national humiliation and decline. (2) In a cultural situation similar to our own, he began by noting his agreement with Lamennais that "everything proceeds from doctrines; manners, literature, constitutions, laws, the happiness of nations and the misfortunes, cultural barbarism and those terrible crises that sweep nations away or else remove them, depending on their level of vitality." (5) He took a historical approach from the outset, noting that historical events "are nothing other than the shapes and contours that reveal the sustained action of the spirit of an age." (5) Thus he sought to demonstrate that events are the historical unfoldings of philosophical principles.

To politically-active evangelicals, who have learned the hard way that all politics are value-laden (local or not), Groen will fortify their resolve. To those who still pine for the idealistic mirage that imagines citizens acting apart from their base-values, Groen is a needed corrective. Of all citizens, evangelicals should embrace the political doctrine that not only do ultimate ideas have ultimate consequences, but moreover, ultimate ideas also spawn very practical consequences.

The two primary ideologies that Groen observed at work in western civilization in his time were the principles of the Revolution and the principles of the Reformation. By the "Revolutionary Principles" Groen referred to the French Revolution of 1789, and to the "general spirit and mode of thinking that is now manifest." (6) For Groen, the singular event of the 1789 Revolution was symbolic, signifying far more than an isolated coup. It represented an entire vein of philosophic thought, which was man-centered and opposed to God's sovereignty. Revolutionary ideas, although associated with the French Revolution, were much more than tools for that one revolt alone. These revolutionary ideas became the philosophic program for western humanism expressed in government.

Among the humanistic offspring of those who ultimately value *libertas, egalitas et fraternitas*, Groen exposes Revolutionary ideas as "the basic maxims of liberty and equality, popular sovereignty, social contract, the artificial reconstruction of society by common consent—notions which today are venerated as the cornerstone of constitutional law and the political order." (6) American evangelicals who seem inclined to embrace democracy as a sacred and inviolable rule may wish to reconsider, in light of Groen Van Prinsterer's critique and our own national abyss.

Moreover, Groen observed that wherever those particular theories and principles gained a foothold the people are "led about in a circle of misery and grief . . . a strict, consistent application of the Revolution doctrine will bring men to the most excessive absurdities and the worst atrocities." (6) Groen Van Prinsterer cites Bonald's putative pathology: "The Revolution began with a declaration of the rights of man; it will end only with the declaration of the rights of God." (7) He says that Revolutionary doctrine is "unbelief applied to politics. A life and death struggle is raging between the gospel and this practical atheism. To contemplate a rapprochement between the two would be nonsense. It is a battle which embraces everything we cherish and hold sacred."(8) Groen spoke of the battle over Revolutionary or unbelieving political principles more than 150 years ago in terms which sound very similar to the cultural war terminology frequently invoked today.

Groen urges Christians to become knowledgeable about the nature and direction of political philosophy in their time. He calls not merely for a general statement of Christian principles, but also insists that a Christian world view penetrate "into the inner recesses of science and the maze of historical events; it is our duty to learn to adore and revere the Lord even here in these His works." (10) Groen is keenly aware that our ignorance of history and constitutional law leads even evangelicals to "advocate very dubious opinions as soon as they enter upon the political terrain." (12)

Groen charges Christians with the duty of being involved in politics. He says that the church, "has been torn from the State only to be turned over to the State. Seceders have been persecuted in the name of modern justice. The government holds itself entitled to hamper Christian education if not to prevent it outright by controlling the public school and obstructing private initiatives towards an alternative." (13) Rightly, therefore, many evangelicals experience *déjà vu* when they read these words at the end of the twentieth century. Inevitably the ideas of either the Revolution or the Reformation work themselves out in practice according to their ideologies: "As the fruit is known by the tree, so shall the tree be known by its fruit." (15)

(2) Antithetical and irreconcilable ideologies are at war.

Groen Van Prinsterer previews this major distinction by contrasting the animating principle of the Revolution and the Reformation. He says:

> The [French] Revolution ought to be viewed in the context of world history. Its significance for Christendom equals that of the Reformation, but then in reverse. The Reformation rescued Europe from superstition; the Revolution has flung the civilized world into an abyss of unbelief. Like the Reformation, the Revolution touches every field of action and learning. In the days of the Reformation the principle was submission to God; these days it is a revolt against God. . . The Revolution proceeds from the sovereignty of man, the Reformation proceeds from the Sovereignty of God. The one has revelation judged by reason; the other submits reason to revealed truths. The one unleashes individual opinions; the other leads to unity of faith. The one loosens social bonds, even family ties; the other strengthens and sanctifies them. The latter triumphs through martyrs; the former maintains itself by massacres. The one ascends out of the bottomless pit and the other comes down out of heaven. (14)

Groen was convinced that just as the underlying premises of any argument determined its outcome, so the underlying premises of social movements could be evaluated as to their validity in light of Scripture. Underpinning all social movement is one ideology or another. At their base, all social and political programs were founded either on God's prescriptions for society, or on man's. Whether or not a movement was founded on theocentric or anthropocentric ordering determines its outcome. In the interim, these two base ideologies are at war.

On the advantage of the Christian ideology, Groen notes, "The Christian knows a principle which gives steadiness to political thought and which, if followed, would be sufficient to restore the tottery political structures on unshakable foundations." (18) On the antiquity of the Christian politic, he says in sum, "The anti-revolutionary or Christian-historical position finds unequivocal confirmation in the unanimous testimony of former times." (22) So, says Groen Van Prinsterer, the written Word of God becomes the "ax that cuts off every root of revolutionary misgrowth." (23) As historian, he chronicles at length the notion that the church and orthodox theology (throughout the ages) have contended in matters of politics, with theology at the forefront, not closeting theological values away like awkward step-children.

Groen asserts that when the Revolution came about, modern secularists had to change not only theology, but history as well. This newer torch of wisdom, this post-1789 history, "projected onto peoples and periods ideas that were wholly foreign to them . . . history became a false witness, and this false witness became yet another powerful means of pressing public opinion into the harness of the revolutionary school. History became a pantheon lined with revolutionary paragons, an arsenal filled with revolutionary weapons for murdering the truth." (24) This resulted in alienation: "We may feel isolated in face of the spirit of our age, but the age itself stands isolated in the history of the world." (29)

A knowledgeable historian, Groen speaks of historical figures like Grotius and others (28), noting their downfall as emblematic of a faulty foundational ideology. The key, according to Groen Van Prinsterer, is this: "Once and for all disposed of the dangerous doctrines of popular sovereignty and an original social contract . . . the newer theories rested on a single untrue assumption: that the state arose from human consent which put an end to the state of nature." (37) This human-oriented consent lies at the heart of the Revolutionary principle. The result of the principle is that an unavoidable and unresolvable conflict arises among these presuppositional ideologies.

(3) The dangers of Rights-ism must be analyzed and exposed.

One of the most dangerous expressions of revolutionary ideas is the preferred status awarded to the notion of individual rights. As our society searches for a rights-centered ethic to guarantee homosexual service in the military, health-insurance for all, and the explosion of rights claims for nearly everything, we can acknowledge Groen's foresight. He predicted the errors of this approach a century and a half ago. Most perceptively he identified the totalitarian expansionism of Rights-ism, which unravels the social fabric, if it is allowed to flourish in a body politic. The claimants to rights-for-everything are the genetic offspring of Revolutionary ideas, not the biblical ethos. A first step to recovering a Christian polity is to refute Rights-ism. In our own time, when justice has become hostage to radical notions of individual rights, the Christian must often return to this theme.

Reminding his readers that "rights" had become more important than justice (45), Groen says, "Justice, in a philosophical sense essential and historical par excellence, was placed above History. It was this dominion of Right over fact that gave rise to a whole series of acquired rights." (46) Whereas formerly respect "for acquired rights meant . . . respect for the highest principles of justice." (47), this was not so after the French Revolution, when a dangerous dogma was created in which men used rights "to demand passivity for subordination, to mistake autonomy for independence, to regard free activity as rebellion, in every respect to subject everything found within the state's territory to the arbitrary will of the state, to oppose on principle any self-government of private persons or corporations . . ." (47)

In sum, Groen alleges that in the revolutionary reconstruction, "Too much attention was paid to questionable historic rights, to the detriment of general principles of justice." (44) At the heart of his criticism is the extension of alleged rights and privileges into nearly every domain. Observing that "Rights have been represented as limitless when in fact they did have limits" (98), he notes that in the very theoretical concepts and definition of the state after the Revolutionary idea took hold, commonwealths were superimposed backwards onto monarchies, thus a "false idea arose that the state must be viewed as an association." (130) Groen diagnoses the historical obfuscation: "[M]onarchical unity was confused with republican union; aggregation was held to be association; every state was made over into a society, a community of citizens; monarchy was reasoned away, and the kingdoms of Europe were delivered up to discord and dissolution." (130)

One of our contemporary critics of rights as an underlying and absolute sub-strata of modern thought has similarly enunciated the same theme. The echo is striking:

> The American rights dialect is distinguished not only by what we say and how we say it, but also by what we leave unsaid. Each day's newspapers, radio broadcasts and television programs attest to our tendency to speak of whatever is most important to us in terms of rights, and to our predilection for overstating the absoluteness of the rights we claim. Habitual silences concerning responsibilities are more apt to remain unnoticed . . . [and some] fail to grasp the other half of the democratic equation . . . personal responsibilities, serving the community, and participating in the nation's political life. . . . The strident

170

*rights rhetoric that currently dominates American political
discourse poorly serves the strong tradition of protection for
individual freedom for which the United States is justly
renowned. Our stark simple rights dialect puts a damper
on the processes of public justification, communication,
and deliberation upon which the continuing vitality of the
democratic regime depends.*[16]

Groen's primary goal is to convince his audience that all
real power is ordained by God: "The powers that be are
not just tolerated. They are willed, instituted, sanctified
by God himself." (51) While not arguing for absolute
divine right ("We do not identify the will of any
sovereign with the will of God." (50)), Groen notes a distinction between power and might or force: "All true
legislation emanates from God. . . . Depart from this, and
I see only arbitrary wills and a degrading rule of force, I
see only men insolently lording it over other men, I see
only slaves and tyrants." (56) If American evangelicals
recognize this fruit in their own civil government, perhaps it is time to consider Groen's analysis of the root.

(4) The limiting of pure democracy is necessary to honor the sovereignty of God.

Groen Van Prinsterer was also prescient in warning
westerners that democracy per se was not a political
panacea. Democracy, although one of the greatest blessings to human freedom in our time, was not the *deus ex
machina* mandated by revelation. Many evangelicals con-
fuse cause and effect, thereby in practice elevating
democracy to an absolute. Although it has brought much
prosperity and liberty, democracy must not — unless
Scripture sanctions — be raised to a political *summum
bonum.* To do so risks elevating corporate human
sovereignty above God's sovereignty. Surely the Christian
may support a limited democracy, ideally one characterized by loyalty to God's rule, even above human plebi-
scite. Jesus's own teaching is applicable to the conflict

between competing political systems: "You cannot serve two masters. For either you will hate the one and love the other, or love the one and hate the other." In political options, such bifurcation may oblige the choice between human sovereignty via democracy, or God's sovereignty. To further support this, merely watch an unrighteous official be chosen by a plurality of voters, and take note of how democracy can be less than felicitous at times.

Groen consistently warns of the danger of a pure democracy. It is unable to deliver righteousness if founded upon the will of unregenerate people. He says, "Whence it follows that there neither is, nor can be, any fundamental law that is binding upon the body of the People, not even the Social Contract itself." (207) He calls the systems of Rousseau and Hobbes monstrous, looking to government as possessing a "provisional mandate, subject to cancellation or modification at the people's pleasure." (208) The result is that "any real distinction between democracy, aristocracy, or monarchy no longer exists" (209). When the "elections are over, they are slaves, they are nothing." (210)

Thus Groen cautions against the danger of unbridled majority rule, reminding us that freedom is founded only in submission to the law and not in submission to the "detestable despotism of the majority." (210) "If freedom means unconditional obedience to the good pleasure of men, then freedom is a fiction." (212)

Groen then reviews the basic historic forms of government and has as the chief focus of his criticism absolutizing the consent of the people. He notes that democracy depended upon an election or mandate of the people for its success. When "the law is made with the consent of the people and by the declaration of the King," proper power begins to diminish. Hence, according to Groen, historians who supported the Revolution necessarily had to reconstrue ancient history in order to democratize the ancient monarchs with a strong dose of revisionism.

In chapter six, Groen speaks at length of the perversion of constitutional law. The very vocabulary of politics had become corrupt. The etymological meaning of words was gradually driven out by revisionist meanings. (126) By such linguistic subterfuge, Groen shows how "monarchies" were transformed into "republics," and "subjects" were translated into "citizens."[17] Language is an important indicator and current of value. He notes that "men lived in monarchies and dreamt of republics . . . since it is a basic need of the human mind to reconcile fancy with reality there was only one solution—to decide that every monarchy, too, is a republic[18] in origin." (129) Thus, Groen Van Prinsterer teaches that the beginning decline into democratism was well underway by his own time.

Groen notes that this was not merely the idea of one Revolution, but that the Revolution of 1789 illustrates that the "theoretic unfolding on every page of its history must have had a theoretic origin." (119) He believes that even the philosophic theory of liberty, which has swept western civilization since 1789, was "born of doctrine," (120) and specifically the doctrine of the rights of man. So he catechizes, "If the king is an autocrat within a republic, whence his authority? By delegation. On the part of whom? The majority of citizens. In what manner? By convention and social contract. To what end? To look after the public interest. On what terms? Joint consultation and responsibility. For how long? Till the favor is forfeited or the mandate revoked." (130) Thus he sees a universal error in which post-revolutionary humanists "accepted a social pact as the precondition of the state" (131), and comments that even the best of scholars have "been sucked into the maelstrom." (131) A false notion "of the state was found everywhere," says Groen, as the social contract thoughts of non-Christian philosophers began to rule the day (135). He notes that whatever one's view of the state in a post-revolutionary construction, the social contract "leaves but two avenues: anarchy or tyranny, depending on personal inclination, character, and circumstances." (136) Oddly, many evangelical prognosticators are sounding the self-same alarm, warning against these two paths in our own day, reminiscent of others who have warned, "Without God society can be constituted only by the artificial authority of the special interests or the passions of the moment."[19]

If Groen Van Prinsterer has begun to sound like Burke it is no wonder. He acknowledged his indebtedness to Burke, who similarly had denounced:

> *If I recollect rightly, Aristotle observes that a democracy has many striking points of resemblance with a tyranny. Of this I am certain, that in a democracy the majority of the citizens is capable of exercising the most cruel oppressions upon the minority whenever strong divisions prevail in that kind of polity, as they often must; and that oppression of the minority will extend to far greater numbers and will be carried on with much greater fury than can almost ever be apprehended from the dominion of a single scepter. In such a popular persecution, individual sufferers are in a much more deplorable condition than in any other . . . those who are subjected to wrong under multitudes are deprived of all external consolation. They seem deserted by mankind, overpowered by a conspiracy of their whole species.[20]*

Burke also recognized that Aristotle (cf. *Politics*, book iv., chap. 4) realized the same dangers:

> *The ethical character is the same; both exercise despotism over the better class of citizens; and decrees are in the one, what ordinances and arrets are in the other: the demagogue, too, and the court favorite are not infrequently the same identical men, and always bear a close analogy; and these have the principal power, each in their respective forms of government, favorites with the absolute monarch, and demagogues with a people such as I have described.[21]*

After discussing Thomas Hobbes's view of the social contract, Groen criticizes the government that becomes the tool of arbitrary will as a devouring monster, a Leviathan. So he finds that various acts, including criminal acts and ownership of property, become beholden to common consent. On the other hand, Algernon Sidney held that the association "is and remains the true Sovereign," (138) thus illustrating Groen's point that once the Revolutionary principles are assumed there are two and only two options: the options of statism under the control of a tyrant, or rank anarchism. Groen Van Prinsterer consistently maintains that the Revolution is the result of the perversion of constitutional law. The attendant Revolutionary theories flow from that font of perversion. He means that Revolutionary theories such as "popular sovereignty, social contract, responsible government, and, as soon as there is popular displeasure, a sacred right to revolt" (142) inescapably ferment: "The Revolution simply realized the republican ideas under constitutional forms, while eliminating whatever used to stop them from being implemented in full." (143)

A profound misconception—that the blame for this non-authoritarianism derived from Calvinism's spread—had taken root at the highest level of principle. Groen carefully points out that this blame cannot be laid at the feet of reformational Calvinists. In Lecture Six he defends the Reformation as not culpable for this newfound freedom: "Calvinism assuredly never led to any sort of republicanism. . . . Calvinists evinced the opposite" (148) in calling for submission. Rather than rebellion, the Reformation principle called for order, submission and an embrace of divine schemes of authority. Repeatedly, Groen defends the Reformation principle. He says that its basic premise was not unrestricted liberty, but a "liberty that is grounded in submission." (156) Furthermore, Groen notes: "A doctrine that points to the total depravity of man is little suited to foster self-exaltation." (158) A theologically informed view of civil government will heed Groen Van Prinsterer's warnings concerning the effect of human depravity.

According to Groen, "the Reformation . . . stemmed the tide of revolutionary unbelief in the sixteenth century . . . only through the flagging of the spirit of the Reformation did revolutionary unbelief gain the upper hand, in the eighteenth century." (165) The germ of unbelief was strong and continued to grow. Groen spoke of this unbelief as "political atheism." He extolled the virtue of the Reformation in intervening: "Into the midst of unbelief and insurrection it flung the principle of faith and obedience, so conducive to wholesome order through the marriage of freedom and submission. . . . The fundamental principle of submission to God both shored up the tottering authority of governments and shielded the liberties of subjects, thereby arresting the advance of the republican theories with their revolutionary leaven." (168–169) He argues that the Reformation could not possibly cause the Revolution, "since it sprang from an antithetical principle: from objective unity of faith rather than diversity of subjective opinions; from the infallibility of Revelation rather than the supremacy of Reason; from the sovereignty of God rather than the sovereignty of man." (176) Groen notes that once faith departed, Christian Europe was dechristianized (178): "Indeed, the last state was worse than the first. The reign of unbelief had arrived. Revolution was now inevitable. For the principle of unbelief, once admitted, propels men from consequence to consequence, ever further down the path of ruin. Once the bond is cut asunder that ties mankind to heaven, none can stop the rush to the abyss." (179) A century and a half later, many American evangelicals utter the "Amen" to that in our own country.

Even earlier, Richard Baxter, for example, had sensed the possible incongruity between pure democracy and honor to God's sovereignty. Baxter, in opposition to the Ranters, Seekers, Levellers and other sects of the seventeenth century, warned that pure democracy would invariably lead to heresy (as well as political disaster): "That the major[ity] vote of the people should ordinarily be just and good is next to an impossibility . . . All this stir of the Republicans is but to make the seed of the Serpent to be the sovereign rulers of the earth . . . The greatest heresy of all was that . . . all [men] had a spark of the divine in them, and so, that all men were equal."[22] Unlimited democracy is incompatible with a Christian allegiance to the sovereignty of God. Thus, evangelicals involved in politics must necessarily place limited trust in democracy alone as a cure for the ills of society.

(5) The fruit of systemic unbelief is seen in our modern western governments.

In Lecture Eight, Groen describes unbelief as "the force of an irresistible march of events" (181) founded upon the Revolutionary principles. He says that the "real formative power throughout the revolutionary era, right up to our own time, has been atheism, godlessness, being without God. . . . From the unbelieving nature of the Revolution one can predict its history. Conversely, in the facts of its history one can discern the constant tokens of its un-believing origin." (182) That Revolution would stem from atheism and return to it, Groen warned, was a "necessary consequence" (182), "a matter of plain logic that atheism in religion and radicalism in politics are not only not the exaggeration, misuse or distortion, but in fact the consistent and faithful application, of a principle which sets aside the God of Revelation in favor of the supremacy of Reason." (183)

Groen's argument is that "where unbelief is free to run its natural course in religion and politics, it cannot but lead to the most radical doctrines." (183) The basic credo of the Revolution is "the sovereignty of man, independent of the sovereignty of God," which Groen considers radically false: "Once orthodoxy failed to preserve this rich heritage, it fell into the hands of the philosophers." (187) Moreover, says Groen, "Revolution is in its entirety nothing other than the logical outcome of systematic unbelief, the outworking of apostasy from the Gospel. My argument will be concerned with religion and with politics . . . Since religion and society have the same origin, God, and the same end, man, a fundamental error in religion is also a fundamental error in politics . . . the Revolution doctrine is the religion, as it were, of unbelief. It is the negation of everything resting upon belief . . . The principle of this vaunted philosophy was Reason, and the outcome was apostasy from God and materialism." (191–192)

Painfully, evangelicals have come to recognize that indeed while there is organizational separation of church and state, there can be no divorce between religious belief and the values of civil government. The predominant religion of our age is still that of systematic unbelief, and Atheism does intrude and impose itself in government. Seeing that these stem from the humanist revolution may be the beginning of political wisdom.

(6) Theology is necessary both for a correct ethic and a correct politic.

Evangelicals, of all groups, should realize the unavoidable theological foundation for ethics and politics. It may be most clear in the latter twentieth century, as we see the blossom of humanism in our own government, that we cease debating whether or not all politics are theological in both root and fruit. One can certainly analyze various political ideas and programs in light of their ultimate principles, which are hardly theologically neutral. Religious belief is inseparably connected to social and political proposals.

Groen Van Prinsterer notes that "Without belief in God there is no basis for morality." (195) Later he says, "Atheism cannot tolerate the truth, because it cannot be tolerated by the truth. It recognizes a mortal enemy in every belief. It puts up with the least hint of that religion only that keeps silent, that bends its neck, that submits to the rules and regulations of unbelief. Atheism equalizes all religions all right—provided all are equally destitute of the signs of vigor and life." (199) In addition he cites Burke: "They who do not love religion, hate it. The rebels to God perfectly abhor the author of their being. They hate him 'with all their heart, with all their mind, with all their soul, and with all their strength'. . . . Indeed, the defining feature of the Revolution is its hatred of the Gospel, its anti-Christian nature. This feature marks the Revolution, not when it 'deviates from its course' and 'lapses into excesses,' but precisely when it holds to its course and reaches the conclusion of its system, . . . the Revolution will never be able to shake it off." (200) Revolutionary humanism does have a religious root, a root embedded in the ancient soil of hideous rebellion and repudiation of God. The theology of a politician or advocacy group is detectable. According to Groen Van Prinsterer, they all grow from one root or the other, from systematic belief or unbelief.

The same principle of unbelief, Groen says, "operates in philosophy proper, in elevating the supremacy of reason, which "culminates in atheism and materialism." (201) The mainstays of this philosophy are revolutionary liberty, or the sovereignty of the human will, [which] dissipates itself in the depths of radicalism." (201) So Groen Van Prinsterer argues that it is an inevitable step from "the chimerical idea of making every man's reason independent of all authority, or of destroying all faith completely, to the no less ridiculous project of emancipating men from every temporal ruler" (202). Thus the foundation of all rights and duties lies in the sovereignty of God, he says, and "When that Sovereignty is denied, what becomes of the fountain of authority, of law, of every sacred and dutiful relation in state, society, and family?" (203) Groen Van Prinsterer's answer is that they all deteriorate, noting that:

There can be, despite all social diversities, no real dif-
ference among men. Eliminate God, and it can no longer
be denied that all men are, in the revolutionary sense of
the words, free and equal. . . . Henceforward the state is
conceived as a multitude of indivisible particles, of atoms.
. . . From the standpoint of unbelief, to liquidate every
form of independent authority means to remove an abuse
that is degrading to humanity. And from that standpoint
the judgment is correct, since unbelief knows only human
authority. It is the denial of the divine right of authority
that we find the source, not only of liberalism, but of the
perfervour which it generates. (203)

In contrast to the Christian emphasis on historical continuity, the neophilic Revolution holds that "innovation
is the only wisdom available" (205), and furthermore,
"Through mutual consent alone" . . . is the state founded.

(7) An anatomy of the conquest of systemic unbelief is a starting point for evangelical political involvement.

Groen gives hope by arguing that an ill-founded politic
will inevitably run its course because there is an "unavoidable collision of truth and law." (223) Sounding
similar to one recent observation regarding the Com-
munist collapse, that "Reality is resilient,"[23] moreover,
Groen also advises that despite attempts to modify these
reality-induced correctives, such that the extremes are not
felt, nonetheless the ideas will bear fruit. Of their consequences, Groen lists the following: "First it will try as
much as possible to get rid of every notion of the Divine,"
(226); it will turn to "superstition and idolatry" (228); and
"it will falsely conclude that it will be as ridiculous to
believe in God as it is today to believe in ghosts; the day
will come when we shall believe only in ghosts." (228)
Groen Van Prinsterer then identifies the five stages of
this unfolding Revolution: (1) a period of preparation; (2)
a time of development, in which the champions of
progress are compelled to move forward with their refor-

180

mation and are largely successful; (3) a period of reaction; (4) a period of renewed experimentation when the reaction ends; and (5) a period of despair regarding liberty and indifference about justice. This phase, Groen calls "despondent resignation."

Thus, the French Revolution in its declaration of the rights of man destroys civil liberty, property, political liberty, freedom of religion and a number of basic values which are necessary for a sturdy civilization. Any system founded on that same philosophical root will yield similar results.

In the next three Lectures Groen Van Prinsterer seeks to chronicle historically his earlier enunciated thesis about the phases inherent in the Revolution. In Lecture Eleven he summarizes that, "the germ of error and corruption, must in theory and practice culminate in atheism and radicalism." (260) He notes that he finds this confirmed in practice and that the Revolution is a major idea which develops into "a systematic rebellion against the revealed God." (262) Groen Van Prinsterer assesses the Revolution as a European Revolution which had as one of its outcomes the overturning of Christendom (263), while at the same time destroying the foundations of law (264). He moreover notes that the Revolutionary principle had an organic relationship connecting Jacobinism, Bonapartism, and Constitutionalism all as branches of the same tree. He asserts again that the only remedy for this is that those citizens must "turn to God whose truth alone can resist the power of the lie." (271)

Groen depicts the Revolution as the "systematic application of the philosophy of unbelief; with its crimes and massacres and devastation; with its self-deification and its adoration of Reason on the ruins of the ancient state." (293) Moreover he says, "What happened in 1789 had to happen" (294), a clear example of the ideological determinism apparent in his work. Groen says that once the Revolution has begun, "ceaseless forward movement, amid a progressively more vehement struggle; release of every moral and legal bond; compulsory unity under the iron yoke of an increasingly more violent centralized government" (296) is unleashed. The Revolution, then, was not an anomaly but a typical analogy (321), characterized as a "symphony of hell, a harmonious chord and a most worthy finale . . . [a] political descent into Inferno." (329–330)

Groen concludes, "Such is the final fruit of liberalism, that men, having lost liberty, also lose the love of liberty and the belief in liberty!" (394). As to possible solutions, he recommends: "Only from a revival of Christian charity and Evangelical spirit can we draw strength to match unbelief and derive the confidence without which no self-sacrifice, no progress, no improvement is possible. Only through faith in the Son of the living God can the Revolution be vanquished." (396)

Groen characterized the life of post-revolutionary Europe as dominated by "revolutionary autocracy." He noted the totalitarian impulse of the modern democratic state: "We do not really live in a monarchy, nor in a republic, but under a centralizing, all-controlling government which is either exercised personally or else conveniently distributed among high state officials. We are living under the almighty power of a revolutionary government under one head, a government limited *de jure* in a variety of ways, *de facto* in no way whatsoever." (414)

In many ways, Groen Van Prinsterer was a predictor of things to come in the next 150 years. He predicted trends such as the rise of socialism, the dominance of rights-centeredness, and the ills of relativism in political ideals. If the governmental system advocated by Groen (culminating with Abraham Kuyper) is compared with our own present system, and if Jesus' standard, "By their fruit ye shall know them" is applied, evangelicals cannot help but embrace this anti-revolutionary principle. To do so is to link arms across space and time with the reformers, and to pursue reformation according to Scripture once again. Such might even contain unifying promise for those of disparate backgrounds, who are united in their disdain of humanism in its political manifestations.

Certainly Groen is not without criticism. His major work was criticized by his contemporaries as one-sided, immoderate, derivative, internally contradictory and selective.[24] Later critics have attacked his method as aprioristic and partisan. He is also open to criticism for style, but more substantively for his apparent identification of the Kingdom of God too closely with a particular movement. Certainly specific historical conclusions may be challenged, Groen's monarchical bias may be questioned, and his methodology scrutinized. Indeed criticism of Groen's work is now possible, and will certainly be profitable. Yet, along with such criticism will also come a familiarity that will be beneficial.

It is also imperative that we take stock of potential evangelical forays into politics in our own times. Have we been very successful, while not benefitting from the counsel of the likes of Groen Van Prinsterer? It is hard at this time to empirically show much advance for all the evangelical efforts in the past two decades. If we see that even tenuous gains can lapse in a few months, we must wonder at our foundation. If we have failed, then "Whither?" In light of the recent exhibitions of Rights-ism run amok, it may be an opportune time to review Groen Van Prinsterer and begin to reconstruct a more enduring form of evangelical politics on some other basis.

Moreover, a proper acquaintance with Groen can serve as a proper hermeneutic to clarify much of the intrinsic thought of Abraham Kuyper. And this instructive model from the past is equally capable of serving as a predictive model for the future. Will evangelicals continue to build on sandy foundations? Or are we ready to reconstruct a new and more viable Christian political platform? It may depend on how desperate we become. In any of these scenarios a familiarity with Groen Van Prinsterer is long overdue. As a leading Kuyper student, McKendree Langley predicted, "If evangelicals neglect to concern themselves with this political aspect of sanctification, they will increasingly find themselves socially impotent to bring a healing influence upon American life."[25]

Endnotes

[1]Summarized in Ibid., p. 5.

[2]Ibid.,

[3]Ibid., p. 7.

[4]Ibid., p. 6.

[5]Ibid., p. 7.

[6]Ibid.

[7]A brief summary of Groen's thought is provided by McKendree Langley in "The Witness of a World View" in *Pro Rege*, December 1979, Col. VIII, No. 2, pp. 3–6. Also in 1976 Lectures XI and VIII–IX were published as separate monographs by the Christian Studies Center (Memphis, TN). Prior to the 1976 centennial, which revived efforts to publish Groen in English, mere summaries were available (see Van Dyke below, pp. 206–207). W. Robert Godfrey in "Church and State in Dutch Calvinism," *Through Christ's Word*, ed. by Godfrey and Jesse L. Boyd III (Phillipsburg, NJ: Presbyterian and Reformed, 1985) gives a succinct summary of the thought and importance of Groen. He also refers to a 1956 translation of Groen Van Prinsterer by J. Faber.

[8]*Guillaume Groen Van Prinsterer: Selected Studies* by J.L. Van Essen and H.D. Morton (Ontario: Wedge, 1989), p. 8.

[9]Published by Wedge Publishing, Ontario, 1989. The references in parentheses in the remainder of this essay are to enumerated paragraphs (which format was selected by the translator, rather than pagination) in the 1989 Van Dyke version.

[10]Harry Van Dyke includes a readable and thorough biographical sketch in *Lectures on Unbelief and Revolution* (Ontario: Wedge, 1989), pp. 39–83, from which most of this summary is taken.

[11]Ibid., p. 27.

[12]Ibid., p. 48.

[13]Ibid., p. 56.

[14]Ibid., p. 54.

[15]According to Van Essen (op. cit., p. 44), 152 writings of Groen were annotated in a 1973 doctoral dissertation.

[16]*Rights Talk: The Impoverishment of Political Discourse* by Mary Ann Glendon (New York: The Free Press, 1991), pp. 76, 171.

[17]For a thorough treatise on this idea, see *Citizens: A Chronicle of the French Revolution* by Simon Schama (New York: Knopf, 1989).

[18]No doubt, Groen Van Prinsterer meant a democratic body-politic by this phrase.

[19]McKendree Langley paraphrasing Lamennais in "God and Liberty" *supra*, p. 16.

[20]*Reflections on the Revolution in France* by Edmund Burke, ed. by J.G.A. Pocock (Indianapolis: Hackett, 1987), pp. 109–110. For the latest in modern revisionism, one might consult *The Great Melody: A Thematic Biography and Commented Anthology of Edmund Burke* by Conor Cruise O'Brien (Chicago: University of Chicago Press, 1993), to see an argument that Burke was not really very conservative.

[21]Ibid., p. 110.

[22]Cited in *The Century of Revolution* by Christopher Hill (Edinburgh: Thomas Nelson, 1961), p. 167.

[23]Michael Bauman in *Man and Marxism* (Hillsdale, MI: Hillsdale College Press, 1991), p. 4.

[24]Van Dyke, op. cit., pp. 4–5.

[25]"The Political Spirituality of Abraham Kuyper," op. cit., p. 9.

The Kingdom of God in George Eldon Ladd as a Theological Foundation for the Role of the Church in Society

by Brad Harper

*T*he concept of the kingdom of God has traditionally been an important means of understanding the relationship between Christ and Caesar. Louis Berkhof noted in his 1951 work, *The Kingdom of God*, that the theology of the kingdom has increased dramatically as a topic of debate since the end of the nineteenth century. More recently, George Eldon Ladd functioned as a theologian of the kingdom of God par excellence. Not only did Ladd dedicate his career to the development of the theology of the kingdom, but a recent survey showed him one of the most influential theologians of any era in the minds of evangelical scholars today.[1] In addition, Ladd's paradigm of the kingdom of God is often cited in the search to form a theology of the role of the church in society.

As a theologian of the neo-evangelical movement, Ladd rejected the dispensational view of the kingdom, which had dominated fundamentalist eschatology. He departed from its idea that the kingdom was completely apocalyptic and in no way present in the church age. Ladd also rejected the idea which dominated early twentieth century liberal theology, that the kingdom of God was an ethical reality to be slowly realized in human society. Ladd argued that Scripture supports the idea that the kingdom is both present now and not yet present, and that in Jesus it invaded human history—with its final eschatological form still to come.

This essay will consider Ladd's "now and not yet" view as a foundation for the role of the church in society. I shall discuss Ladd's theology in light of five key issues in the current debate.

Issue # 1: The Task of the Kingdom in Relation to Culture

Ladd's view of the kingdom of God reflected his self-conscious position as a mediating figure between liberal/critical scholarship and dispensationalism. Ladd rejected the tendency of the liberal/critical school to demythologize the future earthly aspect of the kingdom in favor of immanence. Such a position robbed the message of the kingdom of the biblical expectancy of an apocalyptic act of God that would establish and enforce his ethical standards once and for all. The effect of the dispensational position was just the opposite. It robbed the message of the kingdom of its intended influence on life in this age by postponing the ethical demands of the kingdom to a future millennium. Dispensationalist writers despaired of any hope that the ethics of the kingdom would impact society. They rejected the idea of moral progress for this world, concluding that the expectation of Christ and the apostles was utterly pessimistic.

According to Ladd, both the majority of dispensationalists and critical scholars made unwarranted separations between eschatology and ethics. The critical scholars separated the ethics of the kingdom from the future. Thus, they lost the sense of hope that comes from the expectation of a righteous kingdom to be brought suddenly into history by the power of God. The dispensationalists separated the ethics of the kingdom from the present. Thus, they lost the power of the kingdom to have a significant impact on society.

Ladd's solution to this problem is found in the "already and not yet" character of his theology of the kingdom, in which ethics must be interpreted in light of the dynamic presence of God's rule, which has already manifested itself in Jesus, and will be fully consummated in the eschatological hour. The eschatology of Jesus was both apocalyptic, in that it looked forward to a future deliverance of God's people into a completely righteous and ethical kingdom, and prophetic, in that it spoke to society and called for ethics that reflected the character of a kingdom that was only to come fully later.

The task of the kingdom in relation to culture is a function of the relationship between the kingdom and the church. Ladd found the fundamental issue in the relationship between the kingdom and the church in the definition of the kingdom as God's rule itself. The kingdom is the rule of God, and God's rule has a people, which is the church. "However," remarked Ladd,

> *The church is not the kingdom. The church is the people of God, while the kingdom is primarily the rule of God, and only secondarily the blessings of his rule and the sphere in which these blessings are enjoyed. The church is the instrument or the agency of the kingdom.*[2]

As the agency of the kingdom of God, the church has several key roles to play. Among those roles, it is the church's job to witness to the kingdom. This role was illustrated by the commission Jesus gave to the twelve and the seventy to preach the kingdom. The church is also to be the instrument of the kingdom. After the departure of Christ and the formation of the church, the disciples not only preached the kingdom, but also were instruments of its power as they healed the sick and cast out demons. And in their preaching, they were instruments of the kingdom to bring assurance of ultimate victory over death. As such, the church was an instrument of the power of the kingdom over the power of Satan.

For Ladd, the kingdom and the church were not identical, but were inseparably related. The church exists now as the realm in which the kingdom of God is presently active. The kingdom creates, works through and is proclaimed by the church.

Ladd contended that his dynamic concept of the kingdom of God suggested several principles for social ethics. First, the kingdom of God does not allow for the idea of a social utopia. "If the kingdom of God belongs to the age to come, we are never to expect that this age will see the full realization of God's rule."[3] The ideal social order will only be attained at the apocalyptic consummation of the kingdom at the return of Christ to earth. Because the kingdom is, at present, only partially realized, society can only partially reflect its character. Social utopias are also impossible in this age because of the radical nature of evil. While Ladd could affirm along with early twentieth century liberals that God is the Lord of history, he could not share the prevailing views of liberalism that evil was but one stage in human development. Evil is a terrible enemy of human well-being and will never be outgrown or abandoned until God intervenes to purge it from the earth. It is so radical that it can only be eradicated by the mighty intervention of God.

However, Ladd did believe that evil has a social character and that this age is characterized by evil. But evil is essentially personal, not structural. Goodness and evil are not impersonal entities. They inhere in persons and only in persons. Such a perspective separated Ladd unalterably from any social interpretation of the kingdom. If evil is at the root of human nature and is personal, it cannot be eliminated by human power, nor by the progress of society.

The second principle suggested by Ladd is that the rejection of a social interpretation of the kingdom should not lead to apocalyptic pessimism. In contrast to late Jewish apocalyptic, which was entirely pessimistic about any manifestation of the kingdom in this age, Jesus taught that the kingdom of God has invaded the present age. The powers of evil have been attacked and defeated. The kingdom of God is presently in conflict with Satan and should manifest its power in history through the church. Ladd saw the influence of the kingdom upon society as a function of Christ's disciples, who are to be salt and light. They are to expose evil in every quarter and to make an impact on society according to the character of the ethics of the kingdom.

Third, the presence and power of the kingdom of God must not be relegated to spiritual realities. Ladd believed that "the presence of God's kingdom in Jesus was concerned not only with the spiritual welfare of men but also with their physical well being."[4] The eschatological kingdom will mean both the resurrection of the body and the transformation of the social order. The kingdom of God is concerned with suffering that takes place on a physical level, both in the lives of individuals and within the structures of society.

In Ladd's view, the power of the kingdom over physical effects of evil in this age is part of the meaning behind the exorcisms performed by Jesus. He addressed the pain and suffering of human experience in order to rebuke the evil that caused it and deliver people from its effects here and now. He came not only to bear human sins, but its diseases and infirmities as well. Jesus' disciples not only preached the gospel, but healed the sick. These acts were signs of the presence and power of the kingdom they proclaimed and have clear implications for the ongoing activity of the kingdom in society. "Those who are instruments of the kingdom can never limit their interest to the souls of men and their eschatological salvation. The Kingdom of God is concerned to rescue men from every possible influence of evil, for it is concerned not only with the soul, but with the whole man."[5] Thus, the agents of the kingdom must be concerned with the physical and social well-being of those to whom they preach.

In summarizing these principles, Ladd at once showed his commitment to a social application of the theology of the kingdom of God and, at the same time, revealed that he would take his own work on the subject no further than to elucidate these foundational ideas:

> *In these principles is implicit a "social gospel," for the reign of God in the lives of his people must be concerned with the total man and with the conquest of evil in whatever form it manifests itself. The church is the people of God, the instrument of the kingdom of God in conflict with evil. Here is an incipient theology which needs far more study and attention than it has thus far been given.*[6]

Ladd's greatest contribution to the issue of the role of the church in society is his demonstration that although the kingdom has not fully arrived, its power is present to address and bring healing to physical and social issues and that it is the responsibility of the church, as the agent of the kingdom, to act according to that power. Ladd's kingdom model integrates the spiritual and the material, the personal and the social regarding the Christian mission.

But his self-limitation is the most glaring weakness in Ladd's approach. In declining to go beyond his foundational principles he failed to show us exactly how the church is to be engaged in society to bring the power of the kingdom to bear in the present age. On a related note, his approach does not provide us with a "way in" for commending kingdom ethics to those who are not members of the kingdom. As Oliver Barclay noted, the fact that social ethics are inherent in God's revelation of the kingdom does not provide an adequate basis for those who reject God's revelation. There must be another, perhaps more utilitarian, way of commending kingdom ethics to unbelievers.[7] Ladd does not help us with this.

Issue #2: The Relationship Between Evangelism and Social Action

In the discussion among evangelicals concerning the task of the Kingdom of God in relation to culture, there is no more vigorously debated issue than that which concerns the relationship between evangelism and social action. There is perhaps no area where there is a greater diversity of opinion. Tokunboh Adeyemo, in his helpful article on the subject, listed nine options open to evangelicals.[8] On the one end of the spectrum is the view of some dispensationalists, such as Charles Ryrie, that social action is not a part of the message of the church. The societal benefits of the kingdom must wait for the establishment of the kingdom, which has not yet occurred.[9] On the other end of the spectrum is a group of evangelicals, including Samuel Escobar and Ronald Sider, who contend that social action *is* evangelism.

Ladd's position on this issue was clear. The most important task of the church is to proclaim the message of the kingdom. As clearly as he saw social implications in the presence of the kingdom, Ladd affirmed that the mission of the church is to preach the gospel of salvation, to evangelize the world. The reasons for the primacy of evangelism are several. First, sin is essentially religious because it is rebellion against God; it is only secondarily ethical. Satan's basic desire is not to make the world an immoral place, but to keep people from Christ. Thus, "a man may be a cultured, ethical and even religious person and yet be in demonic darkness."[10] Only the message of salvation offered through Christ can bring people into the kingdom. Entrance into the kingdom comes by a decision to repent of sin and follow Christ, not by a decision to live a moral life.

A second reason for the primacy of evangelism over social action is because of the primacy of the spiritual over the physical in salvation. The miracles of Jesus were not ends in themselves; they were not the highest good of the messianic mission. Although Ladd considered exorcisms to be powerful evidences of the presence of the kingdom, they were only "preliminary to God's taking possession of the vacant dwelling. . . . Healings and exorcisms were the negative side of salvation. The positive side was the incoming of the power and life of God."[11] Of ten lepers who were confronted with the power of the kingdom, nine experienced only physical healing, which was temporal. Only the one who returned in faith received eternal salvation.

Third, the command of Christ to preach the good news of the kingdom was connected to the fact that the kingdom would not be consummated until the gospel was preached to all nations (Mark 13:10). Ladd saw this reality as a powerful motive for the proclamation of the gospel. It is not the church's responsibility to save the world, but to bring to the world the message of salvation. Nor does the church decide when the job is completed; only God will know when the world has been "evangelized." "I only know one thing," remarked Ladd, "Christ has not returned; therefore the task is not done. When it is done, Christ will come."[12]

But the church is responsible for more than evangelism. The message of the kingdom is not only a religious message, it is also an ethical message. In spite of Ladd's contention that evil will characterize society until the end of the age, he still argued that, as the instrument of the kingdom, part of the mission of the church was to oppose evil in society. In Ladd's words,

> *The mission of the Church is not only that of employing the keys of the Kingdom to open to both Jew and Gentile the door into the eternal life which is the gift of God's kingdom; it is also the instrument of God's dynamic rule*

194

*in the world to oppose evil and the powers of Satan in
every form of their manifestation.*[13]

The church is the focus of a battle between the kingdom
of God and satanic evil. Essentially, it is a conflict in the
spiritual realm, but the conflict manifests itself in the
arena of human society. Therefore, the church must battle
evil in the world until Christ returns.

For Ladd, the relationship between evangelism and social action is understood by way of their mutual connection to the mission of the kingdom of God. The kingdom
of God is entirely soteriological, and that salvation means
the "restoration of communion between God and man
that had been broken by sin."[14] But this salvation also includes deliverance from the physical results of sin. Because the nature of the kingdom is never only
apocalyptic, but always also prophetic, the power of the
kingdom to address the societal results of sin is not
postponed to a future age, but is displayed now before the
consummation of the kingdom.

The strength of this position is that, even in the midst
of Ladd's conviction of the priority of evangelism, social
action can never be seen simply as a tool of, or means to,
evangelism, for it is independently connected to the message and power of the kingdom of God. But, Ladd's emphasis on the completion of the proclamation of the
gospel as the *sine qua non* of the consummation of the
kingdom begs the question as to whether social action
could ever truly stand on its own as an act of the
kingdom.

Issue #3: The Problem of Premillennialism as a Deterrent to the Advancement of the Kingdom in Society

The premillennial perspective of the kingdom of God
has historically been criticized as inherently detrimental
to the advancement of the kingdom in society, and for no
small reason. Clearly, the most extreme forms of premil-

lennialism have fostered significant social disengagement. Some dispensationalists have gone beyond claiming that kingdom social ethics do not apply in this age and have suggested that to practice them might even be sinful. In *What You Should Know About Social Involvement*, Charles Ryrie posed this hypothetical question: "If God should judge some area by withholding rain and bringing famine, could it be possible that well meaning Christians might be dulling the sword of God's judgment if they attempted to alleviate famine?"[15] Even to ask such a question moves us beyond pessimism to the fear of doing good in the name of God and creates a kind of "Christian Karma" attitude towards human suffering. Could not the same logic be used to warn Christians about sharing the good news with someone who might not be one of the elect?

Nevertheless, other current writers have claimed that any form of premillennialism is a deterrent to the application of kingdom principles in society. David Bosch places premillennialism at the top of his list of issues that have clouded our understanding of social responsibility.[16] Vinay Samuel and Chris Sugden remarked that premillennialism on its own "gives no adequate theological undergirding for critiqueing or directing Christian social responsibility."[17] They do not deny that premillennialists work for the betterment of society; they deny that they can be motivated by their eschatology.

However, Ladd would disagree with such generalizations about premillennialism. His commitment to the idea that the struggle against evil in society is inherent within the biblical message of the kingdom runs contrary to the pessimism that characterized premillennial thought in the first half of the twentieth century. He believed that too much stress was laid upon persistence of evil to the end of the age. It was his opinion that, "Sometimes so much stress is laid upon the evil character of the last days that we receive the impression . . . that the faster the world deteriorates the better, for the sooner the Lord will come."[18]

The truth that evil persists is no excuse for abandoning contemporary society to Satan. Ladd was no dualist. The power of the kingdom is greater than the power of evil and has defeated it. The message of the kingdom has the power to destroy evil, whether spiritual and societal, in every place it is preached, even in the last days when the power of evil will be most acute.

Issue #4: The Kingdom of God in Society Apart from the Church.

Another important aspect of the current evangelical debate about the kingdom of God in society concerns the suggestion by some that it is active apart from the church. Chris Sugden makes the disturbing suggestion that the transformation of the status of women in society is the work of the kingdom, even when it is accomplished by unbelievers.[19] Such ideas are not far from those of Harvey Cox and other radicals, who contend that the Kingdom of God is found in every act of benevolence.

But according to Ladd, the kingdom of God is at work in society through the church exclusively. The kingdom of God is not inherent within the historical process, nor is it connected with the divinely appointed authority of secular government. As the kingdom was operative in the world through Jesus and then his disciples, it now is operative through the church. Only at the consummation of the kingdom will it become inherent within the socio-historical structure. "Now, the Kingdom works in history; then, history will become the Kingdom."[20]

Yet, this very limitation of the church as the sphere of kingdom activity inclines Barclay and others to contend that the kingdom of God is an inadequate foundation for social action, since the ethics of the kingdom are meant only for the church.[21] But again, Ladd disagrees. Though the church is the only legitimate agent for kingdom activity in society, the ethics of the kingdom, as found for example in the Sermon on the Mount, are absolute ethics. They are binding on all people everywhere. However, only the members of the kingdom receive both the ethical demand of the kingdom and the power of God to live according to those demands.

Issue #5: Confusion Between the "Now" and the "Not Yet."

Among the criticisms leveled against those who see the Kingdom of God as a way of understanding the role of the church in society is that such a position does not adequately distinguish between the "now" and the "not yet" of the kingdom. Robert Saucy contends that views which see the kingdom as having invaded history to bring redemption in some way to all areas of life "fail to discriminate sufficiently between the future of the kingdom and the nature of the kingdom today."[22] Another critic claims that such a position does not distinguish between the *de jure* rule of Christ over all people and the *de facto* rule where His sovereignty is acknowledged.[23]

But Ladd attempted to make just such a distinction in principle. The kingdom is present now by persuasion and must be received by faith; then, it will be present in power as all will be confronted with its irrefutable sovereignty. The current victories of the kingdom over evil are selective and occasional; then they will be comprehensive. Obedience to the standards of the kingdom now is practiced in principle; then obedience will be complete. But as he often did, Ladd left the practical outworking of these principles to others.

Conclusion

In 1957, George Ladd wrote a brief article entitled "Why Not Prophetic/Apocalyptic?" After decades of extremists fighting to cram the kingdom of God into only one of these concepts, Ladd was one of the first evangelicals to suggest that perhaps the truth lay not in antinomy, but in dialectic. Conceivably, the most biblical solution to the nature of the kingdom was in the coexistence of opposing ideas in tension. And, like the other classic tensions of biblical truth, the tension between the prophetic and apocalyptic, the here and the not yet, of the kingdom of God leaves us looking through a glass darkly concerning the ways in which to implement its principles in a practical way in the human society. Yet, the very elusiveness of such a profound truth causes us to press on in the struggle.

Ladd did not allow us the privilege of witnessing his own struggle to implement the social implications of the kingdom. Perhaps that is because during his peak years of writing, evangelicals in general were still rather disengaged from society. Perhaps it is because, as a biblical theologian, he believed that while the foundational principles were clear, their practical outworking was as much the task of sociologists as theologians. But for Ladd, the kingdom of God was the central concern and message of Christ to the world. Christ's vision for the world, both in this age and the age to come, was a product of the kingdom. If George Eldon Ladd were alive today and attempting to work out a practical perspective of the role of the church in society, he would do it by way of the kingdom.

Endnotes

[1] See Mark Noll's survey in *Between Faith and Criticism* (Grand Rapids: Baker Book House, 1986).

[2] Ladd, "The Kingdom of God and the Church," *Foundations* 4.2 (1961): p. 168.

[3] George E. Ladd, *The Presence of the Future* (Grand Rapids: Eerdmans, 1974), p. 303.

[4] Ibid.

[5] Ladd, "The Kingdom of God and the Church," op. cit., p. 170.

[6] Ladd, *The Presence of the Future*, op. cit., p. 304.

[7]Oliver Barclay and Chris Sugden, "Biblical Social Ethics in a Mixed Society." *Evangelical Quarterly* 62.1 (1990): p. 13.

[8]See his "A Critical Evaluation of Contemporary Perspectives," *In Word and Deed: Evangelism and Social Responsibility.* ed. Bruce Nicholls (Exeter: Paternoster, 1985), pp. 41–61.

[9]Charles Ryrie, *What You Should Know About Social Responsibility* (Chicago: Moody, 1982), pp. 22–24.

[10]George E. Ladd, *The Gospel of the Kingdom* (Grand Rapids: Eerdmans, 1959), p. 31.

[11]George E. Ladd, *A Theology of the New Testament* (Grand Rapids: Eerdmans, 1974), p. 77.

[12]Ladd, *Gospel of the Kingdom*, op. cit., p. 137.

[13]Ibid., p. 121.

[14]Ladd, *A Theology of the New Testament*, op. cit., p. 74.

[15]Ryrie, op. cit., p. 24.

[16]David Bosch, "In Search of a New Evangelical Understanding." *In Word and Deed: Evangelism and Social Responsibility*, p. 72.

[17]Vinay Samuel and Chris Sugden, "God's Intention for the World: Tensions Between Eschatology and History." *The Church in Response to Human Need*. ed. Tom Sine (Monrovia: Missions Advance Research and Communications Center, 1983), p. 201.

[18]Ladd, *The Gospel of the Kingdom*, op. cit., p. 138.

[19]Samuel and Sugden, op. cit., p. 212.

[20]Ladd, "The Kingdom of God and the Church," op. cit., p. 170.

[21]Barclay, op. cit., p. 66.

[22]Robert Saucy, "The Presence of the Kingdom and the Life of the Church." *Bibliotheca Sacra* 145: 30–46 (1988): p. 32.

[23]Michael Schluter and Roy Clements, "Jubilee Institutional Norms: A Middle Way Between Creation Ethics and Kingdom Ethics as the Basis for Christian Political Action." *Evangelical Quarterly* 62.1 (1990): pp. 37–62.

The Dangerous Samaritans: How We Unintentionally Injure the Poor

by Michael Bauman

*W*e thought we were doing the right thing. We thought that if we passed laws to raise their wages and lower their rent; if we gave generously to help support mothers without husbands and children without fathers, we could aid the poor in their flight from poverty and alleviate much of their distress while they were still in it. We were wrong.

We forgot that good intentions are not enough, and that virtually all government programs of any significant scope at all carry with them great loads of unintended consequences. We forgot that aiming is not hitting, and that meaning well is not doing well.

First, we thought that if we passed laws mandating higher wages for the lowest paid workers, we could increase their income and thereby aid the industrious poor in their escape from poverty. We forgot that the lowest paid workers were normally those with the least skill and experience, and that, in the marketplace, they are the least desirable of all workers. By artificially elevating their wages, we made them even more undesirable, making it increasingly unlikely they could ever get or keep a job. We forgot that a wage is not merely a purchase price for an employer; it is a selling price for a worker. We passed laws preventing the least desirable workers from selling their services at a price their prospective employers, and ultimately the consumer, can afford to pay.

We forgot that all workers work not merely for their employer, but also for the consumer, and that consumers wisely try to make the most of their money. Nevertheless, due to our desire to be moral and compassionate people, we pass laws requiring employers to pay higher wages to their least desirable workers while, as good stewards of the resources God has given us, we choose not to buy the overpriced products of those who do as the law demands. We put them out of business, which creates more unemployed workers and more poor, whom we then foolishly try to help with more minimum wage laws.

If you have little or no skill and experience, and yet the government requires you to sell your services at an artificially inflated price, you will not find anyone to purchase them because, in order to pay for your overpriced services, your employer must raise his own selling price. In turn, this means that your employer is increasingly likely to go out of business and that all his current employees, who are more skilled than you, more experienced than you, and more worth the money he pays them, lose their jobs because those companies who were wise enough not to hire you at the legally mandated price can produce the same product your company produces, but at a lower cost both to themselves and to their customers.

Perhaps the point can be made more graphically at the corporate level. Imagine that, in an effort to aid portions of our lagging auto industry, we decided to prop up the profits of our weakest auto manufacturer in Detroit by passing a law that put a minimum price of $25,000 on each vehicle it sold. This would dramatically increase the profits it enjoyed from every sale. But, despite our good intention, indeed because of it, that manufacturer would soon go out of business. No matter how much consumers want to "buy American," very few can or will pay $25,000 for automobiles comparable to those available elsewhere for half the legally mandated price. The same principle holds when that which is being sold is not an automobile but an unskilled employee's overpriced labor. When minimum wages laws are in effect, the choice often is not between the legally mandated wage and some other wage, but between the legally mandated wage and no wage at all. In every sector of the marketplace where they have been instituted, minimum wage laws have caused unemployment to soar. We never seem to notice that, judging by their effects, minimum wage laws are anti-black, anti-woman, anti-young, anti-elderly and anti-immigrant —the very people we intend to help.

To such harmful, but well intentioned, legislative conniving, no thinking Christian ought to consent. If we want to make the marketplace more moral, or if we want to be agents of effective compassion, minimum wage laws are not the answer. Indeed, as economist Charles Van Eaton has carefully argued, we ought to encourage more entrepreneurship like that of marketplace giants Ray Kroc or Dave Thomas, who, far more than any government program ever has or could, aided the cause of the poor, both as consumers and as workers. Kroc and Thomas, the founders of McDonald's and Wendy's, provided all-important entry level jobs that permit unskilled workers to gain necessary experience and to learn critical marketplace lessons, ranging from the importance of appearance, punctuality, deference, teamwork, integrity and dependability to more sophisticated management and public relations skills. They also offer a modest wage to boot.

Entrepreneurs like Thomas and Kroc understood that *you cannot climb the ladder of success without first getting on the ladder.* They invited the poor to step onto the first rung and begin climbing. Literally millions of people prospered in precisely this way, all without spending even one tax dollar. Quite the opposite, in fact, for these novice workers themselves, as they rose from poverty, actually paid into public coffers. At one time or another, nearly one-eighth of the entire American work force has been employed by the fast food industry. From such jobs, millions of previously poor workers, many of them minority workers, went on to better jobs and to a level of prosperity that otherwise would have remained unattainable. Some went on to own fast food franchises themselves, which in turn helped others stepping onto that first rung. Thus, while these entry level jobs are not a career, nor ever can be, they are the blocks upon which millions of Americans have built careers. But for millions of the poor, minimum wage laws bar the door to opportunities of this sort because they create unemployment. In the marketplace as in all of life, you cannot take step two until you have taken step one.

Second, we thought that if we passed laws holding down the costs of urban housing, we could aid the poor by making many more inexpensive lodgings available to them than before, and perhaps diminish homelessness in the process. We forgot that a purchase price for renter is a selling price for a landlord. The more attractive a price is for the one, the less attractive it is for the other. When landlords are forced to reduce their rents in the face of burgeoning tax and maintenance costs, they wisely decide to allocate their investments in other ways. For example, when rent-control ceilings make it unprofitable for landlords to rent their apartments, they often sell those apartments as condominiums, and thus escape real estate taxes and the high cost of urban upkeep. Because the supply of condominiums then increases, their selling price tends to go down, thereby aiding wealthy urban dwellers, the only ones who can afford to purchase them. Meanwhile, the price of the apartments remaining on the market now rises because their supply has shrunk.

In order to prevent this dire consequence, we occasionally pass laws prohibiting landlords from taking recourse to condominium conversion. This legislative ban predictably proves counter-productive because it often means: (1) that landlords seek additional payments under the table from their renters, thus making life more difficult for the poor, who can scarcely afford the extra cost; (2) that landlords defer needed maintenance on their decaying buildings, again making life more difficult for the poor; and (3) that landlords get out of the housing business altogether, tear down their apartments, and build a parking lot—a low maintenance, high yield investment that serves only those wealthy enough to afford the high cost of owning, operating and insuring an automobile in an urban setting.

We forgot that, human nature being what it is, people respond to incentives. Therefore, rather than passing rent control laws in order to aid our poorer neighbors, perhaps we ought to give substantially reduced public utility rates and increased tax breaks to those who establish urban rental housing, thus making such housing more plentiful, more affordable and more comfortable. In short, if we do anything at all by means of the state, we should do all we can to promote the supply side of the supply and demand equation. The greater the incentives for property owners, the better it is for landlords. The better it is for landlords, the greater the supply of apartments. The greater the supply of apartments, the lower the price. The lower the price, the better it is for the poor. Furthermore, the increase in urban rental units not only results in lower rental prices for renters, it also provides more jobs for those who construct apartment buildings, as well as for those who service them and who maintain them.

Third, we thought that by transferring money as generously as we could afford to the mothers of illegitimate children, we could soften the pains of kids without fathers and of mothers without husbands. We forgot what insurance companies often call "moral hazard," which is insuring against a disaster in a way that actually encourages the misfortune in question. That is, insurance companies know that because people respond to incentives, if an insurance policy pays off too handsomely, calamity occurs. If the fire insurance policy on a sagging business pays more money to the owner than the owner can get from operating the business, that business is likely to burn. The temptation seems sometimes too great to resist. Likewise, if a life insurance policy pays off so lucratively that the insured's beneficiaries are better off if the insured is dead, death sometimes results. If medical insurance covers too great a portion of medical expenses, people tend to apply for treatment of illnesses that are hardly illnesses at all, thus tying up doctors, clinics, hospitals and pharmacies with cases that too often are trivial. In other words, when we reach the point of moral hazard, fire insurance causes fires, life insurance causes death and medical insurance causes illness. Not surprisingly, insurance companies try very hard to avoid the moral hazard inherent in insurance. They learned the hard way that the threshold of moral hazard is reached very quickly. Our governmental approaches to welfare have not learned that lesson.

In our rush to do well for households without a male bread-winner, we forgot that welfare is poverty insurance and, as result, we actually helped cause the problem we were intending to alleviate. By making illegitimate children a credential for increased financial support, we make certain more illegitimate children are born. And we do so in a particularly shocking way. As Patty Newman, author of *Pass the Poverty*, relates: "Can you imagine my shock when I went into a welfare department and said, 'Do you mean to tell me that a woman can come in here every nine months and begin to get checks for another illegitimate child?' The welfare man said, 'Oh, no, Mrs. Newman, she has to claim a different man as father every time or else she doesn't get the money.' "

Tragically, however, the more illegitimate children a woman has, the more deeply she becomes mired in poverty, and the less likely it becomes that she can ever extricate herself from it, despite the money she is given by the government. As is all too clear, poverty circles around single parent homes, especially when the single parent is a woman. But single motherhood is what we decided to pay for, and it is what we got. As Robert Rector observed, this sort of welfare program is an incentive program from hell. As long as we pay the poor to continue doing the very things that help make them poor in the first place, poor they shall remain. As long as illegitimate children remain the chief breadwinners in welfare homes, more illegitimate children shall be born.

Put differently, what you pay for is what you get. Because single motherhood is what we decide to pay for with our tax money, more single mothers are what we get. The tragic fact is that in the last decade or so in America, up to 80 percent of the children born in the urban black underclass were born out of wedlock and without an adult male to accept any financial responsibility for them. Of course, rising illegitimacy is neither a distinctively black nor a distinctively American problem. Sweden, for example, which subsidizes its unwed mothers even more generously than we do, has the highest rate of illegitimacy in the world. Just as when you tax something, you get less of it, when you subsidize it, you get more. Today, we are subsidizing immoral behavior on a grand scale. As a result, immoral behavior flourishes all around us, while those who practice it are harmed. This is no way to bring morality to the marketplace.

Another unintended consequence of our effort to aid single mothers and their children, is that low-income husbands become extraneous. Welfare actually drives them from the home. The average total relief package for a single mother with three children is more than $19,000 a year, after taxes. By comparison, a traditional two-parent family of four with a higher income, of say $22,000, has only about $18,000 left after taxes. Poor women might be poor, but they are not stupid. Neither are poor young men, many of whom quickly realize that by their own efforts and means they are unable to provide as well for their families as does their rich Uncle Sam in Washington.

Uncle Sam is exceedingly tough competition. Too many mothers decide not to marry the fathers of their children; they marry welfare instead. Thus government makes cuckolds of millions of American men. As George Gilder, author of *Wealth and Poverty*, once observed, the modern welfare state has persuaded poor fathers that they are dispensable. They believe it; so do the mothers of their children. By means of our so-called compassion and generosity, we send the signal to many thousands of women—especially poor, young women eager to get out of their parents' home and away from their parents' control—that poor men are most useful as procreators, not as providers.

To poor young men, who tend to live more for the moment than the future, that same signal had a different but equally devastating effect, for it served to detach their actions from those actions' attendant consequences. We taught those young men that, if they wanted it, sex was a game they could play for free. No longer was there heavy pressure upon them to face up to the consequences of sex outside marriage. No longer did young men feel compelled to work long hours at difficult jobs in order to provide food, clothing and shelter for the new lives they were creating or for the financially dependent women who helped create them. That tab, they soon learned, could be picked up by their rich Uncle Sam, who worked in government—*provided that they did nothing to help the mother or to assume responsibility.*

With no compelling need to channel time and energy into acquiring useful skills and into applying those skills profitably in the marketplace, increasing numbers of poor young men simply took to the streets, where life got boring and then got worse, much worse. Without work, there is no economic prosperity, and without incentives, there is no work.

In our misguided efforts to be good Samaritans, to help those lying in the ditch of poverty, we forgot that whatever undermines traditional family values, roles, and ties undermines society itself. To such moral and social degeneration, we ought never to subscribe. Our first priority, as well as the first priority of any government program of poverty relief, ought to be to stabilize traditional family roles and responsibilities.

Fourth, by giving money to the poor, we thought we were simply aiding and comforting the unfortunate in their time of difficulty. We forgot that giving good gifts is an exceedingly difficult endeavor and that poverty is not always itself the problem; it is often the symptom of another prior problem. That is, if poverty (the lack of money) really were what ails the poor, supplying vast amounts of money would surely alleviate it. After nearly thirty years of Great Society-like welfare programs, however, programs that transferred countless billions—yes, billions—of dollars to the poor, poverty is still winning the war we wage against it. In the last 30 years, we gave $3.6 trillion (in 1990 dollars) to America's poor, yet poverty is still winning. We ought to think about that fact for a minute: In the last 30 years, we gave a million dollars to America's poor nearly *four million* times over, yet all the while poverty got worse. If the money earmarked for the poverty relief in this year's federal budget alone were given directly to the poor, we would have enough funds to raise every man, woman and child in America above the poverty line and have a cool $60 billion left over to celebrate our victory.

Poverty is not primarily a lack of money; it is a lack of something else. While we throw record amounts of money at the problem, we forget that of the many reasons why people are poor, relatively few truly lie outside their own control or require external remedy. And because of this lapse, we fail to convince the poor that the surest way to get ahead in modern America is precisely the way their forefathers did it: Get a good education (which includes a mastery of English and math); work hard; save money and invest.

Instead, we tell the poor that in order to get ahead they need to demand more money from government, as if financial improvement were a public entitlement, not a private achievement, and as if the modern poor were somehow incapable of succeeding by using the same means countless other Americans have used in the past. Then, apparently in an effort to allay some of the responsibility the poor themselves have to make their own lives better, and to lighten the burden that such responsibility inevitably entails, we tell them that they are poor because the wealthy oppressed them. In other words, we teach the poor to blame their poverty on prejudice.

In a perverse sort of way, we are right about the connection between prejudice and poverty. Indeed, prejudice *does* lead to poverty, though not in the way we expect. We convinced the poor that the prosperous prosper only at someone else's expense and usually by deceit and because of greed. Not only are such insulting generalizations not true about the wealthy and are instances of bearing false witness against our neighbors, they are crippling to the poor. If the poor believe that the wealthy are exploitive thieves who squash other people into poverty for their own gain, they will not likely climb the ladder of economic success. They will remain poor because they do not respect or try to emulate the achievement of others and because they are blind to the real path the wealthy typically take to success—hard work, postponed gratification, sacrifice and diligence.

At our hands the poor were too easily convinced that they were poor primarily because of reasons which they could not change and over which they had no control. We taught the poor to be prejudiced themselves—prejudiced against the prosperous. That prejudice proved morally and economically debilitating. We blamed poverty on prejudice and then promoted prejudice among the poor. In the wake of that false and crippling bias, too many of them simply gave up.

We forgot not only that ideas have consequences, but that bad ideas have bad ones. We forgot that real poverty is at least as much a state of mind as it is a state of income. We also forgot to tie our charity more securely to the sincere efforts of the recipient. We mistakenly decided to give aid to the poor, not to *the deserving and industrious poor*, that is, to those who are poor through no fault of their own, or whose escape from poverty can never be produced by their own efforts. In doing so, we ignored St. Paul's prudent scriptural principle: "If a man will not work, he shall not eat" (2 Thess. 3:10).

We should have remembered that love does not squander either its resources or itself in reckless disregard of people's character and actions. By obliterating the distinction between the deserving and the undeserving poor, we ran contrary to the will and practice of God, who treats the undeserving poor as objects not of mercy but of wrath. In other words, we forgot that real love helps those who cannot help themselves. It refuses to subsidize sluggardliness or indolence by doing for others what they can and ought to do for themselves. Christian love operates upon the premise that the defeat of poverty is a joint effort, or common endeavor, between the haves and the have nots, not a unilateral thrust by the haves only. The recipients of Christian charity ought to be either diligent workers or else unable. The unwilling and the slothful must get nothing from us but exhortation. To subsidize them is to do them moral injury, something Christian love does not do.

As long as we fail to distinguish between the deserving and the undeserving poor, we teach others that poverty is an entitlement, a credential, and that the blessings of life and labor are available merely for the asking or for the demanding, regardless of one's contribution.

Finally, in this regard, our indiscriminate giving created a culture of dependence, one in which the connection between effort and prosperity was severed. By failing to distinguish the deserving poor from the undeserving, we told the economically disadvantaged that the diligent application of their private means to the alleviation of their personal distress is either unimportant or ineffective. This misconception implies that if the impoverished are ever to escape poverty it can only be by someone else's doing. This message, coupled with the notion that the poor are poor because of the perverse machinations of the rich, leads the poor to conclude that they are not responsible either for their poverty or their extrication from it. By sparing the poor the challenge of their own success, we consign them to state-funded dependency. We lead them in a direction quite the opposite of that articulated in John Kennedy's memorable challenge: "Ask not what your country can do for you."

The welfare state not only tempts its recipients with nearly irresistible perverse incentives, it seduces those outside it as well, especially those who seek to administer it and those who pay for it. As German economist Wilhelm Röpke wrote:

> *To expand the welfare state is not only easy, but it is also one of the surest means for the demagogue to win votes and political influence, and it is for all of us the most ordinary temptation to gain . . . a reputation for generosity and kindness. The welfare state is the favorite playground of a cheap sort of moralism that only thoughtlessness shields from exposure. . . . Cheap moralism is anything but moral.*

We appear to be virtuous when we really are rather lazy "do-gooders" content to let the welfare bureaucrats handle all that "poverty unpleasantness" for us. More frequently than we care to admit, our poverty programs are thinly veiled efforts to enhance our self-esteem and to assuage our consciences by means of state programs. To imagine that by such shallow and self-gratifying efforts we can eliminate human poverty is shameless hubris, not charity and grace. The size of the federal budget is by no means an indicator of Christian compassion.

On many fronts and in many ways, our poverty programs fail to reduce poverty. What is worse, they tend to injure the very persons they are designed to aid. Because we fail to incarnate our good intentions with effective, well-conceived public policy, because (in the words of economist Walter Williams) we fail to realize that truly compassionate public policy requires dispassionate analysis, and because we choose to think with our hearts instead of our brains, much of the blame is ours. We must realize that real prosperity is created from the bottom up, not from the government down. Wealth must be created, not redistributed.

And if we think the outcomes of the marketplace are not up to our moral standards, we must never again forget that true charity does not lead to the welfare state. The kingdom of God and the Great Society lie in opposite directions. We can help the poor, but we must do so as good, rather than dangerous, Samaritans. Our first tasks are:

1. *Put welfare programs in the hands of contributors, not recipients or bureaucrats.* Welfare recipients and bureaucrats who profit from the enlargement of the welfare state actually have banded together to form lobbies on Capitol Hill, hectoring legislators to redistribute even greater shares of other people's money. They do so as if access to other people's money were their God-given right. Gone is the notion that welfare is a form of charity or that escape from it is the responsibility of the poor. Welfare is now viewed as an entitlement. But if the poor have a natural right to the money earned by others and can confiscate it under threat of government coercion, then charity, which is voluntary giving, is impossible.

Rather than assigning control of welfare payments to the poor or to bureaucrats, we ought to give increased discretion over charitable contributions to the donors themselves. This is done best by giving tax credits (not income deductions) for all documentable charity of, say, up to 40 percent of one's total tax bill. This has the effect of making government charity compete for our philanthropy dollars, which will tend to make government programs more effective, more efficient and less expensive.

2. *Redefine Poverty.* Nearly 40% of those the U.S. government defines as "poor" own their own homes—homes that have more living space than that enjoyed by most middle-class Europeans. Nearly 70% of America's poor own at least one car. "Poor" ought to retain its earlier definition: the lack of food, shelter or clothing. And while we are engaged in the task of redefining, we ought to remind ourselves that the definition of compassion is not increased control of private income by government.

3. *Re-educate the politicians and the poor.* We must remind politicians that to promote the general welfare is not the same as promoting welfare generally. They ought to think not in terms of dollars but in terms of morality and responsibility. They ought always to keep in mind that welfare payments can prove psychologically addictive and debilitating both to those who receive them and to those who provide them. They also must remember that pride in including more and more people on the dole is misplaced. Politicians are not political saints but political pushers when they encourage addictive government paternalism.

As for the poor, we must remind them that it is not a shame to be poor; it is a shame to be lazy and unproductive. Generations of Americans knew how to be something many of today's poor do not: how to be both poor and proud—proud of their modest but hard-won earnings, and of the natural human dignity that does not depend upon a bank account. Nor should the poor shun honest wages for honest work. Too many of today's poor are not proud, they are arrogant. They consider themselves too good to do the menial labor one must perform in order to begin climbing the ladder to success. Yet they are not too proud to take welfare; they are too proud only to flip hamburgers. We must remind them that they have to begin at the bottom and do the jobs no one else wants to do if they wish to stop being poor.

4. No perfect solutions are possible. Poverty cannot be eradicated; it can only be ameliorated. But at least we can keep it from getting much worse and prevent ourselves from making it so. The good news is that there is a lot we can do, and we do not need government help to do it.

5. Abundance can be wrenched from scarcity only by following the Golden Rule of doing unto others as we would have them do unto us. The important question is not how poverty is begotten but how wealth is achieved. To become poor and to stay that way is quite easy. But to become prosperous, you must learn to supply your neighbors' wants and needs at a price he can afford to pay. If you cannot supply your neighbors' wants and needs, you cannot succeed. You cannot supply your neighbors' wants and needs unless you walk in his shoes and see the world through his eyes. Unless you learn to sympathize and empathize with your neighbor, prosperity will elude you.

Biblical Considerations Relevant to Homosexuals in the Military: A View from Inside the Pentagon

by Daniel R. Heimbach

*F*ew Americans are unaware that a battle has been waged recently over the issue of homosexuals in the military. Military personnel policy, a dull subject on the best of days for most American citizens, has recently raged as one of the hottest topics of discussion from the halls of Congress to the family living room, from TV talk shows to college campuses, from newsrooms of the media giants to casual conversations with neighbors across the back fence. But, while most have heard the claims by which homosexual militants are seeking to persuade the public that theirs is a case of simple justice, and while most also have heard these claims countered by arguments about what it takes to build and maintain effective combat forces, much less has been heard about the conflicting moral views driving each side. Even less is known about the degree to which convictions regarding biblical moral standards have affected the public policy battle.

It is my thesis that convictions about what the Bible does or does not teach on the immorality of homosexual behavior and the accountability of persons drawn by homosexual desires, have in fact been a major factor in the recent policy debate over homosexuals in the military. I come to this partly on the basis of what has been written and partly from direct involvement as a policy player; first as an official at the Pentagon responsible for manpower issues and then as a strategist who helped contribute to the public debate and lobbying effort with Congress.

The Bible in the Larger Social Context

I do not intend to develop a detailed analysis of battles now waging in American society at large spurred by homosexual militants intent on attacking traditional views on family, gender and appropriate sexual behavior. I intend, however, to take brief notice of three battles waged in the larger social context that directly impact the military, and to do so with a view to understanding the stake that biblical teaching either has or might have. These battles are being waged to capture and redirect the public message of three sources of cultural authority: history, science and the U.S. Congress. Each battle has been initiated by a dedicated army bent on replacing one fundamental morality or world view, with another—an army that will not be satisfied with tolerance but that insists on social legitimacy, public approval and legal sanctions to guard against moral censure of any kind in the public square.

The Battle to Capture History

The first of these is a battle to capture history, to redefine the sexual conduct of persons in history, and to recast the moral standards of historical leaders. An example is found in an article by Congresswoman Patricia Schroeder (D-CO). Published as an opinion piece in *Legal Times*, she seeks to portray the founding fathers in general, and George Washington in particular, as tolerant of homosexual behavior and unconcerned about its impact on soldiering.[1] She begins by stating, "What was good enough for George Washington is good enough for me," and proceeds to discuss the service of Friedrich Wilhelm von Steuben, a Prussian professional who helped train Washington's inexperienced volunteers. Von Steuben, she claims—without explaining the basis of her assertion—was gay, and it mattered not at all to the men and officers of the Continental Army, including George Washington himself. Unaddressed, of course, is how men, all raised on a more or less strict Protestant sexual ethic and most of whom were church members, could have had such a cavalier attitude toward homosexual conduct. If she had done a more thorough job of historical research, it surely would have undermined her objective.

A more accurate picture of George Washington's views regarding homosexual conduct among his soldiers is found in the following account:

> At a General Court Martial whereof Colo. Tupper was President (10th March 1778) Lieutt. Enslin of Colo. Malcom's Regiment [was] tried for attempting to commit sodomy, with John Monhort a soldier; Secondly, For Perjury in swearing to false Accounts. [He was] found guilty of the charges exhibited against him, being breaches of 5th. Article 18th. Section of the Articles of War and [we] do sentence him to be dismiss'd [from] the service with Infamy. His Excellency the Commander in Chief approves the sentence and with Abhorrence and Detestation of such Infamous Crimes orders Lieutt. Enslin to be drummed out of Camp tomorrow morning by all the Drummers and Fifers in the Army never to return; The Drummers and Fifers [are] to attend on the Grand Parade at Guard mounting for that Purpose.[2]

As to the role of Scripture in shaping the moral understanding of early American leaders, we need not be in doubt. Although the Bible was not quoted in proof text fashion, it was never far from conscious thought when standards of moral conduct were in view. Washington's judgment that Lieutenant Enslin's homosexual behavior did in fact render him guilty of an "infamous crime" deserving of "abhorrence and detestation" was consistent with an edict of the Continental Congress issued in 1775 to the effect that Commanders of the Continental Army were "strictly required . . . to be very vigilant in inspecting the behavior of all such as are under them, and to discountenance and suppress all dissolute, immoral, and disorderly practices."[3] Noah Webster, who had himself been a soldier in the Continental Army through the Revolution, defined the term "immoral" according to its usage at the time as: "Immoral: Inconsistent with moral rectitude; contrary to the moral or divine law. . . . Every action is immoral which contravenes any divine precept, or which is contrary to the duties which men owe each other."[4]

The historical evidence, taken objectively, leads to two related conclusions: (1) for the founding fathers the Bible was a major determinant of moral standards; and (2) their understanding of biblical doctrine on the subject of homosexuality was firm as evidenced by their consistent condemnations.

The Battle to Capture Science

A second battle in the larger social context that has direct bearing on military personnel policy is the battle to capture the authority of science pertaining to homosexual desires and conduct. It is now de rigueur in the media and most other institutions of public discourse to presume that modern science has determined that homosexual behavior is biologically predetermined, irreversible and though different from heterosexual behavior is nevertheless equally natural, at least for persons "born that way."[5] Not only is this perception spread by individuals outside the medical community, it is often encouraged by medical authorities and scientists as well. For example on March 30, 1993, Edward Martin, a Clinton Administration political appointee then still awaiting Senate confirmation to be Assistant Secretary of Defense for Health Affairs, issued an information memorandum for all secretaries of the military departments stating in part:

> *Homosexuality was once medically defined as an aberrant sexual behavior. However, years of medical, psychological and sexual research consistently failed to demonstrate the presence of any specific . . . clinical syndrome and/or psychosocial profile in practicing homosexuals of either sex.*
>
> *By 1975, the American Psychological Association no longer considered homosexuality an aberrant sexual behavior. By 1976, the American Psychiatric Association enacted the same resolution and removed homosexuality from its Diagnostic and Statistical Manual . . .*
>
> *We are not aware of any scientific evidence that individual sexual preferences, in and by themselves, be they homosexual, heterosexual or bisexual, affect . . . disease incidence, medical costs or crime rate in the population at large. . . . homosexuality, per se, cannot scientifically be characterized as a medical issue . . . .*[6]

In fact, nothing is further from the actual records of scientific research and the history of medical treatments. Nevertheless, bald claims are made in the name of science and backed by the aura of authority granted by position and a medical degree. The overwhelming weight of scientific evidence favors the longstanding view that homosexuality is aberrant behavior, is largely a matter of social conditioning and acquired taste and is not an irreversible condition determined by biology. Homosexuality is significantly related to education, family environment, religious beliefs and culture. As such, it is behavior for which persons can and should be held accountable and for which they can be treated with success.

What transpired as the American Psychiatric Association was being pressured to change its designation of homosexuality, as well as the manner in which a shift in designation was achieved, is a revealing story. In 1973, homosexual activists persuaded members of the Board of Trustees of the American Psychiatric Association (APA) to remove homosexuality from its list of mental disorders. In its place they were persuaded to create a new category, "sexual orientation disturbance." This, they were told, would satisfy advocates seeking to promote the idea that homosexuality might be a natural sexual variant, but it would not require members of the association to change their medical views on the subject.[7] Thus, the change was conformed to an intense political campaign and was not based on the discovery of new scientific evidence. Action was rushed through by a few advocates who circumvented normal channels because the leaders of the field were deemed opposed to the desired alteration.[8] Finally, the manner by which the change passed the APA was not by direct vote on the issue. Rather, wording to change the nomenclature of homosexuality was linked to a statement supporting civil rights and members were forced to adopt the strategy for change or put themselves on record as opposed to civil rights. Consequently, the APA vote to change the nomenclature of homosexuality was made contrary to the professional judgment of most scientists working in the field, against the position of leaders in the professional study and treatment of homosexuality, and without regard to the medical evidence.

While much energy and expense has gone into the search for a biological cause for homosexuality, scientists have found no evidence able to withstand testing.[9] Over this same time period, the study of gender identity has added strength to the body of accumulated evidence showing homosexuality to be a learned behavior shaped and strengthened by external factors. The scientific evidence supporting the traditional view is extremely strong and includes important factors such as the possibility of reversal,[10] the insufficiency of associated biological traits,[11] the power of cultural factors to affect incidence rates[12] and the inability to maintain favorable genetic indicators through reproduction.[13]

At the heart of the battle to capture science is the struggle to shift the terms of the larger moral war from arguing the morality of discipline, accountability and treatment for aberrant behavior to the morality of civil rights that ought to protect a normal biological trait from discriminatory prohibitions. Although the Bible is rarely addressed in debating the exploration of new medical hypotheses or the framing of possible conclusions, the import for biblical morality is enormous because there is now such a strong ideological incentive driving researchers to reach conclusions that might be used to shift the terms by which society judges the morality of homosexual behavior. The presuppositions of such medical research often determine claims made at its conclusion. Increasingly these are raising doubts (at least in popular perception) about how science can be consistent with traditional biblical norms. For example: Does the Bible allow a distinction between homosexual status and behavior such that being precedes doing? Does God make homosexuals the way they are? If homosexuality is a natural variation of human sexuality, would it not make sense to allow a responsible venue for such behavior? If these issues are joined and answered in the affirmative, then biblical norms traditionally understood are judged in error or hopelessly out-of-date. Indeed, we already are well into a battle that seeks to use the aura of a politicized science to marginalize, privatize or demonize biblical morality on homosexual behavior wherever it is found to have had influence in the public square.

The Battle to Capture Congress

The third battle in the larger social context bearing on homosexuals and military personnel policy is a cultural battle being waged on the floor and in the halls of Congress. I do not refer here to the general business of political deal-making, constituent representation and party organization. Rather, I intend to draw attention to a cultural-moral aspect that has been injected into the political process in which the Bible and perceptions about its proper interpretation have been used in efforts to capture the moral high ground with Congressional colleagues. Indeed the ramifications of theological and biblical scholarship are here more immediate and direct than in either of the battles already described. Two examples will be given, one from each side of the battle line, but both were generated by the debate over whether to require a change in military personnel policy to accommodate persons inclined toward homosexual behavior.

On March 30, 1993, Gerald Solomon (R-NY), wishing to show that military policy banning service by homosexuals is not arbitrary, based his argument before the House of Representatives on the fact that the ban is "rooted in our Judeo-Christian heritage."[14] He then argued that lifting the ban "would suggest a rejection of those roots" and had inserted into the *Congressional Record* a theological paper written by John Mulloy entitled "Homosexuals in the Military: A Moral Issue." The paper was an explicit and traditional review of classic biblical doctrine regarding the immorality of homosexual behavior, starting with the account of God's judgment on Sodom and Gomorrah given in Genesis 18 and 19 and ending with the New Testament indictment against homosexuality recorded in Romans 1.

A contrary but equally direct attempt to use biblical authority to sway members of Congress was given by Steve Gunderson (R-WI) on September 28, 1993.[15] Mr. Gunderson started by explaining that in the realm of morality "a single truth for everyone . . . does not in fact exist," and that moral issues would be made less difficult if people would only stop thinking their standards of morality had to apply to everyone else. He then addressed the Bible and sought to explain its place in American life and its proper scholarly interpretation, basing his remarks on the work of John Boswell's *Christianity, Social*

Tolerance, and Homosexuality. The Bible, said Mr. Gunderson, is a "living document" that evolves with "social change." In fact, contrary to the confused beliefs expressed by many of the "sincere constituents" who had motivated his speech, the Bible never really condemns homosexuality per se because "there actually is no such word as homosexual in either the Hebrew or Greek languages." Accordingly, "the Bible . . . provides no specific judgment one way or the other on this issue, then or now." He ended by saying we can only take guidance from the Bible's basic message of love and tolerance.

Little comment is needed except to point out that both Congressmen, despite their very contrary policy positions, felt it beneficial to discuss the Bible in order to make a case on the morality of homosexuality before their colleagues and the American people. Each relied heavily on a favored biblical scholar to build his case for the proper morality.

Behind the Scenes at the Pentagon

We have thus far discussed the role of the Bible as it touches three cultural-moral battles now taking place in American society at large. Together, these have caused heavy erosion of the moral foundations on which the military services have been fixed. Despite the conservative nature of these institutions and the generally conservative moral convictions of professionals who serve in the U.S. armed forces, the moral resistance of military leaders to homosexual behavior has been showing signs of stress. What follows are reflections based largely on personal experiences as a Pentagon official serving in the Department of the Navy during the last two years of the Bush Administration and in the transition to the Clinton Administration.

The Standing DOD Policy on Homosexuals

Prior to the arrival of the Clinton Administration, with its agenda to revise radically military policy regarding the acceptance and treatment of homosexuals, Department of Defense policy regarding homosexuals was well established and clear. As legal questions began to be raised in civilian courts challenging the military exclusion and discharge policies in the 1960s and 1970s, the services were made to explain and clearly justify specific limits and procedures used in relation to service members claiming to be homosexual or convicted of homosexual acts. During the Carter Administration, the services and the Office of the Secretary of Defense conducted a series of studies responding to a challenge by the U.S. Court of Appeals in Washington and produced a well articulated directive that met and exceeded all requirements for a clear defensible position in a court of law. That policy, signed into law by President Carter and maintained without change through the present time, states that:

> *Homosexuality is incompatible with military service. The presence in the military environment of persons who engage in homosexual conduct or who, by their statements, demonstrate a propensity to engage in homosexual conduct, seriously impairs the accomplishment of the military mission. The presence of such members adversely affects the ability of the Military Services to maintain discipline, good order, and morale; to foster mutual trust and confidence among service members; to ensure the integrity of the system of rank and command; to facilitate assignment and worldwide deployment of service members who frequently must live and work under close conditions affording minimal privacy; to recruit and retain members of the Military Services; to maintain the public acceptability of military service; and to prevent breaches of security.*[16]

Although never explicitly stated as such, standing Defense Department policy on homosexual behavior has been based on a moral tradition rooted in the Bible and mediated through the support of the people of the United States as expressed by their elected representatives in Congress. The morality that gave definition to the disciplinary standards of the Continental Army have continued in place, and although definitions and procedures have been made more precise, the fundamental moral framework has continued without alteration — that is until recently. Starting a few years ago, and beginning well before Clinton was elected to office, cracks began to show in the level of confidence military leaders had in maintaining convictions about the immorality of homosexual conduct and the accountability of persons inclined to engage in homosexual acts.

Recoupment Policy under the Bush Administration

In February 1991, when I arrived at the Pentagon as Deputy Assistant Secretary of the Navy for Manpower, I found that serious questions were being asked regarding the recoupment policies of the various military services. "Recoupment" has to do with a requirement that persons awarded publicly funded military scholarships — in exchange for a commitment to serve — must reimburse the government for the used portion of their scholarship if they quit their program of study or voluntarily become disqualified for military service. Despite the fact that the issue was one that pertained directly to my appointed responsibilities, information was so closely guarded by my immediate superior, that I would have known nothing at all if I had not probed her staff and embarrassed them into giving me relevant materials. I discovered that a review was well underway and was nearing completion that was heading toward changing the way recoupment policy would be applied to students who became disqualified for military service on announcing a discovery of homosexual identity.

It must be remembered that this was well before the rise of the Clinton Administration and any discussion of changing acquisition policy pertaining to homosexual identity. The standing policy treated such cases as a matter of personal responsibility and volition. Candidates for scholarships have always been, and continue to be, screened for service eligibility. At that time they were required to answer direct questions on whether they considered themselves homosexual or bisexual (defined to include sexual desire for a person of one's own sex) and whether they intended to engage in homosexual acts. Affirmative answers meant automatic disqualification.

The review I discovered did not pertain to students who had *known* they were homosexual on accepting a military scholarship. Such cases fell into the category of fraudulent enlistment, a category that automatically warrants disciplinary discharge with recoupment of scholarship benefits fraudulently received. Rather, the review was undertaken pertaining to students who purported *honest* enlistment as heterosexuals but later announced a discovery of their hitherto unknown homosexual identity. Should the Defense Department policy on recoupment continue to treat the disqualification in such cases as something over which the individuals concerned *have control* and for which they can and should be *held accountable*? Or, should the disqualification be treated as something over which individuals have *no responsible control* and for which they cannot and should *not be held accountable*?

The policy review was launched because the Navy was facing the prospect of multiple court challenges to the standing policy, including at least three recent graduates of the U.S. Naval Academy who had been awarded commissions and sent to the fleet before announcing their "discovery" of homosexual identity. Lengthy challenges in court fueled by the growing militancy of homosexual activists were clearly anticipated. Despite our well settled policy on the exclusion of homosexuals, this aspect turned on judgments regarding the nature of homosexuality—and perceptions were changing. Vice Admiral Boorda, then Chief of Naval Personnel, was feeling the pressure and felt unsure about how defensible the existing policy would be if challenged in court. As a result, he began a push to have it changed. Barbara Pope was put in charge of reviewing the policy and recommending an appropriate response to Secretary of Defense Richard Cheney that would then be implemented consistently across all military services.

When I discovered the review, I found no effort had been made to defend, much less strengthen, the existing policy against possible challenge. Rather, there was going to be a single recommendation with pragmatic justifications all based on accepting as legitimate the basic premises of the homosexual activists: that homosexuality is determined by biology; that biologically based conditions are irreversible; that no matter how late in life a person "discovers" his or her homosexuality it is still a matter determined by their biology; so becoming homosexual is not a choice for which individuals can be held responsible even if they reach full adult maturity all the time thinking themselves heterosexual.

Having come directly from working domestic policy at the White House for President Bush, I was aware of his strong traditional views on the subject, and it greatly concerned me to find an effort underway that appeared headed in a direction directly contrary to the personal convictions and political commitments of the President. To address the matter and hopefully head it back in a more responsible direction, I wrote a memorandum to Barbara Pope explaining the moral and ideological conflict surrounding the challenge to military policy, discussing the scientific record, reviewing the political stakes for the President, and recommending that we keep the existing policy. What I received in return was a compliment on good writing style and a dressing down for spending valuable professional time doing my own analysis of the issue when someone at my level of seniority ought to be relying on work produced for them by more junior members.

Subsequently, my analysis was ignored and my recommendations rejected. The review went forward with no dissent, and the recoupment policy for homosexuals was changed with the approval of Secretary Cheney. I found out later that Barbara Pope had already preset the policy direction with David Addington, Special Assistant to Secretary Cheney. It was all highly controlled and secret. The President was never involved, even though the policy change was completely inconsistent with his values and political commitments.

Consistency with the President concerned me deeply, but what concerned me most was the failure of key policy makers—political appointees who were given their authority by President Bush—to express appreciation, much less concern, for the moral stakes involved as viewed from the moral tradition on which the preexisting policy was framed. There seemed to be a total lack of awareness that changing presumptions to accept the legitimacy of homosexual claims would actually entail rejection of a morality that not only happens to be consistent with the Bible, but is the moral tradition held once by the founding fathers, held then by President Bush, held still by most men and women in uniform,[17] and held still by the overwhelming majority of the American people. A different moral perspective was already operative and evident in the value judgments and policy directions provided by the individuals who were given control of the policy process—Barbara Pope and David Addington. They were the key political players whom Cheney put in charge and trusted to set a proper course, and it was clear from Barbara's response to my analysis and recommendations that she saw no legitimacy whatsoever in the traditional moral perspective on which it was based. It was not her own and she had an ally in Cheney's office who could see it through. Consistency with the President, with the majority of the American people, with most of the men and women in uniform, with the founding fathers and with objective science did not matter. She was convinced that she knew the right thing to do, and she knew how she was going to get it done. The problem was she had already adopted a new

230

moral perspective, a perspective that accepted the legitimacy of homosexuality and that judged it immoral to hold anyone accountable for becoming involved in homosexual behavior even though they had never thought of themselves as homosexual before they entered military service.

The War Goes Hot with the Clinton Transition

For their part, most of the senior military leadership did not realize the moral stakes. The differences seemed small, pragmatic and essentially political. It was not until the shock of Clinton's election and his commitment to lifting the military ban on homosexual service that the military leadership really awoke to the danger of applying homosexual presuppositions and arguments to the military situation. When it did, their resistance to the proposed changes was both moral and practical. And, as their moral convictions were stirred, so was their interest in the biblical origins of the traditional moral perspective on which they continued to operate. In the transition period between Clinton's election and the end of the Bush Administration, a Navy chaplain serving the Marine Corps, Commander Eugene Gomulka, produced a paper sharply attacking the pressure to change long-standing policy excluding homosexuals from military service. His analysis was eagerly copied and distributed through senior military circles and, not because he was considered an expert on military personnel policy per se, but because his views commanded moral respect, respect for the traditional side in the moral war that could no longer be ignored by people in uniform.[18] Also during this time an outline of what the Bible teaches on homosexuality was distributed and eagerly copied. This outline even made it into some official briefing books prepared for senior military officers needing to become more knowledgeable on what suddenly had become the hottest concern in the building. When the need for moral foundations became urgent, biblical teaching on the issue suddenly became

231

important, not for all, certainly, but for many. Although the demand for biblically based instruction could never be official, it was nevertheless felt and accepted on an individual level, and that in turn steeled convictions that could be expressed in practical, social and military terms.

Strategic Areas for Theologians and Bible Scholars

Americans live in a country where biblical teaching, or at least perceptions about biblical teaching, still can be a major influence on the moral judgments of public policy decision-makers. The failure of theologians and biblical scholars to speak with clarity and relevance in support of classical biblical norms leaves public policy decision-makers without sufficient information or the needed moral fiber to face the onslaught of new and contrary claims demanding removal or reversal of policies derived from a biblically consistent moral perspective. The converse is also true: the opportunity for clear teaching by theologians and biblical scholars can yet have strategic influence on public policy decisions as pertaining to persons promoting homosexual desires and conduct. Their influence is not, and has never been, direct. But many decision-makers are listening. For such, the assurance of confident biblical scholars conversant with the battles of the public policy moral war, as well as with Scripture, is imperative to settle their convictions and stiffen their resistance. As a result, biblical scholars and theologians must offer strategic commentary in three key areas: the progressive and morally corrosive spread of homosexual conduct through culture and society; the nature of homosexuality and attendant issues thereto; and finally, the progression involved and consequences following from shifting moral paradigms.

The Prevalence and Spread of Homosexual Conduct

The first key area on which biblical scholars must concentrate concerns the manner in which homosexual behavior will grow and spread through a culture that ceases to resist it, then comes to tolerate it, and finally arrives at celebrating it. Much can be gleaned and learned on this subject from a careful analysis of the two Old Testament accounts in which whole communities were overcome by militant, celebratory homosexual behavior. The first regards the cities of Sodom and Gomorrah and is recorded in Genesis 18 and 19. The second regards Gibeah of Benjamin and is recorded in Judges 19 and 20. We should consider, for example, the rather sobering claim made in Genesis 19:4 that the crowd of militant males demanding homosexual sex with Lot's visitors were, in fact, "all the men [of Sodom]." Lest we take this all inclusive statement too lightly, the passage underscores what "all the men" really means by adding "from every part of the city" and "both young and old." Apparently "all" is indeed meant to be all—all in the sense of geographic distribution as well as all across the spectrum of possible ages.

It would appear that once all moral and cultural restraints are broken down, social pressures throughout a community will reverse. Culture and social pressure turn from barriers restraining homosexual expression into forces in its favor. It can spread until it reaches 100%, or virtually 100%, of the local population. This historical account being true, it has serious implications for those who currently find comfort and safety in scientific studies showing a low incidence rate for homosexuals in American culture. Present figures may not be reliable if they are only measuring the early stages of a progressive social cancer. While cultural tolerance of a fixed and tiny minority may seem magnanimous, acceptance and promotion of a malignant cancer will promote moral and cultural death.

Status vs. Behavior: The Nature of Homosexuality

The second key area that biblical scholars and theologians must address surrounds the nature of homosexuality. A struggle is now taking place in the courts, in the Congress, in the departments of the Executive Branch of government and in our schools over whether or not homosexual status can be distinguished from homosexual behavior, and whether or not they are indistinguishable because homosexuality is a status defined by behavior. Does the Bible speak to this issue? Is homosexuality first something that one is before it becomes something one does, or is it something one becomes because of something one does? Here the battle to capture science must be followed and engaged by non-scientists who nevertheless are knowledgeable enough about science to discern good science from bad, and to discern politicized science-talk from tested and repeatable findings of scientific fact. The theological and moral implications of new claims made concerning the nature of homosexuality are indeed enormous. Does the biblical account of creation allow for variations of human sexuality other than male and female? Can the institution of human sexual relationship following from the creation of Eve and her introduction to Adam be legitimately stretched to allow sexual knowledge of men with men, and women with women? Does the institution of marriage that follows the creation of Eve for Adam include the blessing of same sex marriages? If homosexuality is a biological status before it is expressed in behavior, does that make God responsible for creating homosexuals? And, if so, how can it be immoral for persons to behave according to the way they were created? Biblical scholars and theologians who take the Bible seriously simply cannot ignore such questions, for biblical interpretation is already being stretched and revised to arrive at just such conclusions.

In addressing the nature of homosexuality from a biblical foundation, theologians must not only develop teaching taken from the creation account in Genesis, but must also study the statement of the Creator in Leviticus who, in dictating the law to Moses, not only rules against all homosexual behavior but goes on to say that those caught deserve punishment and have no one to blame but themselves—"their blood will be on their own head" (Leviticus 20:13). This appears to be the Creator himself stating in audible words recorded by Moses that homosexuals, without exception of any kind, cannot shift blame or moral accountability for their behavior to the Creator. Can biblical scholars take the Bible seriously and still find room here to support cultural-moral trends that wish to recognize a status that might make homosexual conduct moral or that makes homosexuality a divine creation for which individuals should not be fully responsible? To this must be added the words of Paul in First Corinthians 6:11, in which he uses the term "homosexuals" (*arsenokoitai*) to characterize something that some of his readers *had been*, but no longer *were*. The verb tenses here are clear and precise and would appear to rule out anything like an irreversible biological condition.

Shifting Moral Paradigms

The final key area on which biblical scholars must concentrate if they are to respond strategically to the moral war in public policy over the treatment of homosexuals has to do with helping policy makers understand the progression involved in shifting moral paradigms and the way it relates to the acceptance and practice of homosexual behavior at the individual and cultural level. Special attention must be given to the progression listed in Romans 1:18–32, for it reveals much about the manner in which moral paradigms are shifted as well as what follows once the shift of moral paradigms has taken place. What begins with a failure to be thankful for what God has given, moves to adopting a false moral compass and the rejection of true moral light based on God's self-revelation. It continues through successive stages to an eventual embrace and celebration of aggressive homosexual behavior, culminating with active efforts to recruit others into acceptance of homosexual morality and participation in the homosexual lifestyle. There are lessons here that are immediately relevant to current public policy battles. Responsibly engaged biblical scholars and theologians must work out and apply insights from Romans 1 and apply them in ways relevant to decision-makers caught up in the public policy moral war. Work of this sort will be strategic and could be determinative if disseminated before public policy decision-makers are wholly overcome by the mounting chorus of new voices who simply presume the legitimacy of the new homosexual morality and press policy makers to respond to demands that only make sense if the new moral paradigm is accepted and the old one is set aside as irrelevant.

To conclude, the Bible and its interpretation has, in fact, played a relevant and strategic role in affecting public policy decision-makers who have been engaged in the rejection of homosexuality by the military services. Its influence has been felt where it has affected the convictions of senior military officers as well as civilians in political positions affecting military policy. But this influence has not been all on one side. The biblical influence has divided as policy opinions have reflected contrary lines of biblical interpretation. Furthermore, while it has been noteworthy, the effect that biblical teaching has had on public policy in general, and on military personnel policy in particular, has never been direct. Nevertheless, its influence has been substantial at the level of fundamental moral convictions and operative moral paradigms—the orientation of world view presumed in policy decisions. These in turn have and continue to determine perceptions concerning the nature of the stakes involved as well as their relative level of importance. As a consequence, battles have been waging in American society at large between competing moral paradigms, each seeking to capture strategic sources of moral-cultural authority such as history, science and the U.S. Congress.

These battles and their outcome in favor of one side or the other will determine the final direction of specific policy issues, such as military personnel policies touching on persons who engage in or who are attracted by homosexual behavior. Because these battles are shaped at the level of competing moral paradigms, the Bible and its interpretation has and will continue to play a strategic role in affecting the moral convictions and judgments of policy players. Theologians and biblical scholars who take the inspiration and historic authority of the Bible seriously must not ignore the impact their work can have on the treatment of moral issues in public policy, and they must not fail to address the moral stakes involved in matters such as the rejection of homosexuality by the military services. Their impact will be felt one way or the other. Let it be the impact of strategic and intelligent engagement, and not the impact of ignorance and neglect.

Endnotes

[1] Patricia Schroeder, "Fears, Not Facts, Fuel Opposition: Gay, Lesbian Soldiers Have Served with Valor," *Legal Times*, February 15, 1993, pp. 27, 33.

[2] George Washington, *The Writings of George Washington*, ed. John C. Fitzpatrick, vol. I (Washington: U.S. Government Printing Office, 1934), pp. 83–84.

[3] *Journals of the Continental Congress*, vol. III (Washington: Government Printing Office, 1905), p. 378.

[4] Noah Webster, *An American Dictionary of the English Language* (Springfield, MA: George and Charles Merriam, 1949).

[5] Charles Socarides, "Sexual Politics and Scientific Logic: The Issue of Homosexuality," in *Hope for Homosexuality* (Washington: Free Congress, 1988), pp. 46–64.

[6] Edward Martin, "Memorandum for Secretaries of the Military Departments: Medical Implications of Homosexuals in the Military," 30 March 1993, The Pentagon, Washington, D.C.

[7] Robert L. Spitzer, "The Status of Homosexuality," *American Journal of Psychiatry* 138, 2 (1981): 210.

[8]For more detail see R. Bayer, *Homosexuality and American Psychiatry: The Politics of Diagnosis* (New York: Basic, 1981); and Charles W. Socarides, "Sexual Politics and Scientific Logic: The Issue of Homosexuality," in *Hope for Homosexuality* (Washington, DC: Free Congress, 1988), pp. 46–64.

[9]Several good analyses have treated this issue. For example see: Robert Knight, "Sexual Disorientation: Faulty Research in the Homosexual Debate," *Family Policy* 5/2 (Washington: Family Research Council, June 1992); Joe Dallas, "Born Gay?: How Politics Have Skewed the Debate Over the Biological Causes of Homosexuality," *Christianity Today* (June 22, 1992): 20–23; also an unpublished paper by Stanton L. Jones, "Doesn't Modern Science Teach That Persons of Homosexual Orientation Are Born That Way?" Fall 1990, Wheaton College, Wheaton, IL.

[10]Every study performed on conversion from homosexuality to heterosexuality has produced significant results. Bieber (1976) and Socarides (1978) reported 33% and 50% success rates by psychoanalytic treatment. Masters and Johnson (1979), using sex therapy and behavior methods, reported a 50% to 60% success rate even after a five year follow-up period. Many others have had similar results. According to Dr. Armand M. Nicholi, Department of Psychiatry, Harvard Medical School, these include Anna Freud, Bergler, Bychowski, Lorand, Hadden, Oversey, Eber, Socaidles, Glover, Bickner, Hatterer, and there are more. Biologically predetermined conditions, such as gender and race, cannot be reversed. But learned behavior can be unlearned.

[11]Scientists have found certain biological traits that are statistically associated with increased manifestation of homosexual behavior. Even so, none of these associated traits (i.e., prenatal hormones, postnatal hormones, psychological anomalies) have been found to either be necessary or sufficient, either alone or in combination, to fix a homosexual orientation. Many individuals with these traits do not become homosexual, and some individuals become homosexual without having any of these traits present. Identical twins have identical constitutions, but one may become homosexual while the other is firmly heterosexual. Whatever influence these traits may have, they do not determine that homosexual behavior will take place. For example, see John Money, "Sin, Sickness, or Status? Homosexual Gender Identity and Psychoneuroendocrinology," *American*

Psychologist 42 (1987): 384–399. Indeed, the weight of scientific evidence indicates that, although certain biological traits are associated with increase rates of occurrence, homosexual behavior is not predetermined by such factors and is not fixed except by additional factors such as external conditioning and choice.

[12]A cross-cultural analysis by Carrier documented strong evidence that the view of homosexual behavior embraced by a society has a powerful shaping effect on subsequent behavior. See: "Homosexual Behavior in Cross Cultural Perspective," in Marmor, ed., *Homosexual Behavior* (New York: Basic, 1980). Gadpaille, of the University of Colorado Medical Center in Denver, also concludes that the cross-cultural data clearly show that adult homosexuality "does not naturally develop . . . in human cultures or families in which the innate heterosexual bias is allowed expression and is fostered." See: "Cross-Species and Cross-Cultural Contributions to Understanding Homosexual Activity," *Archives of General Psychiatry* 37 (1980): 355. The fact that homosexuality is so widely affected by cultural conditioning is strong evidence of learned behavior. Even Richard Green, "Homosexuality as a Mental Illness," in A. Caplan, ed., *Concepts of Health & Disease* (Reading, MA: Addison-Wesley, 1981), who supported the APA removal of homosexuality from its list of mental disorders, recognizes that homosexual behavior "appears to be related to religion . . . educational status, and residence." All these are factors that would not pertain if homosexuality were biologically determined from birth.

[13]From the view of biological development, the notion of an inherited, biologically predetermined cause for homosexuality as a naturally occurring variation like race or gender simply is not possible. Members of a species that are not biologically suited for reproduction do not reproduce themselves and soon die out. Few if any individuals are born from parents who practice bisexuality. No one ever is born of parents who practice homosexuality exclusively, and their genes are not passed on. On the other hand, learned behaviors can vary widely from generation to generation, and may go in directions completely contrary to behaviors necessary for the preservation of a species.

[14]Gerald Solomon, *Congressional Record*, 30 March 1993 (Washington, DC: Government Printing Office), pp. E809–E810.

[15]Steve Gunderson, *Congressional Record*, 28 September 1993 (Washington, DC: Government Printing Office), p. H7071.

[16]Department of Defense Directive 1332.14, "Enlisted Separations," 28 January 1982.

[17]A survey for the Defense Readiness Council showed 95% of all retired flag and general officers to be opposed to lifting the ban on homosexuals serving in the military. See: *Survey of Retired Flag Officers*, by the Robertson Group (Defense Readiness Council, 15 June 1993). While this figure does not separate moral from pragmatic motivations, moral views were clearly a major determining factor.

[18]Chaplain Gomulka's paper was later published as "Why No Gays," *Naval Institute Proceedings* (December 1992): 44–46.

Rush Limbaugh: Politically Incorrect, Biblically Correct?

by Daniel J. Evearitt

*C*laiming to have talent on loan from God, Rush Limbaugh has staked out a claim on the airwaves of American radio and television. For three hours daily, he holds forth, reaching 20 million listeners weekly on over 600 radio stations. And many of his listeners display a devotion and loyalty bordering on the religious.

By far the most listened to radio talk show personality in the nation, he also has a daily half-hour television show which has at times been the third highest rated late-night show in the nation. His first book, *The Way Things Ought to Be*, released in 1992, spent nearly a year atop the hardcover, non-fiction *New York Times* bestseller list. Over 2 million copies have been sold in hardcover alone. His second book, *See, I Told You So*, was also on the bestseller list. His newsletter has a paid circulation of nearly 500,000. An estimated 300 restaurants nationwide set aside "Rush Rooms" for interested diners who cannot bear to miss his lunchtime radio broadcast. Merchandise bearing his name and likeness can be seen from coast to coast.

Part showman, part commentator and decidedly out-spoken, Rush Limbaugh espouses political conservatism. On his call-in radio show, in his writings and on television, he boldly states what he believes is wrong with the country and who is to blame. His programs counterattack what he calls the liberal political bias of "the dominant media culture." He often exaggerates, to the point of distortion, the views which he opposes. Repeatedly he makes the claim that he need not give equal time to opposing viewpoints, because the other side has the television networks, news magazines and countless newspapers advocating the liberal slant on the events of the day. He sees himself as the alternative and frequently asserts, "I am equal time!"

Rush Limbaugh has gained respect as a conservative political spokesman. Occasional appearances on public affairs programs have contributed to his stature. Former president Ronald Reagan has called him "the number one voice for conservatism in our country."

Who is Rush Limbaugh? Rush Hudson Limbaugh III was born in 1951 in Cape Girardeau, Missouri, where his family was active in Republican political circles. His grandfather, a lawyer, was ambassador to India during the Eisenhower administration. His uncle was appointed to a federal judgeship by Reagan. His father, a successful lawyer appears to have been the major influence on his sons and their friends. Rush's younger brother, an attorney, handles some of his legal matters.

Although he came from a family of lawyers, Rush Limbaugh chose radio as his vocation. When Limbaugh dropped out of college after a disappointing freshman year and left for a radio job in Pittsburgh, his father's plans for another lawyer in the family were thwarted. Fearful of what would become of him, his father warned him what a lack of social standing could mean in life. As Limbaugh went from job to job in Top-40 radio, it must have seemed at times as if his father was right. There are reports of angry confrontations between Limbaugh and his father over the direction of his life.[1]

Talk radio became his road to success, first locally at a station in Sacramento, California, then nationally since 1988, based in New York City. Limbaugh proudly chronicles his transition from local phenomenon to mega-stardom in the early chapters of *The Way Things Ought to Be*.

Ultimately, his father knew his son had arrived when, shortly before his death, he saw his son on ABC's *Nightline*, in November of 1990. Having heard his son's national radio show, his father was concerned that Limbaugh's joking around had always detracted from his political message. But here he was on a major network television show, offering serious opinion on the troop build-up before the Persian Gulf War. The elder Limbaugh was clearly proud of his son. Limbaugh wrote later, in his book, that his father had been the source.[2]

While Limbaugh claims to be nothing more than an entertainer, he is far more. He effectively communicates a conservative political worldview day after day. His way of looking at the world, people and government is of interest to the Christian believer. It is difficult to determine just how many evangelical and fundamentalist Christians tune in to Rush Limbaugh on a regular basis. According to one report, advertisers estimate that 20 to 25 percent of his 20 million weekly audience is made up of evangelical and fundamentalist believers.[3]

Limbaugh firmly believes that America was built on a Judeo-Christian foundation. He admits that the role of religious beliefs in the history of this country is not taught in our schools today and believes it should be.[4] He affirms his personal belief in "one God" and holds that this country was established with belief in God at the core of its founding principles.[5]

Unfortunately, according to Limbaugh, anti-religious forces have worked to remove prayer and Bible reading from the classroom. Crowding religion out of public life,

Supreme Court decisions have narrowed the rights of those who wish to practice their religion in public places.

The public arena is the main focus of Limbaugh's comments on religion. That is where he sees a real battle underway. What he labels an "assault" is being made upon the religious foundations of the nation. The dispute centers around how to interpret the First Amendment of the Constitution. The separation of church and state, he maintains, was not written to protect the people from religion, but to prevent government from establishing one as the state religion. He strongly objects to interpretations of the First Amendment that seek to remove religion from active inclusion in the public life of the nation. He contends that the framers of the Constitution did not intend to push God and religion aside, only that no church be given a formal preference over all others.[6]

Limbaugh is in favor of bringing religion back into America's classrooms. Like many others, he wonders if it is merely coincidental that the quality of education has declined since religion began to be removed from schools 30 years ago.[7]

He rejoiced when the Supreme Court ruled that religious groups must be allowed to use school property after hours, just as can any other group. The Supreme Court case allowing prayer at commencement ceremonies, if led by students and not clergy, was hailed a triumph by Limbaugh. He called it a victory for the faithful and God-fearing.[8]

He wonders why creationism cannot be taught in schools, since it comes from God. It takes faith to believe in creationism, he told his radio audience. Yet, Limbaugh notes, no one has been able to prove cross-species evolution, which also must be accepted by faith. It puzzles him that faith in God is deemed wrong, whereas faith in science is alright.[9] This faith in man rather than God raises questions for Limbaugh about the ultimate value of human life. He has told his listeners that though it was an impossibility for man actually to succeed, if man thinks he can create life out of nothing, there is a reduction in the value of life.[10]

The origin and sanctity of human life matters greatly to Limbaugh. The Bible clearly teaches that God created life and that human destiny is in his control. While advances in medical science have made tremendous changes in the treatment of the human body, there are limits to human knowledge. Matters of life and death are still in God's hands, not man's. Limbaugh laments the notion that all mysteries will be worked out by human intellectual development because it leads to a human-centered view that excludes the Creator from the picture.

One of the reasons many evangelicals and fundamentalists are attracted to Rush Limbaugh is because he considers God's existence an important truth.[11] God's creation of human life has implications that impact how we view ourselves, others and all of life. This notion appears to be lost to most of the media establishment. As they see it, religion is a peripheral matter. But to Limbaugh, belief in the existence of God and the importance of religion influences his attitude toward man in relation to nature and the animal world and his attitude toward religion's role in fostering morality.

Because Limbaugh calls to attention the religious heritage of our country's history and for a more active role for religion in today's society, he finds supporters from the Religious Right. This is evidenced, among other ways, by his appearance at a Republican National Coalition for Life event, held in conjunction with the Republican National Convention, with Pat Robertson, Jerry Falwell and Phyllis Schlafly, all long-time prominent leaders of the Religious Right. They share with him the agenda of moving the country in a conservative direction politically. But does he share their theological commitment?

The "gospel" that Rush Limbaugh preaches is heavy on the implications of religion, while light on a theology of personal redemption. He does not discuss religion as religion on his radio or television shows, reportedly because he does not want his shows to be categorized as religious talk shows. He has confessed to being a Christian on the air more than once.[12] However, he seldom attends church.[13]

Limbaugh's message is theologically incomplete. He trumpets the role which religion has played in the shaping of our nation's founding documents and history. He notes that belief in God is important. But teaching that America's founders were religious and that one should believe in God will not get at the core of the human problem. Important as our religious roots and belief in God are, standing alone they are insufficient to remedy man's malady. The fundamental issue of human sin must be dealt with, on an individual basis, by repentance for sin and acceptance of salvation through Christ.

Limbaugh views religion primarily as the teacher of morals and values. While some of our moral standards come from the Bible, he told his radio audience, other moral standards have developed over the centuries. They were not merely imposed by the brute force of the majority, but developed because certain standards worked best. Morality cannot be defined by the individual, he added, otherwise there are no standards.[14] Thus, religion is to be supported primarily for what it does for society—providing moral undergirding. An attack upon religion or a lessening of the free reign for religion in public life he sees as a threat to the moral fabric of the nation.

Limbaugh makes the charge that many liberals are out to remove religion not only from our history but from all of our public institutions.[15] Religion is not to be allowed in "liberal America," he said on the radio. Therefore, liberals must come up with their own religion to transmit their values.[16] In *The Way Things Ought to Be*, he identifies that substitute religion as secular human philosophy coupled with belief in the state.[17]

Secular humanism teaches that man is fine on his own. He needs no help from any power outside his own intelligence and strength. Certainly this teaching presents a clear and present danger to the biblical teaching that God has acted in history on man's behalf. By making man the focus of attention, secular humanism displaces God. There is no place for the Creator in the humanist's world. Man is good enough on his own. Sin is not a problem. Men might do bad things, but they are not really evil. There is no need, therefore, for salvation, and no need of a Christ to redeem mankind. Those who advocate this view appear to be winning the day in America. They seem to be successfully convincing many that they really do not need God.

It is refreshing and reassuring to hear someone reaffirm belief in God—especially in the public arena. When Rush Limbaugh highlights the importance of religion and belief in God, we take notice. There is a danger though. The gospel that Limbaugh presents may be a truncated gospel. It is a gospel that sees what religion can do to modify social behavior, but stops there.

We are warned in Galatians that people will come along with "false gospels" (Galatians 1:6–9). Obviously, secular humanism is wrong. But so also is any partial gospel that attempts to reduce the Christian message to social and political policy only.

Rush Limbaugh's gospel is a political gospel. He aggressively lays out a conservative political agenda. His agenda must not be mistaken for the full gospel. Where it supports the Christian message, as found in the Bible, it should be applauded. Where it diverges, it should be judged. We should be cautious about wedding the gospel of Christ to any particular political ideology. God's program is spiritual in nature. While it has political ramifications, if it is reduced only to politics it runs the danger of pulling us away from the true gospel and from God's true mission for his people.

In the last week of his earthly ministry, Jesus told his disciples that he would not always be present with them physically, but that they would always have the poor with them (Matthew 26:11; Mark 14:7). There are always people who need a financial helping hand. Such indeed has been the case since the beginning of human history. Limbaugh believes this, too, as he echoes these sentiments in "The 35 Undeniable Truths of Life," published in his newsletter. Truth 33: "There will always be poor people." Truth 34: "The fact that there will always be poor people is not the fault of the rich."[18]

Human society seems to always have poor people, but what can be done about it? How people respond to the poor says quite a bit about them as persons. What is Rush Limbaugh's approach to the needy poor? Which social theories have helped to shape his attitude toward the poor? And how does his approach to the poor compare to Scripture?

The Bible has significant things to say about the poor, and also the wealthy. The general pattern throughout Scripture is that the needy were to be cared for by those who had the means. The needy were chiefly made up of the orphans and widows of the community. Due to the social system of the day, widows and orphans were unable independently to care for their financial needs adequately. In the structure laid forth by God for the children of Israel, family or clan members were to care for their own needy. In the New Testament, the early church cared for its widows and orphans as well.

Instruction was given in the Old Testament for the care of the poor, whether they were foreigners in need in Israel or Israelites. These were not helpless widows or orphans, but people whose poverty came about by other means. Loans were to be made to the poor, but not at exorbitant interest rates. The poor were then to pay back the loans and be debt free (Ex. 22:25; Dt. 15:7–8). The way out of poverty was work. Even though a jubilee was established by God to allow for the periodic wiping out of debts at 50-year intervals (Lev. 25), in the intervening years the poor person was expected to work at paying off his debts.

While provision was made for granting loans to the poor, so that they might plant their crops and feed their livestock, strong warnings were given about those who sought to avoid work. Various verses in Proverbs label the one who is lazy and refused to work as a "sluggard." Two parallel passages end with the identical saying, "A little sleep, a little slumber, a little folding of the hands to rest, and poverty will come on you like a bandit and scarcity like an armed man" (Prov. 6:10–11; 24:33–34). In one passage, the author walked past the field of a sluggard, found it full of weeds and thorns, its walls fallen down and took this object lesson to heart as a warning not to be like that person (Prov. 24:30–32). In the other passage, the author urged the sluggard to get up from his sleep to go watch an ant storing food, in order to learn industriousness (Prov. 6:6–9). Deliberate avoidance of work had dire consequences, namely poverty. The person who did not plow and plant seed would not have anything to harvest (Prov. 20:4). Work was presented as a necessary ingredient for a successful life.

In the New Testament, Paul warned believers to avoid idleness by following his example. He worked and paid his own way. He expected others to do the same. A firm rule was established, "If a man will not work, he shall not eat." Hearing of some who were idle, Paul urged them "to settle down and earn the bread they eat." If they refused, they were to be shunned and made to feel ashamed, with the expectation that correction would take place (2 Thess. 3:6–15).

Just as laziness was condemned in Scripture, work was applauded. The order and rhythm of life was established by the pattern of God's creation of the world. Genesis records that God spent six days working to create the world and its inhabitants, but on the seventh day He rested. So He mandated that humans work six days but rest on the seventh (Dt. 5:13–14). Built into the system is the sabbath for re-creation and renewal.

The implication of the creation account is that, like his Creator, man has creative ability. He was given the ability to work with his hands and was placed in a setting where work would be necessary (Gen. 2:15). God gave man something to do. Work was assigned to the first human couple. It was part of human self-identity from the beginning.

Proverbs says that, "All hard work brings a profit" (14:23). It is said of Job that God had "blessed the work of his hands" (Job 1:10). Paul told his followers, "Make it your ambition to . . . work with your hands, just as we told you, so that your daily life may win the respect of outsiders and so that you will not be dependent on anybody" (1 Thess. 4:11–12). Work brings self-respect, self-worth and a sense of usefulness. Work is not only important for supplying the daily needs of life, but also has much to contribute to one's self-image. By working, one is carrying out a divinely-intended role. One is functioning within the purposes of the Divine economy. Limbaugh's message ties in with Weber's thesis that Calvinistic Protestantism, with its high regard for work and frugality, is supportive of capitalism. In Limbaugh's world, one apparently gets out of life what one puts into it.

Homelessness is one of the more visible manifestations of poverty. If someone is living on the street or in a park because they have no place to go, we naturally feel compassion toward them. Limbaugh, at times, questions the helplessness of many of the homeless. His solution to homelessness involves dealing with the root cause that brought a person to the point of destitution, rather than creating permanent governmental bureaucracies to care for them. He might be called heartless by some, but over the long haul, his solution is perhaps more compassionate.

Bringing a person in off the street, only to make them a permanent charity case, or to create an ongoing, generational underclass of poor people dependent upon government assistance, hardly seems humane. To be dependent totally on the kindness of others with no hope of ever being able to care for themselves, is personally demoralizing and destructive.

Some of the homeless, Limbaugh claims, choose to be homeless. They do not want to take on the responsibility to work and care for themselves.[19] These persons fall into the biblical category of "sluggards," about which the book of Proverbs warns. Others are homeless because they have drug or alcohol problems. These, he says, should be rehabilitated. Those homeless who are mentally ill, he adds, should be institutionalized. Those who are able to work should be shown the opportunities that are available and be given jobs. Limbaugh sees these as realistic steps to begin solving the problem.[20]

We have established the fact that the poor will always be around, but what about the wealthy? As we have noted, one of Limbaugh's "undeniable truths" is that, while there will always be poor people, the wealthy are not to be blamed. For someone to have more, he would argue, does not mean that it comes at the expense of others. When there is recovery from a recession, someone will get rich. But he insists that to be rich is not a sin. Liberals might see the rich as sinners, simply because they have money. They might want to rob from the rich in order to equalize them with the poor. But Limbaugh maintains that achievers should not be punished merely because they are achievers.[21] Unfortunately, he notes, the successful are under assault. Those who have abided by the law and worked hard for what they own, are now accused of stealing what they have.

The question centers around material gain. Is wealth inherently evil? Biblical examples of wealthy people are numerous. They are never condemned for their wealth alone; they are judged for how they attained their wealth and for what they did with it.

Isaiah warns those who benefit from oppressing the poor: "The LORD takes his place in court; he rises to judge the people. The LORD enters into judgment against the elders and leaders of his people; 'It is you who have ruined my vineyard; the plunder from the poor is in your houses. What do you mean by crushing my people and grinding the faces of the poor?' declares the Lord, the LORD Almighty" (Is. 3:13–15). Those who take advantage of the poor for their own gain stand to be judged harshly by God.

Jesus warned His followers, "Be on your guard against all kinds of greed; a man's life does not consist in the abundance of his possessions" (Lk. 12:15). He then told the parable of the rich fool, a person who lived totally for material gain. God said to him, "You fool! This very night your life will be demanded from you. Then who will get what you have prepared for yourself? This is how it will be with anyone who stores up things for himself but is not rich toward God" (Lk. 12:19–21). If wealth blocks spiritual growth and development, it is condemned.

The danger of losing sight of spiritual matters in a material world is so strong that Jesus warns of it repeatedly. Just after the parable of the rich fool, He tells His disciples to trust in God for their daily needs: "Life is more than food, and the body more than clothes" (23). God, who clothes all of nature, will take care of them as well. He cautions them: "Do not set your heart on what you will eat or drink; do not worry about it. For the pagan world runs after such things, and your Father knows that you need them. But seek his kingdom, and these things will be given to you as well" (29–31). The priority is clear: spiritual matters take precedence over material things. Jesus goes on to instruct His followers, "Sell your possessions and give to the poor. Provide purses for yourselves that will not wear out, a treasure in heaven that will not be exhausted, where no thief comes near and no moth destroys. For where your treasure is, there your heart will be also" (33–34).

Riches, material gain, possessions—can obscure the spiritual dimension of life. We might not think that our possessions own us, but we all need to examine our attitude and our priority.

Throughout Scripture God is considerate of the plight of the poor and oppressed. Perhaps nowhere is this clearer than Jesus' reading of Isaiah and his application of it to Himself: "The Spirit of the Lord is on me, because he has anointed me to preach good news to the poor. He has sent me to proclaim freedom for the prisoners and recovery of sight for the blind, to release the oppressed, to proclaim the year of the Lord's favor" (Lk. 4:18–19).

When the day of judgment comes, our reward or punishment is at least partly related to our treatment of the needy. Our relationship to material possessions helps define who we are as persons. The Scriptures teach the priority of spiritual values over worldly goods. We are taught to work to supply our daily needs, but that life does not end with the physical. Work is a noble endeavor; laziness leads to poverty and is condemned. We are instructed not to gain at the expense of others, yet we live in a competitive society. We must regulate our lives in such a way that we do not add to the oppression of the poor. The poor who are truly in need are worthy of charity to help to get them on their feet and headed toward self-support. Those needy who cannot fend for themselves must be provided for.

True compassion understands that a lasting solution to the problem has been implemented. Limbaugh's criticism of a system that makes people dependent upon the government, when they could and should be supporting themselves, is justified. But we must not blindly ignore those who cannot take care of their own needs. The poor will always be present, but should not be ignored.

Rush Limbaugh is judged as politically incorrect by the prevailing mood of the intellectual community. "Political correctness" is a recently coined term to describe a situation that has developed on many college and university campuses across America. Political correctness asserts that the old standards of what is good and bad in literature,

253

philosophy, art, morals, etc., were set by a restrictive, European-centered, male-oriented system and must now be challenged. To be politically correct an individual must believe that truth is relative. Nothing should be judged as "better" than anything else. Everything is a matter of one's perspective. No absolutes exist.

Political correctness demands tolerance of all points of view. The surety of a statement cannot be assumed simply because civilization handed down a time-tested, well-thought out position. The politically correct will ask, who came up with this idea? What perspective does it represent? What motives stand behind its formulation? Whose place in the societal structure does it enhance?

Taken to its extreme, there can be no absolute standards of right and wrong, or good or bad, in a politically correct world. Cultures are relative, as are all the elements within a given culture. Equality becomes the watchword in a politically correct framework. Everything should be treated equally, objectively and without bias, because everything has the same relative value.

The use of the term "politically correct", PC for short, has spread into general use. One hears it applied to people and statements outside higher education all the time. Limbaugh is a very vocal defender of tradition. He believes that the standards of American society must be upheld because they are under attack by forces that demoralize the nation and lead it into anarchy. Because he feels this threat so intensely, he lashes out against any and all people or forces he thinks contribute to the other side. PC-ese, therefore, is a frequent and well-lit target. Many of his statements challenge the politically correct assumptions that underlie the causes he attacks. Therefore, he would definitely have to be categorized as politically incorrect by today's standards. In *See, I Told You So*, Limbaugh equates political correctness with political cleansing.

When Limbaugh speaks in support of absolute moral values being based upon Divine law, he may be politically incorrect, but he is biblically correct. The politically correct disagree. They say that there are no moral absolutes; everything is relative. These laws, and the Divine authority held to be behind the laws, are the product of one culture among many cultures. It is unjustifiably judgmental to place one set of moral values higher than other sets of values derived from different conditions.

By the same token, arguing that criminals are responsible for the crimes they commit might make Limbaugh politically incorrect, but he is biblically correct. Individual responsibility for one's actions is taught in the Bible. Political correctness seeks to excuse criminals for unlawful behavior because of their upbringing, poor environment, or other factors. Speaking out against abortion might not be politically correct, but it is biblically correct. The Bible supports the sanctity of human life. Condemning homosexual behavior and opposing the allowing of gays in the military is not politically correct. The Bible, however, always condemns homosexual activity. Considering human life superior to animal life might not be politically correct. However, the Bible teaches that man has been given dominion over the earth and is to care for the earth. As beings created in the image of God, mankind is distinctively set above all animal creation, no matter what physical characteristics we might have that are similar to other animals. Believing that there are innate differences between males and females, differences that define certain roles in life, is not politically correct. However, the Bible holds that males and females have different roles to perform in life that make each uniquely responsible before God.

On a number of key points, then, Rush Limbaugh is politically incorrect but biblically correct. There are other issues, however, where the lines are not so clear. His condemnation of those who are pacifists is too broad. Simply because one is opposed to a war in which the United States becomes involved does not mean that one is anti-American. There are good people who are conscientious objectors to all wars. Traditional peace denominations should not be lumped in with others who have opposed any war Americans have engaged in, for perhaps less noble reasons.

Limbaugh's view that man cannot really do anything to destroy the environment overlooks the destruction that nuclear waste entails. While man has been given the earth, we are to care for it. While we are superior to the animal world, we are to be caretakers of the earth and treat animals humanely. The attitude toward the environment that he espouses could lead to callousness and arrogance toward the world we are to superintend. Rather than being caretakers, this attitude tends to make us unwise stewards of the world God has created and in which he has placed us.

Christianity, as a major element of traditional American culture, generally benefits when older established ways are reemphasized. It cannot be denied that Rush Limbaugh speaks out regularly in support of some of the traditional values that evangelical and fundamentalist Protestants also support. As a vocal spokesman for traditional values, he is gaining some attention for important issues. The problem comes with the way in which these issues are being raised and the attitudes which they foster.

Rush Limbaugh prides himself on being an entertainer. He has proven that he can draw an audience in print, radio, television and personal appearances. His adept use of comedy and other entertaining production features prove him a master showman. Simply because he views himself as primarily an entertainer does not mean that he does not also want to be taken seriously, as we have seen. Yet, he cannot hide behind his comedy and excuse things he says simply by saying they were a joke. Some of his humor is off-color, and not just in the minds of the listener. He uses language, on occasion, that must be condemned as vulgar. Making fun of segments of the population, particularly his putting down of radical feminists, homeless advocates, environmental extremists and others, spills over to hurt well-meaning people, whether intentionally or not. By exaggerating the extremes—and then attacking them—he is often unfair to moderate positions. This seems to be an intentional tactic. Extremists are ridiculed as being way off the mark. Then anyone who supports even the mildest form of anything Limbaugh opposes is painted with the same brush and dismissed as entirely wrong.

Part of the problem is the public persona of Rush Limbaugh. He deliberately heralds himself as the defender of all that is good in America. He sees himself as one of the only ones standing up for truth against the distorting forces of the dominant media culture—almost a prophetic posture. He gives his audience the idea that they are not going to discover truth anywhere else. He alone is on the cutting edge; nearly everyone else is off the mark. He repeatedly tells his audience all they have to do is listen to him; he will tell them the truth.

Limbaugh says he is after the truth. But is it the whole truth? Not really, for no one is purely objective; everyone has an agenda. Although he told his radio audience that they only think he is on a crusade to destroy liberalism, that he really has no carefully plotted effort, that he merely gets up every day and answers the phone, it is not that way.[23] While he wants to be seen as an entertainer, which he is, he must be seen as far more than merely a funny fellow, one who says some witty things. He is more than a guy who talks to people on the phone over the radio. In fact, he is the most popular dispenser of conservatism currently on the American scene. His agenda of getting at the truth is getting at his brand of the truth. It is a selective choice of issues. If it means exaggerating his opponents' views to the point of distortion to score his points, he does so. Apparently the means are justified by the ends.

Should evangelicals and fundamentalists get their entire picture of the world only from Rush Limbaugh? No. Each person should read, view and listen widely, always with an eye on what Scripture teaches on an issue. Will they find Limbaugh's views always consistent with the Bible? No, though many are. His main deficiency is in the attitude he takes toward people. We are told to love our neighbors. We are told to love our enemies. Love and genuine concern for people often seems to be missing from Limbaugh's message.

Just as Limbaugh discounts a socialist utopia, those who are expecting a capitalist utopia and a perfect nation to arise in America will be disappointed. A perfect social order awaits the return of our Lord to set up his kingdom. In the meantime, we should be cautioned against too closely attaching our Christian faith to any political party or agenda. We are to be the church. Our mission is always more than any specific political party or ideological movement. We must see changed hearts through the redeeming power of the gospel of Jesus Christ as our primary focus. If we lose sight of this, we have lost our way.

Endnotes

[1] Steven V. Roberts, "What a Rush!" *U.S. News and World Report*, August 16, 1993, p. 31.

[2] Rush Limbaugh, *The Way Things Ought to Be* (New York: Simon and Schuster, 1993), p. 17.

[3] Roy Maynard, "Can We Talk?" *World*, July 17, 1993, p. 12.

[4] Limbaugh, op. cit., p. 274.

[5] Ibid., p. 3.

[6] Ibid., pp. 277–281.

[7] Ibid., pp. 275–276.

[8] Rush Limbaugh, The Rush Limbaugh Radio Show, June 7, 1993.

[9] Ibid., July 15, 1993.

[10] Ibid., July 7, 1993.

[11]See Limbaugh's second list of "Thirty-Five More Undeniable Truths," that "There is a God." (*The Limbaugh Letter*, March 1994).

[12]Jeff Dunn, "Rush Fever in Christian Stores," *Christian Retailing*, July 1, 1993, p. 28.

[13]Roberts, op. cit., p. 30.

[14]Rush Limbaugh, The Rush Limbaugh Radio Show, July 2, 1993.

[15]Limbaugh, op. cit., p. 281.

[16]Rush Limbaugh, The Rush Limbaugh Radio Show, July 14, 1993.

[17]Limbaugh, op. cit., p. 281.

[18]Rush Limbaugh, "The 35 Undeniable Truths of Life," *The Limbaugh Letter*, Vol. 1, No. 3, December 1992, p. 10.

[19]Limbaugh, op. cit., p. 249.

[20]Ibid., p. 252.

[21]Rush Limbaugh, The Rush Limbaugh Radio Show, June 17, 1993.

[22]Ibid., June 10, 1993.

[23]Ibid.

The Secularizing of the Faith: Recent Supreme Court Decisions Regarding Religion

by Richard I. McNeely

*T*he First Amendment to the United States Constitution opens with the brief, emphatic command that "Congress shall make no law respecting the establishment of religion, or prohibiting the free exercise thereof," the purpose of which is clearly to prevent domination of government by religion or domination of religion by government. Though taken for granted by most twentieth-century Americans, S.H. Cobb asserted that,

> *This revolutionary principle, declarative of the complete separation of Church from State, so startlingly in contrast with the principles which had dominated in the past—this pure Religious Liberty—may be confidently reckoned as of distinctly American origin. . . . Here, among all the benefits to mankind to which this soil has given rise, this pure religious liberty may be justly rated as the great gift of America to civilization and the world . . .*[1]

At about the same time that Cobb so eloquently characterized religious liberty in the United States, Mary Baker Eddy (1903) linked God and the Constitution in describing her pillars of faith,[2] while Henry Estabrook, one of New York's most respected attorneys, intoned:

> *Our great and sacred Constitution, serene and inviolable, stretches its beneficent powers over our land—over its lakes and rivers and forests, over every mother's son of us, like the outstretched arm of God himself. . . . O Marvellous Constitution! Magic Parchment! Transforming Word! Maker, Monitor, Guardian of Mankind![3]*

To be sure, Americans continue to share a rather lofty range of affinities for the Constitution, often viewing that "Magic Parchment" as a sacred document. Now, if one accepts the concept of religion as "a collection of beliefs, symbols, and rituals with respect to sacred things and institutionalized in a collectivity,"[4] then there is a civil religion in this country and its clergy are those black-robed, high-benched members of the United States Supreme Court, "domiciled in Washington, D.C., as the Pope is in Rome."[5] And in this respect, note Rothenberg's observation:

> *Appellate judges as a group are, by nature and occupational conditioning, lofty personalities. As Justice Neely of the West Virginia Supreme Court has written, "a more strutting, preening egotistical group of prima donnas than the entire body of senior appellate judges would be difficult to assemble, except in the United States Senate."*
>
> *Preeminent in that group are the justices of the United States Supreme Court, [who] . . . are in positions analogous to that of the Pope. They interpret the nuances of the Constitution and apply them to statutes and lower court decisions. In doing so, they face little danger of being overruled. While his Holiness Pope John Paul II might not agree that his position is analogous, the justices of*

American's highest court always have the last word on any subject. As one of their own, Chief Justice Charles Evans Hughes, put it, "the Constitution is what the [justices] say it is."[6]

Americans have a long history of distrusting pronouncements from their high clergy (witness the present battles over the Pope's latest encyclical), the seeds of which find expression in Rudolph's observation: "Unable to set the world straight as Englishmen in England, the Puritan settlers . . . intended to set it straight as Englishmen in the New World."[7]

So, somewhere between the promises of the Constitution and Supreme Court case law, one may view some present-day Puritans of sorts, still stalking Old Deluder, questioning, skeptical of all authority other than the authority of the sacred scripture (viz., the Constitution), demanding liberty of conscience and the promise of equality of opportunity and individual freedom. These oppose a contempt for a just social order, including law enforcement agencies, schools and colleges, students, business, labor, the military and the poor, no less than the rich—all of whom on occasion seem to outdo each other in breaking the rules and violating the ethics that the Constitution established for society's protection.

As A.P. Stokes observed: "It is one thing to secure 'rights,' a very different thing to see that they are preserved inviolate."[8] And moving closer to the major focus of this paper, Millington implied that the First Amendment's religious guarantees can hardly be listed among America's untarnished constitutional trophies (if there are such things):

Ipse dixit—which would be translated loosely here as, because the First Amendment says it, it must be so—is not a phrase that springs unbidden from the lips of legal scholars when the Constitution's religious guarantees come up. For one thing, the purpose and meaning of these guarantees are like the Colorado River. At the source they are clear and strong. Downstream they become silty and oft-times disappear in the sand. . . . Why is that so? The answer, my friend, lies somewhere in the divine mystery of judicial process.[9]

As is true with most controversial issues, this debate has been accompanied by the surfacing of self-interested and emotion-laden perspectives that have become serious obstacles to rational discussion and understanding. One is reminded of de Tocqueville's earlier observation that "religious insanity is very common in the United States,"[10] as inconsistencies are so manifold. One can get some idea of this "religious insanity" from a few examples, beginning with some items Rothenberg extracted from the media:

ITEM: *A senate hearing in Washington [D.C.] on a bill to define the origin of human life is interrupted by 6 spectators, described as members of the Women's Liberation Zap Action Brigade, who stand on their chairs and shout: "Stop the hearing! Not the church, not the state, women must decide their fate."*

ITEM: *Eugene F. Diamond, M.D., outgoing President of the National Federation of Catholic Physicians' Guilds speaks out in his presidential address at his organization's annual meeting against the legalization of abortion by the United States Supreme Court and states: "We used to be a Christian country, but now are a pagan country."*

ITEM: *A fundamentalist minister in Niles, Ohio, believes that the Easter Bunny is a "pagan god" and who sought to burn a giant fake rabbit in the town square in order to dramatize the true meaning of Easter, is charged with public burning, disorderly conduct and obstructing official business after lighting the fire and calling some 100 per-*

sons watching from across the street, "heathens and dummies."

ITEM: *The American Civil Liberties Union takes out a full-page newspaper ad, headlined: "If the Moral Majority Has Its Way, You'd Better Start Praying," and warned: "the Moral Majority—and other groups like them—think that children should pray in school. Not just their children. Your children. But that's just the beginning. They want their religious doctrines enacted into law and imposed on everyone."*[11]

Though there is always a hue and cry about original intent, it is apparent that such argumentation is of little authority in modern pluralistic society. The religious scene in the United States today bears little resemblance to that of Colonial America. As Shelley and Shelley note, "Americans live with two loyalties in life: one as church members and another as citizens."[12] But they also follow a rather narcissistic bent of life, choosing "churches not so much to meet God and surrender to his revealed ways as to satisfy some personal need."[13] It is akin to what Peter Berger is reported to have observed about religion in the United States, "that if India is the most religious country in the world, and Sweden the least religious, then America is a nation of Indians ruled by Swedes. The ruling philosophy of our Swedes is naturalism."[14]

Notwithstanding, the secularization of religion is apparent in the United States. In defining a secular culture as "a culture reduced to thing and function," Eugene Peterson marks the present trade-off of these for the more important "essentials of human fullness: intimacy and transcendence."[15] Small wonder that such secularization may be characterized as the trivialization of religion, or the idea that religion is hardly to be taken seriously, a theme behind parts of Stephen L. Carter's recent work, *The Culture of Disbelief.*

Recently, Robert L. Wilkin defines secularization as "practical atheism."[16] Raul F. Yanes and Mary Ann Glendon have presented a synopsis of the decisions of the last four religious cases decided by the Court, concluding that "the continued reign of separationism means that the Court remains a collaborator, witting or unwitting, of the cultural forces bent on secularizing America."[17]

A Brief Review of Religious Jurisprudence in the Latter Half of the Twentieth Century

The changes in interpretation of the twin religious clauses in the Bill of Rights, (and changes there have been), can be traced to Justice Black's statement in the majority opinion of *Everson v. Board of Education* (1947), that "In the words of Jefferson, the clause against establishment of religion by law was intended to erect 'a wall of separation between church and State.' "[18] In fairness to him, Black seemed to retreat from that position in *Adamson v. California* (1947)—decided later in the same Court session.

What has happened during the latter half of the 20th century is the bifurcation of the two religious clauses. The result of this has been a setting of the two in opposition to one another. When the Equal Access case, *Widmar v. Vincent* (1981) came to the Court, it was thought by some that there would be some judicial clarification in setting the two clauses as complementary rather than opposed. The direction which the Court took, though it resulted in a victory for the religious interests, made the religious clauses no different from those which followed in the Amendment. The effect was to denigrate the religious clauses.

To demonstrate the thesis of this paper—that recent cases have moved in the direction of secularization—I will first discuss briefly the judicial bases on which "establishment" and "free exercise" issues are decided. Then, I will summarize three cases which demonstrate the move toward the secularization of religion.

Testing the Establishment Clause: The Incorporation Principle

James Madison, early in the deliberations regarding the Bill of Rights, proposed that the First Amendment be worded: "The civil rights of none shall be abridged on account of religious belief or worship, nor shall any national religion be established, nor shall the full and equal rights of conscience be in any manner, or on any pretext, infringed."[19] But Madison added: "No State shall violate the equal rights of conscience, or the freedom of the press, or the trial by jury in criminal cases." He further proposed that this article be included in the original Constitution together with the statement regarding religious tests for office (See U.S. Constitution, Article VI, paragraph 3). This second statement which pertained to the States was defeated by the Senate, but any claims of its death were premature. Indeed, the effect of his original idea was realized when the Fourteenth Amendment was ascertained to have incorporated within it the full Bill of Rights.

The first case to examine critically the question of what constituted "an establishment of religion" was *Everson v. Board of Education* (1947). Arguing from the incorporation principle, the case was a test of a state-imposed regulation which the appellant held was in violation of the First Amendment. Justice Hugo Black, writing for the majority opinion, delineated what he believed "an establishment of religion" to be:

The "establishment of religion" clause of the First Amendment means at least this: Neither a state nor the Federal Government can set up a church. Neither can pass laws which aid one religion, aid all religions, or prefer one religion over another. Neither can force nor influence a person to go to or remain away from church against his will or force him to profess a belief or disbelief in any religion. No person can be punished for entertaining or professing religious beliefs or disbeliefs, for church attendance or non-

attendance. No tax in any amount, large or small, can be levied to support any religious activities or institutions, whatever they may be called, or whatever form they may adopt to teach or practice religion. Neither a state nor the Federal Government can, openly or secretly, participate in the affairs of any religious organizations or groups or vice versa. In the words of Jefferson, the clause against establishment of religion by law was intended to erect "a wall of separation between church and State."[20]

From that point on, the Establishment Clause was to undergo close scrutiny and a new direction. First, there came about a new concept of the meaning of *religion*. Pertaining to the First Amendment, *Black's Law Dictionary* (1979) notes that "the term means a particular system of faith and worship recognized and practiced by a particular church, sect or denomination."[21] This, however, has not been the ruling definition in more recent Court decisions. Tribe (1978) points out that one piece in this is that "within a single religion—Christianity—tremendous diversity has occurred, with some Christian groups formally accepting members who regard the concept of 'God' as irrelevant or even harmful."[22]

The Three-Pronged "Lemon" Test

What has resulted is the three-pronged Lemon test, a procedure that Stephen L. Carter declares is, "a lemon indeed, for it has proved well nigh impossible to apply."[23] This three-fold method of evaluating establishment cases did not arise solely from *Lemon v. Kurtzman* (1971), but rather, in *Lemon*, the three prongs: secular purpose, primary secular effect and the absence of governmental entanglement, were in place.[24] Thus the Burger Court continued the road to secularization begun by the Warren Court, though Chief Justice Burger spoke of the test as providing little more than "a blurred, indistinct, and variable barrier depending on all the circumstances of a particular relationship."[25] The end result of the application of the "Lemon" doctrine has more often than not resulted in the Court's apparent belief that "religion must be tamed, cheapened, and secularized."[26]

McConnell denoted Lemon as "a recipe for intolerance,"[27] and proceeded to demonstrate that each prong of the test contributed to that end. Prong one, the secular purpose requirement, while appearing innocent enough, nevertheless, inadequately addresses the religious beliefs and/or behaviors of the minority religions, the very groups for which the first of the religious clauses was set to protect.

The second prong, the prohibition of a government action which "advances religion" actually works to discriminate against religion, according to McConnell's analysis. This is demonstrated by two results: First, government action which benefits a broad range of activities excludes religious activities or institutions from those benefits. Secondly, "it fails to distinguish between advancing religion and advancing religious freedom."[28]

The third prong, which prohibits an "excessive entanglement" between government and religion fails to comprehend the interaction which religion must have with government if religion is to survive. This is the same point made by Carter as he observed that the religious clauses were not put in place to remove religious discussion from the public arena but to allow it a free voice in such public debate.[29]

Testing A Free-Exercise Claim

That the Free Exercise Clause should have received first attention as being applied to the States through the principle of incorporation is obvious. A violation of the Free Exercise Clause is more directly related to the question of deprivation of rights and would trigger a due process investigation. Furthermore, a Free-Exercise violation often involves freedom of expression (See, e.g. *Cantwell v. Connecticut*, 1940; *Murdock v. Pennsylvania*, 1943; *Schneider v. Town of Irvington*, 1939), or the concept of content-neutrality with regard to expression (See, e.g. *Police Department of the City of Chicago v. Mosely*, 1972). Both freedom of expression and the concept of content-neutrality are closely connected and stand in a privileged constitutional position in any lawsuit.

There have developed, then, two basic tests to govern a Free-Exercise violation. The first is that of "the least restrictive means to a compelling end" (*Cantwell v. Connecticut*, 1940), which by the principle of incorporation made the free exercise clause applicable to the States. The second and much more subjective means of testing a Free-Exercise violation is that of examining the "sincerity and centrality" of the belief. The Court declared its intention not to weigh whether or not a particular belief is true—only that it is sincerely held.[30]

It was, however, *United States v. Seeger* (1965) which provided the litmus test for the principle of a "sincerely held belief," for the Court declared that "belief" was not limited to a theistic belief alone but to any sincerely held belief which occupied "a place in the life of its possessor parallel to that filled by the orthodox belief in God."[31] And that brings us to consider, then, the first of three cases bearing on the subject of this essay.

Widmar v. Vincent (1981)

Widmar (1981) was the culmination of a case which began when the United States District Court for Western Missouri upheld the decision by the Board of Curators of the University of Missouri, Kansas City, to exclude Cornerstone, a student religious organization, from access to university facilities. Though Cornerstone was a recognized student organization and had used university facilities for a number of years, the Board, in 1972, promulgated a new regulation which banned the use of university grounds and buildings from use for the purposes of religious worship or teaching.[32] This action, maintained the Board of Curators, was mandated not only by the Establishment Clause of the First Amendment but also by Missouri's Constitution and the state's long history of strict separation of church and state which "insists upon a degree of separation of church and state to probably a higher degree than that required by the First Amendment."[33]

Yet from 1973 until 1977, Cornerstone regularly received permission to conduct its meetings in UMKC facilities. Their meetings typically included prayer, hymns, a Bible commentary and discussion of religious views and experiences with an avowed purpose "to promote a knowledge and awareness of Jesus Christ on campus, and also, of course, to encourage one another in the faith and to grow in the grace and knowledge of our Lord Jesus Christ."[34]

In January, 1977, the leaders of Cornerstone requested the use of two rooms for two and one-half hours every Saturday night from January 15 through May, 1977. University officials, requesting clarification of the types of activities to be conducted, subsequently refused permission for on-campus meetings—including Cornerstone's request to hold small Bible studies on the lawn of the campus. Cornerstone filed an action with the United States District Court for Western Missouri, (Florian Chess named plaintiff), for declaratory judgment and injunctive relief, alleging generally that the University had unconstitutionally deprived them of their rights to the free exercise of religion, free speech and equal protection of the law.

Named as defendants were Gary Widmar, Dean of Students at UMKC, and the University's Board of Curators, who argued that the State of Missouri's interest in maintaining a strict separation of church and state was a sufficiently compelling interest to justify whatever constitutional infringement, if any, had resulted from the ban.

The district court held in favor of the University. Space does not allow any analysis of the case here.[35] Suffice it to say that there were a number of inaccuracies and ir-

271

regularities in the decision, and as a result it made its way to the U.S. Court of Appeals, Eighth Circuit. The Circuit Court reversed the decision of the district court, arguing principally from the lower court's employment of the Primary Effect test of Lemon. They concluded:

> *We cannot agree, . . . that such a policy would have the primary effect of advancing religion. Rather, it would have the primary effect of advancing the University's admittedly secular purpose—to develop students' "social and cultural awareness as well as [their] intellectual curiosity." It would simply permit students to put their ideas and practices in competition with the ideas and practices of other groups, religious or secular. It would no more commit the University, its administration or its faculty to religious goals than they are now committed to the goals of the Students for a Democratic Society, the Young Socialist Alliance, the Young Democrats or the Women's Union.*[36]

The opinion then focused on the consideration of the University claim that this was in effect "an establishment of religion." Quoting from *Walz v. Tax Commission* (1970), the judge noted that to the framers of the First Amendment, "the 'establishment' of a religion connoted sponsorship, financial support, and active involvement of the sovereign in religious activity."[37] None of these were true of this case. Arguing from the "three-pronged Lemon Test," the Appellate decision marks the most effective use of this procedure in validating the fact that Cornerstone's use of university facilities did not constitute an "establishment."

The case was argued October 6, 1981, with the decision of the Court announced on December 8, 1981. However, opting not to deal with the religious issues, the Court decided the case on the basis of Public Forum doctrine, reflecting directly upon the UMKC's institutional mission as providing a "secular education" of which religion was a part. The "D" word, discrimination, came into the

272

decision as it turned on the requirements for a review which was appropriate for "content-based exclusions."[38] That the Court upheld the decision of the appellate court was not surprising. What was curious was the Court's skirting the attempt to clarify the connection of the two clauses by retreating obliquely into the secular areas of the public forum and free speech, thus removing the religious clauses from effective interpretation.

Thus, the outcome (the right one in the view of this writer) still did not clarify either the meaning of the two religious clauses nor their connectedness. In its failure to decide the case on the special place which religion occupies in the Bill of Rights, the Court based its arguments on the concept of content-neutrality. Rather than settle the question, the case was mired in the slough of secularist doctrine.

Employment Division, Dept. of Human Resources of Oregon, et al. v. Smith et al. (1990)

Probably no case in recent years has caused the furor which this case has spawned. Alfred Smith and Galen Black, Oregon residents and both members of the Native American Church, were fired from a private drug rehabilitation organization, because, as a part of their religious beliefs, they used peyote, a hallucinogenic drug classified as an illegal drug by the State of Oregon. Filing applications for unemployment compensation, they were denied such compensation under a state law which disqualified employees dismissed for "misconduct."

The Oregon State Supreme Court, while holding that "sacramental peyote use violated, and was not excepted from, the state-law prohibition," nevertheless concluded that such a ban was invalid under the Free Exercise Clause. The case then reached the U.S. Supreme Court, and in a 6–3 decision was reversed. Since that decision, the National Council of Churches has issued a memo which synthesizes over 40 subsequent Free Exercise cases affected by *Smith*. Obviously, a discussion of those cases is beyond the scope of this chapter.

Working from the famed Mormon case, *Reynolds v. United States* (1879), Justice Scalia, writing the majority opinion, pointed out that there is a difference between religious beliefs and religious behavior. *Reynolds* confirmed the concept that though beliefs/opinions could not be restricted, behavior could. Therefore, Smith and Black could believe whatever they wished about their religious obligation, but they were not allowed exemption under the state criminal code.

Though concurring with the majority, Justice Sandra Day O'Connor wrote a separate opinion, which, when followed, would have led one to believe that she opposed the decision. Noting that the First Amendment operates in a "preferred position," she nevertheless concluded that the government did have a "compelling interest" that outweighed the religious tenets of the Native American Church. Also, she disagreed with the majority opinion noting "the Court today suggests that the disfavoring of minority religions is an 'unavoidable consequence' under our system of government and that accommodation of such religions must be left to the political process."[39]

In a dissenting opinion, Justice Blackmun presented a seven-point argument as to why the exemption from the Oregon statute should be allowed: (1) the State of Oregon had not enforced the criminal prohibition of peyote, and to honor a law which was not enforced "amounts to a symbolic preservation of an unenforced prohibition"; (2) the Federal Government lists for prohibited drugs did not ban the use of peyote for religious uses, and in addition, 23 other states have exemptions for its religious use; (3) the practice of the Native American Church itself labels the use of peyote outside the ritual as sacrilegious. In fact, the four parts to the ethical code of the Native American Church are of the highest order: brotherly love, care of family, self-reliance, and avoidance of alcohol; (4) the taste and effect of peyote itself would be limited in that it produces nausea and sometimes vomiting; (5) the fear of the "slippery slope" or "domino effect" is purely speculative. Quoting Lupu: "Behind every free exercise claim is a spectral march; grant this one, a voice whispers to each judge, and you will be confronted with an endless chain of exemption demands from religious deviants of every stripe;" (6) though using the "compelling government interest" test, the results may not always be the same when it is applied; and (7) the American Indian Religious Freedom Act, 92 Stat. 469, 42 U.S.C. 1996 (1982 ed.) states:

> [I]t shall be the policy of the United States to protect and preserve for American Indians their inherent right of freedom to believe, express, and exercise the traditional religions . . . , including but not limited to access to sites, use and possession of sacred objects, and the freedom to worship through ceremonials and traditional rites.

And in a footnote, Blackmun concludes, "Oregon's attitude toward respondents' religious peyote use harkens back to the repressive federal policies pursued a century ago."

The *Smith* decision may become moot, for engendering the attention of the President and the Congress, the Senate on October 27, 1993, by a vote of 97–3, passed a bill which would prohibit governmental interference with freedom of religion. In effect, it states, "The measure will prevent any level of government, federal, state or local, from interfering with a person's exercise of religious freedom unless it can show a compelling governmental interest in doing so."

There is another possibility for *Smith*. Rather than turning on the free exercise principle, it may, as Glendon points out, "come to be seen as explicable mainly in relation to a strong national policy for dealing with a severe social problem," i.e., "Smith may turn out to be primarily a drug case—a detour, rather than a landmark, in First Amendment case law,"[40] thus secularizing the decision.

Zobrest et al v. Catalina Foothills School District (1993)

James Zobrest attended a school for the deaf for his first five years of formal education. Then for the next three years he was a student in a public school, during which time he was furnished a sign-language interpreter at government expense. His parents opted to send him to a Catholic high school to complete his undergraduate education. Requesting the public school district to furnish him an interpreter at the Catholic school, the district refused on the grounds that such a benefit would amount to a violation of the Establishment Clause. His parents then sued for relief on the basis of (1) the federal *Individuals with Disabilities Education Act* (IDEA), and (2) that the Free Exercise Clause required the public school authorities to provide such assistance.

First heard in the district court, the court decided in favor of the school district, and in appeal, the Court of Appeals affirmed. Appealing to the Supreme Court, the decision was reversed. An *Amicus Brief* was filed for the Zobrests by groups including the Christian Legal Society, the National Association of Evangelicals, the National Council of Churches of Christ in the USA, the Catholic League for Religious and Civil Rights, the Southern Baptist Convention's Christian Life Commission, the Association of Christian Schools International, The Family Research Council, the Church of Jesus Christ of Latter-Day Saints, Joni and Friends and the Lutheran Church-Missouri Synod.

The argument presented in the *Amicus Brief* turned on four arguments: (1) that the two religious clauses should be read as complementary rather than contradictory; (2) the inconsistency is caused by the Ninth Circuit's understanding of the Establishment Clause; (3) as interpreted by the Court below, the three-part test of *Lemon v.*

Kurtzman is the source of the conflict between Free Exercise and Non-establishment; and (4) *Stare Decisis* permits reconsideration and reformulation of the *Lemon* test.

Chief Justice Rehnquist wrote the majority opinion. He first pressed for the nonconstitutional questions, noting that it was "a familiar principle in our jurisprudence that federal courts will not pass on the constitutionality of an Act of Congress if a construction of the Act is fairly possible by which the constitutional question can be avoided." However, the case as coming from the appellate court was based on the religious clauses, so it was on that basis that the Court made its decision.

Citing *Bowen v. Kendrick* (1988), Chief Justice Rehnquist declared, "We have never said that 'religious' institutions are disabled by the First Amendment from participating in publicly sponsored social welfare programs." That was the point. Governmental programs which offer benefits "neutrally," that is, without regard for the "sectarian-non sectarian, or public-nonpublic nature" of the school are acceptable. IDEA created "no financial incentive for the parents to send a youngster to a private school, and the benefit which the school might receive is minimal at most." Unlike other cases, there were no massive programs supplying personnel or equipment. The interpreter was not expressing religious views but was merely a conduit of information from the sectarian instructor to James Zobrest. Rehnquist noted:

> [T]he task of a sign-language interpreter seems to us quite different from that of a teacher or guidance counselor. . . . Nothing in this record suggests that a sign-language interpreter would do more than accurately interpret whatever material is presented to the class as a whole. In fact, ethical guidelines require interpreters to "transmit everything that is said in exactly the same way it was intended."

The dissenting view placed too much emphasis on the religious aspect of the work of the interpreter. Justice

Blackmun, joined by Justices Souter, Stevens and O'Connor wrote that the "duty" of such an employee "consists of relaying religious messages." That seems, to this writer, a bit of overkill.

Certainly the fact that we live in a pluralistic society must be taken into account, and that such society is becoming increasingly secularized is not news. Still, however, the church must resist becoming pluralistic, at least in its doctrines. The church and the society will often be in conflict as our Lord observed (Lk. 6:22; Jn. 15:18–21). If some of our modern futurists are correct in identifying this time in human history as "post-Christian," then there should be no surprise that the constitutional safeguards for religion will continue to be eroded. Though our society is very different from the world in which the religious clauses were framed, it may be that the Church will have to take stands which should be protected by the religious clauses but will continue to be ignored or misused. That is, in a "post Christian" world, the Church may be called upon to stand alone without governmental safeguards, and this will be framed in a desire to maintain order.

The maintenance of order is important, as Carter notes: "Nobody much likes anarchy."[41] But in spite of that, he pursues the heart of the problem in his criticism of Justice Scalia's conception of the Free Exercise Clause in *Smith* as a "neutral" approach, that is, "that the state should not favor religion but also should not oppress it." Building on that, Carter continues:

> *The ideal of neutrality might provide useful protection for religious freedom in a society of relatively few laws, one in which most of the social order is privately determined. That was the society the Founders knew. In such a society, it is enough to say that the law leaves religion alone. It is difficult, however, to see how the law can protect religious freedom in the welfare state if it does not offer exemptions and special protection for religious devotion.*[42]

The key, of course, is not strict neutrality, which, as many have observed, may not be so neutral at all, constituting "neutrality only from the point of view of the state."[43] An accommodation of religion seems to be latent not only in the two religious clauses but in the Court's interpretation of those clauses up until the last decade of this century.

Widmar to many was a breakthrough. The concept of "establishment" as tried by Lemon was found wanting. However, it seems to this writer that the failure of the Court to deal with the questions regarding the two religious clauses was in a sense a "cop-out", and though it seems that religious freedom emerged victorious, that victory may prove to be hollow in that the ground of decision was not the religious issue per se, but rather the content of speech. Mark Tushnet speaks of the doctrine behind the decision as the "reduction principle" of religious freedom, a doctrine holding: "that religious belief is indistinguishable from other kinds of belief, so that neither the free exercise nor the establishment clause constrains governmental action any differently than the free speech clause does."[44]

Smith, because of its effect on Congress, may turn out to be the basis of a return to an understanding of what free exercise of religion meant to the Founders, but the results of that will probably not be acceptable to some rightist groups. A statutory change of *Smith*, could result in the Court's long-standing *Reynolds* polygamy case decision being declared moot. With the growth of Islamic communities in the United States as well as the "blind-eye" given by law enforcement agencies to radical Mormon-type groups, polygamy could become lawful. Blackmun's dissenting opinion in *Smith* partially found its thrust in the fact that the state of Oregon was not enforcing its statute against the use of peyote in religious ceremonies, just as some western states are not enforcing the laws against pluralistic marriage.

What is ahead for the Court can only be surmised, but with the elevation of Ruth Ginsberg to the bench, a proactive agenda may once again be the order of the day. The issues of the contemporary society which pass over into the religious realm are legion, and no one will be totally joyous at the outcome of future cases. What does seem to be pervasive is that a secular mindset will be judge both in majoritarian views as well as from the formal judicial reviews. McConnell averred that "[t]he religious freedom cases under the First Amendment have been distorted by the false choice between secularism and majoritarianism, neither of which faithfully reflects the pluralistic philosophy of the Religion Clauses," and he concluded,

> *Instead, the Free Exercise and Establishment Clauses should protect against government-induced uniformity in matters of religion. In the modern welfare-regulatory state, this means that the state must not favor religion over non-religion, nonreligion over religion, or one religion over another in distributing financial resources; that the state must create exceptions to laws of general applicability when these laws threaten the religious autonomy of religious institutions or individuals; and that the state should eschew both religious favoritism and secular bias in its own participation in the formation of public culture.*[45]

A worthy objective! But if a court operates without a personal understanding of the dynamic of faith in a believer's life or a comprehension by the legal profession of the operative nature of that faith, the secularist view will continue to be the basis of judicial decision and the religious clauses will become little more than vestigial legal apparati.

Endnotes

[1] S.H. Cobb, *The Rise of Religious Liberty in America: A History* (New York: MacMillan, 1902), p. 2.

[2] Mary Baker Eddy, *The People's Idea of God* (Boston: The First Church of Christ Scientist, 1903).

[3] E.F. Goldman, *Rendezvous with Destiny* (New York: Vintage Books, 1952), p. 68.

[4] R.N. Bellah, "Civil Religion in America," in D. Cutter (ed.) *The Religious Situation* (Boston: Beacon Press, 1968), p. 341.

[5] W.G. Millington, "Faculty Employment Rights: Definitions and Limitations," unpublished manuscript, University of Southern California, Department of Higher and Post-Secondary Education, 1986, p. 110.

[6] L.S. Rothenberg, "The Meaning of the Free Exercise Clause: Original Intent, Subsequent Interpretation, and Normative Conclusions," Paper presented at the Conference on Freedom of Religion in America, University of Southern California, April 1981, p. 17.

[7] F. Rudolph, *The American College and University: A History* (New York: Vintage Books, 1977), p. 5.

[8] A.P. Stokes and L. Pfeffer, *Church and State in the United States* (Westport, CT: Greenwood Press, 1964), p. 593.

[9] Millington, op. cit., p. 112.

[10] Cited in P. Fussell, *Class* (New York: Ballantine Books, 1984), p. 173.

[11] Rothenberg, op. cit., pp. 1–3.

[12] Bruce and Marshall Shelley, *The Consumer Church* (Downer's Grove, IL: InterVarsity Press, 1992), p. 59.

[13] Ibid., p. 130.

[14] Phillip Johnson, "The Swedish Syndrome: A Review of Stephen J. Carter," T*he Culture of Disbelief* in *First Things*, December 1993, p. 48.

[15] Eugene Peterson, "Spirit Quest," *Christianity Today*, November 8, 1993, p. 28.

[16] Robert L. Wilkin, "No Other Gods," *First Things*, November 1993, p. 13.

[17]Raul F. Yanes and Mary Ann Glendon, "Religion and the Court," *First Things*, November 1993, p. 30.

[18]*Everson v. Board of Education*, 330 U.S. 1 (1947), p. 16.

[19]Stokes and Pfeffer, op. cit., p. 93.

[20]*Everson*, p. 16.

[21]H.C. Black, *Black's Law Dictionary* (St. Paul, MN: West Publishing, 1979), p. 1161.

[22]L.H. Tribe, *American Constitutional Law* (Mineola, NY: Foundation Press, 1978), p. 826.

[23]Carter, op. cit., p. 110.

[24]For a fuller development of the tests, one must consult: First prong: *Everson v. Board of Education* (1947); Second prong: *Abingdon Township School District v. Schempp* (1963), and the Third prong in *Lemon*.

[25]*Lemon v. Kurtzman*, 403 U.S. 602 (1971), p. 64.

[26]Michael W. McConnell, "Religious Freedom at a Crossroads, *University of Chicago Law Review*, 31:1, pp. 1–80, 1992.

[27]Ibid., p. 14.

[28]Ibid., pp. 14–15.

[29]Carter, op. cit., p. 112.

[30]See also *Fowler v. Rhode Island*, 1953; *United States v. Ballard*, 1944.

[31]*United States v. Seeger*, 380 U.S. 163 (1965), p. 166.

[32]*Chess v. Widmar*, 480 F. Supp. 907 (1979), p. 909.

[33]*Widmar*, p. 917.

[34]*Widmar*, p. 911.

[35]See Richard I. McNeely, *The Widmar (1981) Decision and the Status of Religious Liberty on the Public and University Campus*. Unpublished doctoral dissertation, University of Southern California, 1986, pp. 123–131 for discussion.

[36]*Chess v. Widmar*, 635 F 2d 1310 (8th Cir., 1980) at 1317. Emphasis added.

[37]*Walz v. Tax Commission*, 397 U.S. 664 (1970), p. 668.

[38]*Walz*, p. 270.

[39]*Employment Division, Department of Human Resources of Oregon, et al. v. Smith et al. (1990)*, p. 902.

[40]Terry Eastland, ed., *Religious Liberty in the Supreme Court* (Washington, DC: Ethics and Public Policy Center, 1993), p. 481.

[41]Carter, op. cit., p. 133.

[42]Ibid.,

[43]Richard J. Neuhaus, "The Couture of the Public Square," *First Things*, December 1993, p. 66.

[44]Quoted by Carter, op. cit., p. 130.

[45]McConnell, op. cit., pp. 79–80. As this was originally completed an excellent work was released. For a thorough survey of the past 50 years of the court and religion, cf. Terry Eastland (ed.), *Religious Liberty in the Supreme Court* (Washington, DC: Ethics and Public Policy Center, 1993).

Separation of Guru and State?: Influence of the New Age Movement on Public Education

by Francis J. Beckwith

"Congress shall make no law respecting an establishment of religion, or prohibiting the free exercise thereof. . . ."

*W*ithin the past several decades there has been an increased effort on the part of civil libertarians to broadly interpret the establishment clause of the First Amendment to mean that any public funding or support of any religious activity is constitutionally forbidden. Popularly known as "the separation of Church and State," this doctrine has been broadly applied to such issues as public school prayer, the proselytizing of students by public school teachers, the leading of religious practices in public university classrooms, the placing of nativity scenes and stars of David in public places, and other activities and symbols associated with Western religions (i.e., Judaism, Christianity, and Islam).

Recently, however, Americanized Eastern religious thought, known as the New Age Movement, has made significant inroads on all educational levels. But the problem in terms of public policy is that civil libertarians, who are trained to recognize Constitutional infringement by practitioners of Western religions, are not equally adept in recognizing their Eastern counterparts. For this reason, New Age thought, by disguising itself in most cases in the language of science and the jargon of the educational establishment, has gone virtually unopposed in promoting activities in public education from which adherents of Western religions are constitutionally prohibited.

In May 1991, the Michigan State Senate approved SR 107, which resulted in a bipartisan select committee to investigate parent and teacher complaints that the state's school health education curriculum advocated and inculcated, among other things, New Age religion and practices. In an October 1992 preliminary report, this committee concluded that New Age thought was being taught in state public schools and that such teaching violated the separation of church and state.[1]

However, in contrast, educator Edward Jenkinson argues that the New Age movement is an imaginary movement and that it is impossible to prove that it is a religion.[2] For this reason, this chapter will address the following concerns: (1) what the courts and legal scholars define as "a religion"; (2) the U.S. Supreme Court's view of the separation of church and state and how it applies to the issue of teaching religious doctrine in public educational institutions; (3) the New Age Movement, its fundamental beliefs, and whether or not it is a religion; and (4) New Age thinking in public education and how similar infiltration by Western religions would never be tolerated.

The fundamental thrust of this discussion is quite simple: if the teaching of Jewish or Christian religious doctrine and/or practice in public education violates the Establishment Clause of the First Amendment, then the teaching of New Age religious doctrine and/or practice does so as well, and should therefore be forbidden for precisely the same reason the government forbids the teaching of Judeo-Christian religious traditions.

I. Defining Religion and the Separation of Church and State

Expert on alternative religious movements, Professor Douglas Groothius, begins one of his books with the following story:

> Picture twenty-five normal first-graders peacefully lying in silence on their classroom floor. It's not a fire drill or an air raid, but part of the new curriculum. The children are being guided through a meditation in which they are instructed to imagine the sun radiantly shining toward them. They are then told to gaze into its brightness without being hurt by the light. Next the children are asked to try to bring the sun down into their bodies and feel its warmth, power, and illumination.
>
> "Imagine that you are doing something perfect," the teacher commands, "and that you are perfect."
>
> The children are told to see themselves as resplendent with light; they should feel peace, for they are perfect. They "are reminded that they are intelligent, magnificent, and that they contain all of the wisdom of the universe within themselves."[3]

This "exercise" occurred in a public school in Los Angeles, California. Known as "confluent education," it was federally funded and employed for the express purpose of helping students who need an "expanded view of learning."[4] Designed by the late Beverly Galyean, this meditation is certainly not prayer of Christian or Jewish devotion, for such teacher-led activities under public school auspices are constitutionally forbidden. And yet this activity does not appear to be passing on the fundamentals of reading, writing, or arithmetic. What then was the purpose of this exercise? According to Galyean:

*Once we begin to see that we are all God, that we all have
the attributes of God, then I think the whole purpose of
human life is to reown the Godlikeness within us; the perfect love, the perfect wisdom, the perfect understanding,
the perfect intelligence, and when we do that we create
back to that old, that essential oneness which is consciousness. So my whole view is very much based on that idea.*[5]

If this is the purpose of such a curriculum, why is it allowed in public education? In order to answer this question, we must first answer four questions fundamental to
the issue of religion in public education: (A) What is
religion? (B) Is religion defined differently in the free exercise clause than in the establishment clause of the Constitution? (C) What is the separation of church and state?
and (D) What government-sponsored religious practices
in public education have been deemed unconstitutional
by the U.S. Supreme Court?

A. What is Religion?

Throughout American history, the courts have proposed
different definitions of religion, broadening their definitions as the country increased in religious diversity.
Religion was defined in early decisions "as an organized
body of believers employing religious ceremony and
having a faith in and commitment to a supernatural
Supreme Being."[6] In *Davis v. Beason* (1890), the U.S.
Supreme Court first attempted to give content to the constitutional meaning of religion. Using a theistic definition
of religion, the court said that "[t]he term 'religion' has
reference to one's view of his relations to his Creator, and
to the obligations they impose of reverence for his being
and character, and of obedience to his will."[7]
The modern trend in the courts toward a broader and
more global view of religion began in the Second Circuit
Court of Appeals case, *United States v. Kauten* 133 F.2d 703
(2d Cir. 1943). The court denied an atheist status as a conscientious objector because his refusal to serve in the

military was based exclusively on political grounds. However, in writing for the court, Judge Augustus Hand, in dictum, "dismissed the notion that belief in a Supreme Being is a necessary element of 'religious training and belief' under the statute."[8] That is to say, conscientious objection prodded by conscience could be just as religious as that prodded by theological commitment.[9]

The courts continued to define religion in a broader context, accepting as religious many belief-systems and practices. For instance, in *Torcaso v. Watkins* (1961) the Supreme Court unanimously held that it was unconstitutional for the commonwealth of Maryland to make belief in God a requirement for becoming a notary public. The justices were quite clear in affirming that a belief-system can be religious without being theistic: "Among religions in this country which do not teach what would generally be considered a belief in God are Buddhism, Taoism, Ethical Culture, Secular Humanism and others."[10] In *United States v. Seeger* (1965), the Supreme Court ruled that a belief is religious if it is "sincere and meaningful [and] occupies a place in the life of its possessor parallel to that filled by the orthodox belief in God."[11]

In the *Seeger* decision, the Court consulted theologian Paul Tillich, who has claimed in his writings that most, if not all, human beings, including atheists, have an ultimate commitment of one sort or another, something that serves as a unifying center for their personality and consciousness: a transcendent object.[12] Similarly, philosopher John Dewey, who considered his own espousal of humanism as "religious," defined religion in the following way: "Any activity pursued in behalf of an ideal end against obstacles and in spite of threats of personal loss because of convictions of its general and enduring value is religious in quality."[13] It is evident, therefore, why the Court defined religion as a belief "based upon a power or being or upon a faith, to which all else is subordinate or upon which all else is ultimately dependent."[14]

In October 1977, in *Malnak v. Maharashi Mahesh Yogi*, a New Jersey Federal Court barred the teaching of Science of Creative Intelligence (SCI) and Transcendental Meditation (TM) in the state's public schools. According to U.S. District Judge H. Curtis Meanor, the teaching of SCI/TM, a Westernized version of Eastern religious mysticism, is "religious in nature; no other inference is 'permissible' or reasonable. . . . Although defendants have submitted well over 1,500 pages of briefs, affidavits and deposition testimony in opposing plaintiffs' motion for summary judgment, defendants have failed to raise the slightest doubt as to the facts or as to the religious nature of the teaching of the Science of Creative Intelligence and the *puja* [A Sanskrit prayer used during the initiation ceremony. English translations clearly show its religious nature]. The teaching of the SCI/TM course in New Jersey public high schools violates the establishment clause of the First Amendment, and its teaching must be enjoined."[15] There are several other court cases which clearly establish that a belief-system which excludes a belief in the theistic God of Judaism, Christianity, or Islam may nevertheless be "religious."[16]

In order better to understand how the courts came to their conclusions, let us engage in a brief thought experiment by trying to answer the question: "What is a religion?" This question has been given many answers. For example, some have said that a religion is a belief system that involves belief in a god and life after death. But, as the courts have realized, one problem with this definition is that it excludes systems of belief that are usually considered to be religions but that do not have a belief in God or gods, such as Jainism and some forms of Buddhism. Other religions do not have a full-fledged belief in life after death, as in the case of early Greek religion, though no one doubts that they are religious.

For these reasons, it is better to define a religion as a world-view or comprehensive system of belief that has a goal or ideal, as well as an assumed metaphysical perspective, which "transcends" (goes beyond) the empirical world and to which a believer places ultimate commitment. This definition seems better to capture a notion of religion consistent with both the history of the courts as well as our global and historical observations. It does not exclude some religions which have religious ideals and do not have a concept of God or the afterlife (e.g., early Buddhism), but yet it does include other religions which have a very rich and complex theology (e.g, Judaism, Christianity, Islam).

B. Is religion defined differently in the Free Exercise Clause than in the Establishment Clause of the Constitution?

It is important to understand that the modern legal cases we have gone over actually deal with two different aspects of defining religion. For example, *Torcaso v. Watkins* concerns the *free exercise* of religion. The court ruled that because Secular Humanism served the same function as traditional religion for the prospective notary republic, the state could not inhibit his free exercise of religion by demanding he believe in God. For the sake of free exercise, religion is in the eye of the beholder. Whatever *functions* as a religion in the subjective life of an individual *is* a religion when it comes to free exercise.

By contrast, the *Malnak* case concerns the *establishment* of religion. The court ruled that the state could not prefer one religion over another, including a religion that has its origin in Eastern religious thought and denies the existence of the Judeo-Christian view of God.

But unlike the free exercise clause, when it comes to a court deciding whether the establishment clause has been violated, it cannot rely exclusively on the free exercise criterion that defines religion so broadly as to include that which serves as an ultimate value for the person committed to it (as a traditional religious belief does for the people who believe in it). For this would make nearly every belief propounded in the public arena religious, since in principle nearly every belief can be held religiously, in the sense of being held as an ultimate value. But, as Joel Incorvaia points out, this "would run counter to the realities of public education in America." That is to say, "[i]f the broad functional definition were to be used in the educational sphere, classroom inculcation of democratic values, such as free speech, equality, justice, and majority rule, and moral values, such as honesty, personal integrity, and self-discipline, could be barred as unconstitutional." This would result in "a sterile educational environment marked by moral relativism."[17]

If for establishment purposes one defines religion too narrowly so as to include only traditional Western religions, excluding from the religious some belief-systems that are clearly intended to function in the same way as do traditional Western religions, then practitioners of these traditional religions would be unfairly excluded from influencing the public square while their non-traditional counterparts would be provided with carte blanche permission. This is why "religion should also be given a meaning flexible enough to prevent government aid to modern religious or quasi-religious movements that do not fit into traditional religious categories."[18] Consequently, the courts must provide more objective criteria in order to differentiate "between ultimate values that society deems necessary to impart through the educational process and values that if inculcated through the curriculum would offend establishment norms."[19]

Incorvaia proposes such criteria, based on a careful reading of the history of court rulings on the establishment clause:

> *(1) Potentially functionally religious values necessary for democracy should be permitted to be inculcated.*
> *(2) The establishment clause is violated when:*
> *{A} The challenged practice and/or inculcated belief serves a potentially functionally religious purpose, and either one or both of the following is true:*

292

> *{B} The state aids a group or organization primarily espousing a belief or beliefs in ultimate values; and*
>
> *{C} State action results in inculcation of ultimate values not shared by the vast majority of society's members.*

Let us cover each one of these points in detail.

(1) Potentially functionally religious values necessary for democracy should be permitted to be inculcated. Incorvaia writes that "a solution would be to permit the inculcation of potentially functionally religious values that are consensually shared by society in general and that are essential to effective participation in a democracy."[20] That is to say, it would be permissible for schools to teach that cheating, lying, and stealing are morally wrong as well as to officially encourage students to adopt the precepts of democracy, since it is clear that these values are highly uncontroversial to the public at large.

In other words, the values necessary for the very existence of our society, though potentially functionally religious, cannot be banned from state-supported inculcation on the basis of the First Amendment, since the First Amendment itself would be imperiled by their absence.

(2) When the Establishment Clause is violated {A} the challenged practice and/or inculcated belief serves a potentially functionally religious purpose. In order to be consistent with the recent history of the courts as well to be considered religious for First Amendment purposes, a practice and/or inculcated belief, Incorvaia argues, thought to violate the establishment clause, must *at least* serve a functionally religious purpose. But this criterion alone is certainly not sufficient to prove that the practice violates the establishment clause, since, as we saw above, some beliefs which are potentially functionally religious are uncontroversial and are necessary conditions for the existence of government itself. For this reason, Incorvaia argues that one of either two other conditions must be

present in order for a belief to be considered "religious," and hence, in violation of the establishment clause.

These two conditions, which we will look at below, must be understood in light of the constitutional purpose of the establishment clause. Incorvaia points out that "[c]ourts and commentators have stated that the non-establishment guaranty furthers two goals: the precluding of civil strife among organized religious factions competing for government benefits, and the safeguarding of individual religious liberty." That is to say, "[t]he establishment clause advances freedom of religion by forestalling the religious discrimination, persecution, and coercion that inevitably occur whenever the state throws its support behind favored religious groups or tries to inculcate an official religious orthodoxy." Therefore, in contrast to the free exercise clause, "when assessing establishment claims, the courts need not accept every assertion that a government activity is religiously based but should further examine whether the activity contravenes the underlying values of the establishment clause."[21]

Based on these underlying values, which the courts have appealed to on numerous occasions in establishment cases,[22] Incorvaia offers the following two conditions either of which must be present, along with the first condition above, in order for a belief to violate the establishment clause.

{B} The state aids a group or organization primarily espousing a belief or beliefs in ultimate values. If the state aids a group or organization primarily espousing a belief or beliefs in ultimate values, the establishment clause is violated. That is to say, "the establishment clause would be violated if the government extended aid in any form to" a group or organization whose principal tenets "attempt to supply answers to ultimate questions about Man's purpose and being, thereby forming the supreme life commitment of its adherents." Moreover, "whether a group addressed itself to obedience to God's will, pursuit of universal human brotherhood, or a devotion to the inherent goodness of all men would have no bearing under the proposed test." As long as the group's adherents believed these tenets to be of supreme importance, "[g]overnment support of each group would be unconstitutional."[23]

This prong of the test helps solve the problem that arises when one uniformly applies the free-exercise functional definition in the context of the establishment clause. As I noted above, if the free exercise definition is applied too broadly, then some ultimate values, necessary for the existence of government itself, would have to be stricken from the public square. Under this prong, "[g]overnment programs and policies that actualize such ultimate values are safe from constitutional challenge," since only when their primary purpose and effect would be "to confer benefit on a functionally religious organization would the establishment clause come into play." Consequently, under this test, "government could legislate broadly in the area of public welfare without establishment limitation."[24]

{C} State action results in inculcation of ultimate values not shared by the vast majority of society's members. This part of the test is intended to cultivate the free exercise rights of individuals by shielding them from inculcation through government agencies in a manner antagonistic to their own personal religious convictions. This test "comes into play primarily with the extremely troublesome and complex constitutional issues posed by religious teaching, ceremony, and value inculcation in the realm of public elementary and secondary education." Incorvaia points out that "a great deal of the case law on establishment has cropped up in the educational field, largely because school-age children, emotionally immature and with unsettled internal value structures, are uniquely susceptible to religious indoctrination by their peers and by adult authority figures."[25] Since public education is compulsory in most jurisdictions, consuming most of a child's day, and since the school can no doubt have a weighty influence on the formation of a child's personality and values, susceptibility to religious indoctrination is augmented.

Would this third test also apply to higher education as well? Although it is correctly assumed that a college student is old enough to critically examine differing religious positions, it seems clear that if a public university or college instructor is proselytizing in the classroom and/or leading students in religious activities or ceremonies, that instructor has at least violated the second prong of the criteria (and the third prong if these activities are *required* for a good grade). For by permitting the teacher's religious actions while excluding the religious activities of others the state would be in fact aiding a religious group or organization.

C. What is the Separation of Church and State?

Granted that a belief is religious, when does its presence in public education violate the separation of church and state? As many scholars have come to realize, the history in the United States of the relationship between church and state, as well as the U.S. Supreme Court's interpretation of the Constitution on this matter, is riddled with inconsistencies, the reconciling of which goes far beyond the scope of this paper.[26] However, we can come to some important conclusions which can help us answer the question of whether the teaching of New Age thought in public education violates the separation of Church and State.

In a 1971 case, *Lemon v. Kurtzman*, the Supreme Court provided a three-part criterion that is used by many courts to determine whether a given public policy or law is constitutional. The Court believed that this three-part criterion is based on the history of the Court's decisions on the matter of church and state. If it passes the "Lemon test," then the law or policy in question is constitutional.

Every analysis in this area [church and state cases] must begin with consideration of the cumulative criteria developed by the Court over many years. Three such tests may be gleaned from our cases. First, the statute must have a secular legislative purpose; second, its principle or primary effect must be one that neither advances nor inhibits religion, Board of Education v. Allen, 392 U.S. 236, 243 (1968); finally, the statute must not foster "an excessive government entanglement with religion." Walz, 397 U.S. 664, 668 (1970).[27]

The operative terms in this test are "principle and primary effect" and "excessive entanglement," since the court has ruled that the government may accommodate religion, as Justice Harry Blackmun has pointed out:

> Everson and Allen *put to rest any argument that the State may never act in such a way that has the* incidental effect of facilitating religious activity. . . . *If this were impermissible . . . a church could not be protected by the police and fire department, . . . The Court has never held that religious activities must be discriminated against in this way.*[28]

Blackmun's observation is often ignored by many school administrators, who do not realize that the Free Exercise Clause of the Constitution allows for many types of religious expression on the public school campus, as long as it is not government or school endorsed. According to the courts, to forbid such religious expression, simply because it is religious, is to violate the free speech rights of students and sometimes others. As the Supreme Court stated in the *Mergens* decision, "[T]here is a crucial difference between *government* speech endorsing religion, which the Establishment Clause forbids, and *private* speech endorsing religion, which the Free Speech and Free Exercises Clauses protect" (*Board of Education of the*

Westside Community Schools v. Mergens, 496 U.S. at 250 [1990]).

Among the many activities allowed by the courts are the following: the right of students to distribute literature, wear religious clothing, including T-shirts, and engage in personal evangelism on school grounds; student-led prayer at graduation; the right of valedictorians, salutatorians, or honorary student speakers to give speeches on religious subjects, including reading from the Bible; the right of members of the community or organizations to use school facilities for religious purposes; the right of students to start, attend, and advertise a Bible Club on school property.[29]

But let us now apply the Lemon Test to the *Malnak* case. First, did the teaching of TM have a secular purpose? Yes, for it was intended to help students relax and concentrate on their studies. Second, did the teaching of TM have the principle or primary effect of neither advancing nor inhibiting religion? No, for it advanced the cause of a sect of the Hindu religion by making school children engage in a teacher-led religious activity (TM) while at the same time a teacher-led Judeo-Christian religious activity (e.g., prayer, Bible-reading) was constitutionally prohibited. And third, did the teaching of TM *not* foster an excessive government entanglement with religion? No, for the religious practice in question (TM) is part of a publicly funded school curriculum. Imagine if public schools were teaching Christian systematic theology only from a Calvinist perspective to the exclusion of other Christian theologies and world religions. Would not this foster an excessive government entanglement with religion? No doubt it would. But this is exactly what certain New Jersey public schools were doing when they put TM in public school curriculum to the exclusion of all other theological and religious perspectives. Consequently, the New Jersey schools failed at least two parts of the three-part Lemon Test.

It should be noted that scholars[30] as well as recent Supreme Court opinions[31] have criticized and questioned certain aspects of the Lemon Test. In fact, recent Supreme Court rulings have attempted to supplement (though some would claim "substitute") the Lemon Test.[32] For example, in *Lynch v. Donnelly* (1984) Justice Sandra Day O'-Connor proposed what is commonly called the "endorsement" test. According to this test, if a government action creates a *perception* that it is either endorsing or disfavoring a religion, the action is unconstitutional. The concern of this test is whether the disputed activity suggests "a message to nonadherents that they are outsiders, not full members of the political community, and an accompanying message to adherents that they are insiders, favored members of the political community."[33] It seems, however, as Louis Fischer and Gail Paulus Sorenson point out, that "as we await guidance from the Court in future cases, the three-prong test established in *Lemon* is our most reliable guide."[34]

D. Religious practices the Supreme Court has declared unconstitutional.

Even though there is disagreement about the Constitution and its application to religious teachings and practices in the public square, the U.S. Supreme Court has come to some apparently definitive conclusions about the unconstitutionality of some religious practices in public education. In each one of the following six cases, the government was actively involved in, as well as sponsored, the religious practices under scrutiny:

> *(1) state-directed and required on-premises religious training, in* McCollum v. Board of Education; *(2) state-directed and required prayer, in* Engel v. Vitale; *(3) state-directed and required Bible reading, in* Abington School District v. Schempp; *(4) state-directed and required posting of the Ten Commandments, in* Stone v. Graham; *(5) state-directed and authorized "periods of*

299

silence" for meditation and voluntary prayer, in Wallace
v. Jaffre; *(6) state-directed and required teaching of scientific creationism, in* Edwards v. Aguillard.[35]

One should not erroneously conclude from these cases
that any study of religion is forbidden as part of public
school curriculum. In fact, "[a]ccording to case law, references to religious matters are permissible if (1) they are
presented objectively; (2) no disruption occurs; and, (3)
they are relevant to the subject matter,"[36] such as the
study of religion by way of "comparative religion; the history of religion; art, music, and religion; or other approaches." However, "[r]eligious exercises, rituals, and
celebrations . . . are against the law, whether compulsory
or voluntary."[37]

Consequently, if the New Age teachings and practices
found in the classrooms of America's public educational
institutions parallel any of the above unconstitutional
practices, and/or if these New Age ideas do not pass the
muster of what is permissible, then they should be
declared unconstitutional on the same basis as other
religious teachings and practices that have gone before
them. Of course, even if publicly inculcated New Age
ideas and practices do not exactly parallel these unconstitutional activities, they may certainly be unconstitutional on their own merits.

II. Is New Age a Religion?

Influenced by Eastern religious thought, there is no
doubt that the New Age Movement (NAM) is unified by
certain fundamental assumptions and beliefs that distinguish it from other theistic and non-theistic belief-systems. The central beliefs and practices of NAM are
undoubtedly religious. First, New Agers have concepts of
ultimate reality (monism), God (pantheism), and the
afterlife (reincarnation), which are similar if not identical
to concepts espoused by Eastern religions such as Hinduism and Buddhism. These beliefs and practices serve

300

the same purpose in the lives of believers as do the beliefs and practices of adherents to Western religions. Thus, from a constitutional perspective, New Age thought is a religion.

Second, New Age practices intended to result in an altered state of consciousness, such as yoga, meditation, guided imagery and creative visualization, are saturated in most cases with religious assumptions, because their primary purpose is to help the adherent experience his (or her) presumed oneness with God (or "Higher Self," "the One," "the Self" or any other synonym for the New Age God) by manipulating the universal metaphysical energy that supports and permeates all of existence. Some of these techniques are often practiced under the assumption that the New Age worldview is correct. In other words, even if taught in a context in which the New Age worldview is not readily apparent, the techniques themselves often presuppose the ultimate unity of all reality (monism) and/or the mental ability to manipulate reality since all reality is One (monism).

Third, these beliefs and practices parallel Western religious activities which the Supreme Court has deemed as violations of the Establishment Clause if inculcated in public education. Recall the six practices deemed unconstitutional by the Supreme Court:

> (1) state-directed and required on-premises religious training, in McCollum v. Board of Education; (2) state-directed and required prayer, in Engel v. Vitale; (3) state-directed and required Bible reading, in Abington School District v. Schempp; (4) state-directed and required posting of the Ten Commandments, in Stone v. Graham; (5) state-directed and authorized "periods of silence" for meditation and voluntary prayer, in Wallace v. Jaffre; (6) state-directed and required teaching of scientific creationism, in Edwards v. Aguillard.[38]

Three experts in school law add, "[r]eligious exercises, rituals, and celebrations . . . are against the law, whether compulsory or voluntary."[39]

Consider the chart on the next page, paralleling a forbidden Western religious practice with its New Age counterpart:[40]

There is little doubt that if such New Age practices and beliefs are inculcated in public education, then the establishment clause has been violated. We will now look at specific instances of New Age teaching and practices in public education.

III. New Age Religion in public education

Prior to answering the question of whether or not public institutions teach New Age thought, it is important to define what I mean by *inculcate* and *teach* in this context. For one thing, I do not mean the *presentation* and/or *critique* of ideas in a position of *non-indoctrination*. Obviously, it is essential to education for students, especially in a university or college setting, to explore the arguments for and against particular religious and philosophical viewpoints. An example of this would be a philosophy or religion instructor at a public school or college presenting her own or another's religious viewpoint to her students in the context of an *analytical discussion*. In this context the instructor is not asking for converts, leading students in a religious practice, or proselytizing.

In contrast, when I speak of an instructor *teaching* or *inculcating* New Age thought I mean that the instructor *advocates* the views in question and leads his students in religious practices clearly without the hint of critical discussion. In other words, the lesson presupposes the "truth" of the New Age worldview, and its purpose is to teach the students how to either engage in New Age practices or accept New Age ideas. Such teaching is simply indoctrination and proselytizing and does not allow the students to explore the arguments for and against the New Age viewpoint in a critical manner. This type of New

CHART

Unconstitutional Practice	Religious Purpose	New Age Practice or Belief Purpose
1. School prayer	Petition God	Self-realization/Realize oneness with all
2. Religious training	Inform about ultimate things	Teaching all is one/Inform about ultimate things
3. Teaching creationism	Inform about source of all	Teaching all is energy/Inform about source of all
4. Bible reading	Learn one's place in cosmos	Reading New Age lit./Learn place in cosmos or viewing New Age films

Age religious inculcation, if it occurs, is equivalent to inculcating students in Western religious practices such as attending a prayer meeting, going to synagogue, celebrating a Catholic Mass, or reciting the rosary.

The above is consistent with and is supported by legal precedent: "According to case law, references to religious matters are permissible [in a public education setting] if (1) they are presented objectively; (2) no disruption occurs; and, (3) they are relevant to the subject matter,"[41] such as the study of religion by way of "comparative religion; the history of religion; art, music, and religion; or other approaches." However, "[r]eligious exercises, rituals, and celebrations... are against the law, whether compulsory or voluntary."[42]

Some public institutions clearly offer courses that inculcate students in New Age thought. We shall review examples from two public universities and a community college.

A. University of Nevada, Las Vegas

The Division of Continuing Education at the University of Nevada, Las Vegas offers at least one course that clearly teaches religious doctrine. "Kundalini Yoga and Meditation." The Winter 1992 catalogue describes the course in the following way:

> Each class starts with dynamic breathing and stretching warm ups which lead into a vigorous series of exercises. After winding down you will *tune your mind* as well as your body. Systematically energize and build each system of your body. Learn and apply techniques which maintain health, youthfulness, and flow of life, mentally, physically, and *spiritually*. The teachings of this ancient technology give the ability to tap into your unknown potential and *experience the unity of being within yourself*. Kundalini Yoga stretches the nerves and muscles and makes the blood circulate.[43] (italics added)

According to religious historian, Dr. Ruth Tucker, "Yoga is a Hindu system of mental and physical exercises, the goal of which is to separate the soul from the body and mind in order to release the soul from the endless cycle or reincarnation. It is the avenue that unites the soul with God."[44] Russell Chandler writes that the goal of the Indian religious tradition of yoga "is a state of well-being, the loss of self-identity, and absorption into union with the Absolute, or Ultimate Being."[45] The UNLV course description, however, uses euphemisms to describe this unity when it promises the student that he or she will "learn and apply techniques which maintain . . . flow of life . . . *spiritually*" and "experience the *unity of being within yourself*" (italics added). And this makes perfect sense, since, according to New Age thought, all is One (God).

Although many Westerners may practice Yoga as a means to relaxation, Dr. Irving Hexham, a religious studies professor at the University of Calgary, states "that despite claims to the contrary . . . yoga cannot be practiced in isolation from other Indian beliefs. The whole concept of yoga is based upon a carefully worked out theory of beliefs about the human condition. The terminology used to explain the practice itself involves acceptance of presuppositions with religious origins."[46]

The particular type of Yoga taught in this course, Kundalini, is fundamentally religious: the "kundalini" refers to the "psycho-spiritual power thought by Yogi(s) to lie dormant at the base of the spine. Believed to be a goddess, kundalini is referred to as 'serpent power.' "[47] This is based on the New Age and Hindu belief that there are seven energy points on the human body called *chakras*. " 'Raising' the kundalini up through the chakras is the aim of Yoga meditation. Enlightenment (Samadhi) is achieved when kundalini reaches the 'crown chakra' at the top of the head."[48]

If analogous practices of Western religion were taught in a public university setting, no one would doubt that the wall of Church/State separation had been breached:

> Systematically energize and build each part of your life. Learn and apply praying techniques which maintain love, peace, and joy, mentally, physically, and *spiritually*. The teachings of this ancient practice give you the ability to tap into your unknown potential and *experience the unity of yourself with the divine*. Certain praying postures stretch the nerves and muscles and make the blood circulate.

In light of this, I asked the following questions in a letter of inquiry to the Director of the Division of Continuing Education at UNLV (January 15, 1992):

Question #1: Can a person teach a continuing education course in which students are instructed to participate in a religious ceremony, such as prayer, Catholic mass, rosary, etc.? Why or why not?

Question #2: Can a person teach a continuing education course where religious doctrine is taught as factual in which students are encouraged to believe? Why or why not?

Question #3: Can a person teach a continuing education course where religious doctrine is applied to individuals? For example, can a teacher tell her students, as a factual matter, that certain "sinful" activities will be detrimental to both their current and post-mortem existences? Or that meditative and prayer techniques lead to a unity of being or causing things to come into being? Why or why not?

Attaching a copy of the Bill of Rights to his reply letter (with a check-mark next to the First Amendment), the Director responded in the following way:

> *In my opinion the answer to each of your questions is NO.*
> *The reason is contained in the first ten amendments to the*

306

*United States Constitution as interpreted by the United
States Supreme Court so as to apply to the States. UNLV,
including Continuing Education, is supported by the State
of Nevada and Nevada may not present a religion or the
tenets of a religion as being factual.* I will not approve
any course that requires students to participate in a
religious activity or that teaches religious doctrine as
factual. . . . *There are many interesting and difficult questions to be asked but I think your three are quite straight-
forward and my answers are correct. I'd be happy to discuss them further with you.* [emphasis mine]

But it is evident that religion, of the New Age and Eastern variety, is being taught at UNLV. But because it is not
Western religion, good civil libertarians, such as this Continuing Education Director, make the mistake of not
recognizing it as a religion.

B. Community College of Southern Nevada

The description of "Metaphysical Training," a course offered in the Spring 1993, Spring 1992, Fall 1991, and
Summer 1991 Community Education schedules at the
Community College of Southern Nevada (CCSN), is
thoroughly New Age:

> Discover your inner strengths and become all you can
> be in this powerful 10-week course. Simple techniques
> for learning meditation, *yoga*, and the power behind
> *mantra* and *prayer* will be emphasized. A look into
> *reincarnation* and ESP as additional tools to maximize
> your potential will be explored. . . .[49] (italics added)

This course uncritically promotes religious doctrine as
well as guiding students in religious practice. Although we
have seen that yoga and reincarnation are religious, and
we all know the place of prayer in religion, the concept of
mantra is religious as well. Chandler points out that
mantra is "a 'holy' word, phrase, or verse in Hindu and

Buddhist meditation techniques. A mantra is usually provided to an initiate by a guru who is supposed to hold specific insights regarding the needs of his pupils. The vibrations of the mantra are said to lead the meditator into union with the divine source within."[50]

I sent a letter of inquiry to the Executive Director of Community Education at CCSN. Asking him the same questions I asked the Director of Continuing Education at UNLV, the CCSN administrator responded in the following way in a January 21, 1992 letter:

Question #1. Can a person teach a C.E. course in which students are instructed in a religious ceremony or activity? This depends on the sponsoring institution and what is defined as the community. It would be more appropriate to call this religious education of course but labels in this arena are loose. In general *C.E. sponsored by public institutions (which is the majority) would not provide instruction in specific religious practice.* [emphasis mine]
Question #2 could be answered in the same fashion of course.
Question #3 really raises the same issue.

Although he admits that my "questions raise far deeper issues than can be addressed in this format," it is evident that the administrator at CCSN does not believe it is the place of a public institution to "provide instruction in specific religious practice." Yet his program, which is part of a public institution, offers "Metaphysical Training," a course which "provides instruction in specific religious practice."

In the Spring 1993 Community Education catalogue, twelve other courses are offered which teach particular New Age religious doctrines and divination practices: "Menu Metaphysics—An Overview," "Mastering the Tarot," "Past Life Regression," "The Urantia Book—Planet Earth and the Cosmos," "Astrological Calendar Reading," "Zodiac of Love," "Improving Your Bottom Line with

Astrology," "A Course in Miracles," "Hatha Yoga—Iyengar Method," "Introduction to Kundalini Yoga and Meditation," "Kundalini Yoga and Meditation Sadhana," and "Yoga with Olga."[51]

C. University of Massachusetts at Amherst

The Division of Continuing Education at the University of Massachusetts at Amherst offers the course, "Past Life Regression," in its Spring 1992 schedule. The course description reads:

> Reincarnation is an area that has started to come out of the dark corners of mysticism and into the light of the twentieth century. Through this workshop, participants learn about past lives and their relevance to their lives today. Many will find that through knowing and understanding their past lives, they will have greater insights into and better understanding of this life. This workshop consists of two group regressions and one individual regression. Bring a pillow and a blanket or mat.[52]

As I noted earlier, reincarnation is a religious view, linked to both New Age thought and Eastern religion. It is a proposed solution to the problem of evil and the way in which humans eventually reach "salvation" or Oneness with God. It is evident that a contrasting Western concept, such as the concept of resurrection found in Christianity, if taught in a publicly-funded institution in the same way that reincarnation is taught at the University of Massachusetts, would be seen as a clear violation of separation of church and state. Imagine if the course description had read:

> Resurrection is a doctrine that has started to come out of the dark corners of the Bible and into the light of the twentiety century. Through this workshop, participants learn about the doctrine of resurrection

309

and its relevance to their lives today. Many will find that through knowing and understanding the doctrine of resurrection, they will have greater insights into and better understanding of their life. This workshop consists of two group altar calls and one individual testimony to the truth of the resurrection doctrine. Bring a kneeling pad, some paper, and a pen.

Conclusion

It is evident that certain New Age and Eastern religious practices and teachings are allowed in public education which would not be tolerated by civil libertarians if their Western counterparts were taught in their stead. Of course, some educators, such as Edward Jenkinson, believe that such an observation is the product of the overactive imaginations of right-wing parents.[53] Although I do not believe that Jenkinson is correct, I do believe he raises a point which should be taken seriously: Every accusation of state/church conflict should be examined and analyzed carefully and honestly with a more global view of religion and religious practice. Since I began doing work in this area nearly two years ago, I have run across many claims by parents that they had found "New Age teaching" in their children's schools, which turned out in most cases to be either misinterpretations of professional jargon or reading into curricula things that were simply not there. However, there were some cases where the parents were correct.

I must admit that I am a reluctant participant in this severely neglected area of State/Church conflict. When I first was approached by concerned parents in my community, I did not believe their concerns were valid. I labeled them right-wing reactionaries. However, the fact that they approached me because of my faculty status (I teach religion and philosophy), I felt obliged to listen to their concerns. Although I found some of their concerns hyperbolic and reactionary, I had reluctantly to admit that they were right about a great deal more than I had supposed.

My advice to civil libertarians who want to fortify the wall of separation of Church and State in public education is that they should fight just as vigorously against infiltration of New Age and Eastern religion as they do against infiltration of Western religion. This, I believe, would garner a great deal of respect from conservative and orthodox religious believers who presently perceive civil libertarians as the enemy.

Endnotes

[1] Senate Select Committee to Study the Michigan Model of Comprehensive School Health Education, *Michigan Model for Comprehensive School Health Education: It's Not Kid-Friendly (Preliminary Report)* (October 1992): 32, 41–43, 47–50. In order to understand the broad scope of this study, it should be noted that the committee's criticism of New Age teaching was one of many critical comments on a variety of subjects.

[2] Edward Jenkinson, "How an Imaginary Movement is Being Used to Attack Courses and Books," *Educational Leadership* (October 1988): 74–77.

[3] Doug Groothius, *Unmasking the New Age* (Downers Grove, IL: InterVarsity Press, 1986), p. 13. The final quote in Groothius' story is taken from Frances Adeney, "Educators Look East," *Spiritual Counterfeits Project Journal* 5 (Winter 1981): 28.

[4] Adeney, "Educators Look East," p. 29.

[5] Ibid.

[6] Joel Incorvaia, "Teaching Transcendental Meditation in Public Schools: Defining Religion for Establishment Purposes," *San Diego Law Review* 6 (1978-79): 336–337.

[7] *Davis v. Beason* 133 U.S. (1890) at 342. Incorvaia points out that "*Davis* involved the criminal prosecution of a member of the Mormon church under an Idaho statute disenfranchising persons from voting or holding elected office if they belonged to any organization practicing or advocating bigamy or polygamy.

The Court upheld the statute's constitutionality against a free exercise challenge. It refused to recognize that belief in bigamy or polygamy could be a tenet of a bona fide religious faith, saying, 'To call their advocacy a tenet of religion is to offend the common sense of mankind.' *Id.* at 341–42." (Incorvaia, "Transcendental Meditation," p. 337).

[8] Incorvaia, "Transcendental Meditation," p. 337.

[9] *United States v. Kauten* 133 F.2d 703 (2d Cir. 1943) at 708.

[10] John Whitehead, "The Establishment of the Religion of Secular Humanism and Its First Amendment Implications," *Texas Tech Law Review* 10 (1978): 13.

[11] Whitehead, "The Establishment of the Religion of Secular Humanism," p. 14.

[12] Paul Tillich, *Ultimate Concern*, ed. D. Mackenzie Brown (London: SCM, 1963), p. 106.

[13] John Dewey, *A Common Faith* (New Haven, CT: Yale University Press, 1934), p. 27.

[14] Whitehead, "The Establishment of the Religion of Secular Humanism," p. 14.

[15] United States District Court, District of New Jersey, Civil Action No. 76–341 (October 1977), as quoted in Elliot Miller, "Hinduism: Hare Krishna and Transcendental Meditation (TM)," in *The New Cults*, ed. Walter R. Martin (Santa Ana, CA: Vision House, 1980), pp. 93-94.

An English translation of the *puja* is found in Ruth Tucker, *Another Gospel* (Grand Rapids, MI: Academie Books, 1989), pp. 383–384.

[16] For an overview of these cases, see Whitehead, "The Establishment of Religion of Secular Humanism," and Norman L. Geisler, *Is Man the Measure?* (Grand Rapids: Baker, 1983), pp. 162–165.

[17] Incorvaia, "Transcendental Meditation," p. 349.

[18] Ibid., p. 344.

[19] Ibid., pp. 349–350

[20] Ibid., p. 349.

[21] Ibid., pp. 345–346.

[22] For instance, the Supreme Court asserts in *Abington School District v. Schempp* 274 U.S. 203, 222 (1963): "The wholesome

'neutrality' of which this Court's cases speak thus stems from a recognition of the teachings of history that powerful sects or groups might bring about a fusion of governmental and religious functions or a concert of dependency of one upon the other to the end that official support of the State or Federal Government would be placed behind the tenets of one or all orthodoxies." In addition, the majority in *Engel v. Vitale* 370 U.S. 421, 429–432 point out that the first amendment Framers sought to avoid "the anguish, hardship and bitter strife that could come when zealous religious groups struggled with one another to obtain the Government's stamp of approval. . . . Another purpose of the Establishment Clause rested upon the awareness of the historical fact that governmentally established religions and religious persecutions go hand in hand."

[23]Incorvaia, "Transcendental Meditation," p. 347. "Determining whether such beliefs touch ultimate values would be the most difficult problem encountered by the courts under the proposed definition. However, it should not be too difficult to distinguish, for example, between the NAACP, whose programs are based on ultimate values concerning the inherent equality of the races, and TM/SCI, which claims to hold the panacea to all of society's problems. All groups engaged in social and political action may be expressing some types of ultimate values. Ideals concerning the equality of all men, the moral injustice of war, or the immorality of abortion, for example, are based to some extent on ultimate values about Man's nature and purpose. The distinction, however, between political and social groups and religious organizations is one of degree. One must look to whether the questioned group attempts to provide all-inclusive answers to ultimate questions and to whether such beliefs command an exclusive loyalty or faith from the group's adherents. *See* Ladd, *Public Education and Religion*, 13 J. PUB. L. 310, 324 (1964)." (Ibid)

[24]Ibid., p. 348.

[25]Ibid. Incorvaia cites the following example from case law: "[S]peaking of the inherent coercion involved in released-time programs, Justice Frankfurter perceptively stated that in such programs '[t]he law of imitation operates, and nonconformity is not an outstanding characteristic of children. The result is an obvious pressure upon children to attend.' Illinois *ex rel.* McCollum v. Board of Educ., 333 U.S. 203, 227 (1948) (Frankfurter,

J., concurring)." (*Ibid.*)

See also, *LaRocca v. Board of Education of Rye City School District*, 406 N.Y.S.2d 348 (App. Div. 1978), *appeal dismissed*, 386 N.E.2d 266 (N.Y. 1978); and *Dale v. Board of Education, Lemon Independent School District 322-2*, 316 N.W.2d 108 (S.D. 1982). John Whitehead points out that in the *LaRocca* case a teacher was dismissed "for recruiting students to join her religious organization and using [the] classroom to promote tenets of religious faith." In the *Dale* case "a biology teacher [was] denied contract renewal for devoting excessive instructional time to biblical theory of creation in violation of [the] school board's guidelines." (John W. Whitehead, *The Rights of Religious Persons in Public Education* [Wheaton, IL: Crossway Books, 1991], p. 259).

[26]See Robert L. Cord, *Separation of Church and State: Historical Fact and Current Fiction* (Grand Rapids, MI: Baker Book House, 1982); Whitehead, *Rights of Religious Persons*.

[27]*Lemon v. Kurtzman* (1971) 403 U.S. 602, at 612–13, as quoted in Cord, *Separation of Church and State*, pp. 198–199. However, "prior to 1970, the Supreme Court sought to determine state neutrality [concerning religion] with a two-part test which required that: (1) the action of the state not be intended to aid one religion or all religions and (2) the prinicipal or primary effect of the program be one that 'neither advances nor inhibits religion.' In 1970 the Supreme Court added a third prong to the test, that the state must not foster 'an excessive government entanglement with religion.' Walz v. Tax Commission, 397 U.S. 664, 90 S.Ct. 1409 (1970)." (Kern Alexander and M. David Alexander, *The Law of Schools, Students, and Teachers in a Nutshell* [St. Paul, MN: West Publishing, 1984], pp. 100-101). The Court simply added this third prong in the *Lemon* case.

[28]*Roemer v. Board of Public Works* 426 U.S. 736, 747 (1976). (emphasis added)

[29]For an overview of the court decisions which address these activities, see *Students' Rights and the Public Schools* (Virginia Beach, VA: American Center for Law & Justice, n.d.)

[30]See, for example, Whitehead, *Rights of Religious Persons*; Cord, *Separation of Church and State*, pp. 169–211; Michael W. McConnell, "Accommodation of Religion," *1985 Supreme Court Review* 1 (1985); and Michael W. McConnell, "The Origins and Historical Understanding of Free Exercise of Religion," *Harvard*

Law Review 103 (1990); Michael W. McConnell, "Should Congress Pass Legislation Restoring the Broader Interpretation of the Free Exercise of Religion?," *Harvard Journal of Law & Public Policy* 15 (Winter 1992).

[31]See *Marsh v. Chambers*, 436 U.S. 783 (1983); *Lynch v. Donnelly* 465 U.S. 668 (1984); and *Mueller v. Allen*, 463 U.S. 388, 394 *passim* (1983).

[32]In his dissenting opinion in *Meek v. Pittinger* (421 U.S. 349, at 374 [1975]) Justice William Brennan claimed to have found a fourth prong: ". . . four years ago, the Court, albeit without express recognition of the fact, added a significant *fourth factor* to the test: 'A broader base of entanglement of yet a different character is presented by the divisive political potential of these state programs.' Lemon v. Kurtzman, 403 U.S. 602, 622 (1971)."

[33]*Lynch v. Donnelly* at 688 (O'Connor, J., concurring). O'Connor's endorsement test has been criticized as well. See Smith, "Symbols, Perceptions, and Doctrinal Illusions: Establishment Neutrality and the 'No Endorsement' Test," *Michigan Law Review* 86 (1987).

[34]Louis Fischer and Gail Paulus Sorenson, *School Law for Counselors, Psychologists, and Social Workers*, 2nd ed. (New York: Longman, 1991), p. 203.

[35]Whitehead, *Rights of Religious Persons*, p. 59.

[36]Ibid., p. 100. Whitehead extracted these principles from the following cases: *Abington School District v. Schempp*, 374 U.S. 203 (1963); *Florey v. Sioux Falls School District 49–5*, 464 F. Supp. 911 (D. S.D. 1979), *aff'd*, 619 F.2d 1311 (8th Cir.), *cert. denied*, 449 U.S. 987 (1980); *Parducci v. Rutland*, 316 F. Supp. 352 (M.D. Ala. 1970); and *Zykan v. Warsaw Community School Corporation*, 631 F.2d 1300 (7th Cir. 1980).
See especially the state of California's policy for the teaching of religion, *Moral and Civic Education and Teaching about Religion*, rev. ed. (Sacramento: California Department of Education, 1991)

[37]Louis Fischer, David Schimmel, and Cynthia Kelly, *Teachers and the Law*, 2nd ed. (New York: Longman, 1987), p. 159.

[38]Whitehead, *Rights of Religious Persons*, p. 59.

[39]Fischer, Schimmel and Kelly, *Teachers and the Law*, p. 159.

[40]Although moral relativism is certainly part of much New Age thinking, and in many classrooms moral relativism is taught, I

chose not to place it in this chart for a very important reason: if inculcated in public education apart from the New Age world view, it would be difficult to classify such teaching as "religious." That is to say, moral relativism is not necessarily pantheistic just as moral objectivism is not necessarily theistic. That is, someone can be a moral relativist without being a New Ager or pantheist just as one can be a moral objectivist without being a theist or religious believer. However, if either view is inculcated in the context of its religious worldview in a public education setting, such inculcation would appear to violate the establishment clause.

Confusion over this subtle distinction is quite common. Consider the American Civil Liberties Union's opposition to a 1988 California State Assembly bill, which mandated that abstinence be taught in sex education classes in public schools. In a letter written to the Assembly Education Committee (May 26, 1988), ACLU attorneys Majorie C. Swartz and Francisco Lobaco argue that it is the ACLU's position "that teaching that monogamous heterosexual intercourse within marriage is a traditional American value is an unconstitutional establishment of a religious doctrine in public schools. There are various religions which hold contrary beliefs with respect to marriage and monogamy." (reproduced in James Dobson and Gary L. Bauer, *Children at Risk* [Dallas: Word Publishing, 1990], p. 26). Since one can be an atheist and agree with the assembly bill, it seems ludicrous for the ACLU to assert that the bill advances a religious doctrine. If the ACLU's position were to become law, a teacher would be legally forbidden from telling Johnny that it is morally wrong to steal from Suzie, since such a moral condemnation is found in the Ten Comandments.

[41] Whitehead *Rights of Religious Persons*, p. 100. See note 36 for a list of cases from which Whitehead extracted these principles.

[42] Fischer, Schimmel and Kelly, *Teachers and the Law*, p. 159.

[43] Division of Continuing Education, University of Nevada, Las Vegas, *The Catalogue: Adult Classes, Workshops and Seminars* (Winter 1992): 32.

[44] Tucker, *Another Gospel*, p. 385.

[45] Russell Chandler, *Understanding the New Age* (Dallas: Word Publishing, 1991), p. 330.

[46]Irving Hexham, "Yoga, UFO's, and Cult Membership," *Update: A Quarterly Journal of New Religious Movements* 10 (September 1986): 6.

[47]Chandler, *Understanding the New Age*, p. 333.

[48]Ibid., p. 330. See also, Swami Rama, Rudolph Ballentine, and Swami Ajaya, *Yoga ga and Psychotheraphy: The Evolution of Consciousness* (Honesdale, PA: The Himalayan International Institute of Yoga Science and Philosophy, 1976), pp. 138, 216–280.

[49]Non-Credit Classes, *Community College of Southern Nevada* (Spring 1992): 27.

[50]Chandler, *Understanding the New Age*, p. 333.

[51]Non-Credit Classes, *Community College of Southern Nevada* (Spring 1993): 21,34, and 36.

[52]Division of Continuing Education, University of Massachusetts at Amherst, *Schedule of Courses, Workshops, and Seminars* (Spring 1992): 16.

[53]Jenkinson, "Imaginary Movement," pp. 74–77.

Law and Justice
by John Warwick Montgomery

*I*n his discussion of "Law as the Will of God: The Heritage of the Old Testament," Carl Joachim Friedrich observed that "Jahweh, the god without name of Israel, was clearly distinguished from surrounding gods of other peoples by his preoccupation with law."[1] If the Bible is what it claims to be—not a collection of fallible ancient New Eastern opinion, but the inerrant written revelation of the God of the universe—what does this scriptural "preoccupation with law" mean in the sphere of human jurisprudence? It is the contention of the present essay that a divinely given, biblical philosophy of law offers two overarching contributions to the human search for justice: explicit eternal norms against which positive law can and must be judged; and a redemptive perspective for all juridical activity.

Biblical Jurisprudence and the Quest for Norms

Is human law no more than a sociological product of the *Zeitgeist,* the spirit of the age? If so, the truly clever man is the one who can "get away" with violating it in order to achieve his purposes; after all, law observance is then only a question of the values of some over against the values of others. In W.H. Auden's words,

> *. . . Law-abiding scholars write:*
> *Law is neither wrong nor right,*
> *Law is only crimes*
> *Punished by places and by times,*
> *Law is the clothes men wear*
> *Anytime, anywhere,*
> *Law is Good-morning and Good-night.*[2]

These lines point to the single most important conceptual battle in modern philosophy of law: the struggle between natural law theorists, on the one hand, and the legal positivists or realists, on the other.

The most influential contemporary representative of legal positivism or realism is H.L.A. Hart, a thinker schooled in the best traditions of the analytical philosophy movement. Hart has raised to a level of considerable sophistication the rather simplistic nineteenth century view that law and rights are no more than products of the commands of a sovereign (John Austin) or the results of judicial decision (John Chipman Gray). In Hart's view, law requires a social dimension (rules have an "internal aspect") and can only function by way of "shared morality."[3]

But, as Rosenbaum well observes, Hart's "community" approach to rights does not tell us "how to obtain universal agreement on the essentials of a community" or "how it is possible to experience the sense of community when the competing views around the world on the nature of community seem to thwart the development of a unified concept of human rights."[4] The force of these criticisms becomes particularly evident when we note that for Hart the ultimate "rule of recognition" on which any given legal system is founded is *unjustifiable* outside of the system itself.

> *We only need the word "validity," and commonly only use it, to answer questions which arise within a system of rules where the status of a rule as a member of the system*

depends on its satisfying certain criteria provided by the rule of recognition. No such question can arise as to the validity of the very rule of recognition which provides the criteria; it can neither be valid nor invalid but is simply accepted as appropriate for use in this way. To express this simple fact by saying darkly that its validity is "assumed but cannot be demonstrated," is like saying that we assume, but can never demonstrate, that the standard metre bar in Paris which is the ultimate test of the correctness of all measurement in metres, is itself correct.[5]

We are thus left—as in the case of sociological and anthropological relativism—with no single, unified, justifiable legal standard.[6]

The single gravest problem with all forms of legal realism or positivism is their restriction of the idea of justice to the confines of particular legal systems or jurisprudential orientations. No overriding standard of law and justice is brought to bear on the human situation. As the great Belgian philosopher of law Ch. Perelman succinctly puts it:

This conception of juridical positivism collapses before the abuses of Hitlerism, like any scientific theory irreconcilable with the facts. The universal reaction to the Nazi crimes forced the Allied chiefs of state to institute the Nuremberg trials and to interpret the adage nullum crimen sine lege in a non-positivistic sense because the law violated in the case did not derive from a system of positive law but from the conscience of all civilized men. The conviction that it was impossible to leave these horrible crimes unpunished, although they fell outside a system of positive law, has prevailed over the positivistic conception of the grounding of the law.[7]

In the nineteenth century, legal positivism or realism replaced a much older juridical philosophy, the theory of natural law. And today, the overwhelming difficulties

321

with all varieties of realism are producing still another pendulum-swing in the history of ideas—a swing back to natural law thinking.[8] But the most influential representatives of the current natural law revival do not operate theologically as did their medieval predecessors; rather, they attempt philosophically to establish a ground within human nature for absolute legal norms, a ground allegedly surpassing positive law and cultural relativity.

The most impressive contemporary effort to rehabilitate natural law is provided by John Finnis, fellow of University College, Oxford. Finnis is Roman Catholic and much concerned with the interpretation of Thomas Aquinas vis-à-vis the arguments he presents, but Finnis' great work, *Natural Law and Natural Rights*, is not disguised theologizing. He is thoroughly trained in analytical philosophy and attempts to show in the most general sense that "practical reasonableness" in ordering human affairs requires an approach to the state, law and justice that will preserve and extend human goods (specifically: life, knowledge, play, aesthetic experience, friendship or sociability, religion, etc.). "There are human goods," he writes, "that can be secured only through the institutions of human law, and requirements of practical reasonableness that only those institutions can satisfy."[9] Henry B. Veatch observes:

> *What Finnis is trying to show is how any common enterprise of human beings, aims at achieving a common good, and hence demands something which can only be called political or governmental authority. Nor is the function of such authority to be understood exclusively, or even primarily, in terms of any mere exercise of coercive force. No, it is rather for the necessary and indispensable coordination of the efforts of the different agents of the community that the authority is instituted in the first place; and it is only through the exercise of such a directing and coordinating authority that the common good of the community can even be concretely determined, much less*

achieved. And as for law—human law or positive law—it is nothing if not the indispensable instrument of such a public or governmental authority, aimed at the attainment of the good of the community. Moreover, since the good of the community is not any literally collective good, or even an additive good, but simply the well-being of each and all of the members of the community individually, the law needs to be so constituted as to respect the rights of the individual members of the community. And here again, in his discussion of the rights, i.e., the natural rights, of citizens, Finnis is very careful to construe such rights—e.g., common law rights, such as the right to property, to a fair trial, to protection against self-incrimination, to safeguards against violence—not as absolute rights, in the way in which this term is so often understood nowadays, but rather as rights that are justified in terms of the natural needs and requirements of the individual, if he is ever to be able to live the life of a truly moral and autonomous human person.[10]

Finnis' commendable attempt to establish standards of justice in terms of practical reasonableness and the common good of the community suffers from great difficulties, however. Bankowski has pointed out that, of the several "human goods" Finnis sets forth, only "knowledge" is effectively justified by his retorsive argument such that one cannot argue against it without cutting the ground out beneath one's own feet. Even in the case of knowledge the vital question is still left open: "what items of knowledge we should seek."[11] Indeed, Finnis "is better at showing how law needs to be grounded in ethics, than he is at showing how the principles of ethics are discoverable right in the very facts of nature and reality."[12]

Like every natural law thinker, Finnis must solve the problem of defining what man's nature really is. As Aristotle well observed: "In order to find what is natural we must look among those things which according to nature are in a sound condition, not among those that are corrupt."[13] Granted, man frequently desires knowledge, life and friendship; but it is equally the case empirically that human beings have often sought to deceive, kill and subjugate their fellows. After all, Hobbes—and Machiavelli before him—built his totalitarian social theory strictly on the natural law basis that human life is "nasty, brutish, and short!" A successful natural law theory must be able to say whether the good or the bad in human life is truly "natural" and to what degree—for otherwise no one can determine what values are justly to receive legal sanction in society.

This dilemma connects with the related quandary for natural law thinkers as to how—even if we know what human nature actually consists of—we can justify deriving an "ought" from the "is." The great analytical ethicist G.E. Moore termed this difficulty the "naturalistic fallacy": the false idea that once you know what is natural you will have justified it as a positive value.[14] In reality, even as the natural fact of murder or torture does not justify killing or inhuman punishment, so the natural fact of self-preservation or truth-seeking does not in itself vindicate the alleged right to life or civil liberties.

A fatal error is therefore committed when well-meaning religionists (not excluding some evangelicals) try to solve the root problems of legal philosophy by rejecting positivism in favor of a return to natural law thinking. In reality—though this is almost never recognized—just naturalism and legal positivism have correlative strengths and weaknesses which point directly to the need for *biblical jurisprudence.* Consider the two essential defining elements of all natural law theories, with their corresponding advantage and disadvantage; and the parallel defining elements and strength/weakness of legal positivism or realism:

	DEFINING ELEMENTS	ADVANTAGES/ DISADVANTAGES
NATURAL LAW THEORY	N-1. Insistence on an ideal standard of judgment above positive legislation or case law	a. *Advantage:* Ethical judgment is brought to bear on existing positive law
	N-2. The conviction that only law which conforms to this ideal is truly law	b. *Disadvantage:* Bad law is not recognized as law at all, thus opening the doors to anarchy
LEGAL POSITIVISM OR REALISM	P-1. Absence of any ideal standard of judgment above positive legislation or case law	a. *Disadvantage:* No standard of ethical judgment is brought to bear on existing positive law, thus leaving demonic legal systems (e.g., National Socialism) untouched
	P-2. The conviction that all societal rules with the formal, official sanction of the body politic are law	b. *Advantage:* Even bad law is seen to be law, thus preserving the rule of law

What is needed for a sound jurisprudence is a *combination of defining element (N-1a) of jus naturalism with defining element (P-2b) of legal positivism*—and the rejection of the corresponding disadvantageous elements of the two positions ([N-2b] and [P-1a]). *This is precisely what the biblical jurisprudence offers.*

Thus, Romans 13 plainly asserts that "the powers that be are ordained of God," that "whosoever resists the power, resists the ordinance of God," and that we are to be subject to constituted authority "not only for wrath but also for conscience sake." Scripture clearly holds that even bad law is nonetheless law and that there is something worse even than bad law, namely anarchy. The positivist concern with the preservation of the rule of law (P-2b) is thus vindicated.

Even more important, Holy Writ provides, from cover to cover, innumerable declarations of God's normative standards for human life. These norms are exactly what natural law theory gropes for (N-1a) but is unsuccessful in defining apart from a clear and unambiguous Word from God. In the Genesis vs. evolution area of evangelical discussion, where the non-inerrantists have claimed that the "law of nature" must be placed on an equal footing with Scripture (since, admittedly, God is the source of both), consistent believers in the inerrancy of the Bible have rightly pointed out that Holy Scripture, being already in verbal, propositional form, has a tremendous advantage in clarity and perspicuity over "nature." The same point applies jurisprudentially: God has unambiguously set forth his normative standards in the pages of Scripture, and the "natural law" cannot hope to compete with, much less contradict, its asseverations. As Sir William Blackstone well put it: "Man, considered as a creature, must necessarily be subject to the laws of his Creator. . . . No human laws should be suffered to contradict these."[15] It is Scripture that has the final word on what the eternal laws in fact are, thereby preserving us from oral and jurisprudential chaos and relativism.

How does biblically revealed law relate to the laws "written in men's hearts" (Hebrews 8:10, etc.)? Principally on the basis of Romans 1 and 2 (in particular, 1:20 and 2:14–15), the Reformers maintained that even after man's Fall into sin, a limited general knowledge of the universal principles of morality remained, indelibly inscribed on man's heart. This was Luther's position, and Calvin's also.[16] In the twentieth century, following the collapse of the old modernism or religious liberalism—which in effect jettisoned biblical revelation in favor of a saving view of general revelation—a powerful reaction set in. Karl Barth in particular cried *Nein* to Emil Brunner's relatively mild endeavor to maintain natural revelation (as in the case of the Reformers, not as a means of salvation, but only as a partial and imperfect knowledge of divine standards for human life and thus an objective judgment on man's sinful conduct toward his fellows).[17] Brunner's position was in fact little more than a restatement of the classic Reformation doctrine of the *Schopfungsordnungen* (Orders of Creation), declaring on the basis of Scripture that even after the Fall, God in his grace structured human life through government, the family, education, etc., to prevent sinful man from destroying himself through unrestrained selfishness.[18] The weight of evangelical scholarship has concluded that Barth's total rejection of natural theology—and, with it, natural law theory—is scripturally unwarranted.[19]

But even if a biblical natural law theory is accepted, does it provide the necessary grounding for human jurisprudence? Norwegian theologian Einar Molland contends that:

> It is enough to believe in the value of man and in a written law which is valid for all mankind at all times, that is, in the law which ancient thinkers called the natural law. This is not what the natural sciences understand by natural law, since the law they refer to raises us above nature. The law in question here is concerned with man and

corresponds to man's nature. For human co-existence, it is
enough to believe that such a natural law exists and that
we can all more or less clearly discern it.[20]

We doubt very much that this is "enough for human co-existence." The problem is not that formal natural-rights structures or orders are absent from human society. The trouble is that, though ubiquitously present, they *are* "formal," lacking in universal or justifiable substantive content. Perrott's theory of fundamental rights highlights the root difficulty, when he concludes that "there are what may be called Natural Areas of Legal Concern rather than Natural Law principles with a specific content," and that "the precise content of the rules, within limits, does not matter very much; what does matter is that legal discriminations should be drawn, and then generally adhered to. We *do* need to decide which side of the road to drive on; the choice of sides is, within limits, arbitrary."[21]

With respect, this is simply inadequate. In a footnote to the passage quoted, Perrott states that "of course, it [the choice of substantive legal content] matters enormously from an evaluative or emotional point of view." Does it only matter emotionally? Is it just an arbitrary question of which side of the road one drives on? A little earlier in his essay, Perrott declares that "a number of different definitions of murder may be equally acceptable!" In point of fact, the substantive definition of legal standards is all-important, and it is these clear definitions which natural law fails to provide. Carl Joachim Friedrich noted that the formula of the Justinian Code is so "imprecise" that it does little more than to underscore the need for "some kind of equity."[22] I observed at the Buchenwald death camp that the *Digest's* vague expression, "Give to each his own," was inscribed in German translation (*Jedem das seine*) on the metal doors leading into that place of horror.

This is not in any sense to deny the reality of natural rights; it is only to say that their content is left undefined by natural law thinking, and it is precisely their content which is essential to solve the jurisprudential dilemma. C.S. Lewis is correct that all human societies operate—and must operate—with ethical values;[23] but in order effectively to oppose the myriad variations of man's inhumanity to man, we must be able to determine *which* ethical values are good, bad and indifferent. (Is torture wrong? What about cannibal environmentalists cleaning their plates?) The Orders of Creation are a reality; but it is not enough to know that the family has been instituted by God: one must be able to determine whether polygamy and polyandry are an asset or a liability to human dignity.

The best that can be said of religious natural law theories is that, like John the Baptist, they point beyond themselves. They point to God's special revelation of Himself in the Living Word (Jesus Christ) and the Written Word (the Bible). God's inerrant special revelation yields concrete eternal norms of divine law by which human laws can and must be evaluated and judged.[24] This is the first of the two great contributions of biblical religion to man's quest for law and justice. The second is no less important, and to it we now turn our attention.

Biblical Jurisprudence and the Centrality of Redemption

An inerrant catalog of divine norms for jurisprudence is of incalculable value, for it makes fundamentally impossible the reduction of human law to mere sociological consensus—to

> . . . *the clothes men wear*
> *Anytime, anywhere.*

But revealed norms are not enough, for the profoundly practical question remains: Granting that we know or are in a position to learn God's will in the sphere of normative jurisprudence, *what is law supposed to accomplish?* What are its proper functions? What is it supposed to do and what is it incapable of doing? Without an answer to

329

this basic functional question, we are like workers who have been given a perfect tool but are unclear as to how the tool should properly be used.

The God of the Bible has not left us in such a quandary. The Scriptures make clear what the law's proper functions are and what they are not. Here is a summary expression of biblical teaching on the subject, in terms of the classic doctrine of the "three uses of the law":

> *The Law has three uses, the Political, the Elenchtico-pedagogical, and the Didactic. By the Political use is meant the use of the law as a curb to hold in check wicked men, and to protect society against their aggressions. By the Elenchtico-pedagogical use is meant its use to convict men of sin and thus indirectly to lead them to Christ (Gal. 3:24). This use of the Law refers primarily to the unconverted. But there is an Elenchtico-pedagogical use of the Law even for the regenerate, inasmuch as the Christian's life should be a daily repentance, and the law enables him to see his daily shortcomings and his need of Christ more and more clearly. The Didactic use of the law is its use as a guide for the Christian mind and conduct.*[25]

Politically, the law is regarded as a restraint for the wicked, not as a means of building the "perfect society." Christian faith has no illusions about man: "There is none that doeth good, no, not one" (Psalms 14:1, 3; 53:1; Romans 3:12). To be sure, the Christian should strive to maximize good through the existing legal system and employ all legitimate efforts to change that system for the better where it falls short; but no legal system will be perfect, for it is administered by imperfect men, and even if it were perfect, it could not make men good. Is the lawyer's task therefore an unimportant one, viewed politically? Hardly, for without it society would literally explode, since the conflicts of self-interest among sinful men will be resolved either within an ordered, legal framework or in an anarchical conflict. But the attorney or judge must see his work in this respect as more analogous to that of the policeman (ponder the double meaning of the term "lawman") than to the endeavors of the social reformer.

At the same time, the Christian in the legal sphere has a positive role of the most powerful nature—one far more significant than the (often naive) role of the social activist. The Pedagogical use of the law, which Luther regarded as its primary function, is that of "schoolmaster [Greek, *paidagogos*]: the slave who took the schoolchild to his master] to bring us to Christ." The law shows us where we fall short, and therefore continually reminds us of our need of Christ's redemptive work on the Cross. Lawyers and those who administer the law have, not so incidentally, an ideal vantage point from which to drive home to others this central truth of the gospel. They are constantly in contact with those in trouble—whether because the latter have personally displayed a *mens rea* or because they are caught in the machinery of a sinful world. What better time or opportunity to help them to see that Christ is the only ultimate answer?[26]

As for the third, or Didactic, use of the law, the most important thing to note about it is that, unlike the Political and Pedagogical uses, which apply to non-Christian and Christian alike, it has meaning solely for the believer. Only those who have experienced the forgiveness of sin in Jesus Christ can look at the law (revelational or civil) as something more than a threat. Only the Christian believer can say *ex corde*: "O how I love Thy law" (Ps. 119:97, 113) and "Thy law is my delight" (verses 77, 92, 174). Christ's presence alone is capable of transmuting law from a terror (*lex semper accusat*) into an expression of God's loving will.[27]

Having seen what law is from the standpoint of biblical revelation, we must now state with equal precision what it is *not*. As noted in our comments on the Political and Pedagogical uses of the law, law is *not gospel*. Indeed, the proper distinction between law and gospel can be regarded as the key to all sound theology and Christian life.[28] In his great New Year's sermon of 1532, on Galatians 3:24–25, Luther—who had read law for a year before taking up theological studies—declared:

> The difference between the Law and the Gospel is the height of knowledge in Christendom. Every person and all persons who assume or glory in the name of Christ should know and be able to state this difference. . . . To be sure, both are God's Word: the Law, or the Ten Commandments, and the Gospel; the latter first given by God in Paradise, the former on Mount Sinai. But everything depends on the proper differentiation of these two messages and on not mixing them together. . . . Therefore place the man who is able nicely to distinguish the Law from the Gospel at the head of the list and call him a Doctor of Holy Scripture, for without the Holy Spirit the attainment of this ability to differentiate is impossible. . . . By "Law" we should understand nothing but God's Word and command by which He tells us what we are to do and not to do and demands our obedience or work. . . . The Gospel is such a doctrine or Word of God as does not demand our works or command us to do anything but bids us simply receive the offered grace of the forgiveness of sins and eternal salvation and be satisfied to have it given to us as a free gift.[29]

The essential difference between law and gospel is not that gospel comes from God while law comes from man; both have their origin in the Divine will. The distinction between them is not genetic but functional: law *commands*, while gospel (OE *godspel*, "good news") *bestows a gift*. Law and gospel are differentiated on this basis throughout the length and breadth of Scripture, but the distinction can be seen with particular clarity when the Bible speaks of the way of salvation or provides salvatory examples. When the people asked our Lord, "What shall we *do*, that we might *work the works* of God?" (thereby confusing gospel with law in thinking that salvation comes by fulfilling the law), Jesus answered in terms of pure gospel: "This is the work of God, that ye believe on Him *whom He hath sent*" (Jn. 6:28–29). Similarly, Jesus taught this to the rich young ruler (Mt. 19:16–22), and Paul to the Philippian jailer (Acts 16:29–34).

The Apostle states this principle in formal terms again and again; indeed, it constitutes the very theme of his epistles to the Romans and the Galatians. For example, in Romans 3:20–22 he draws the line between law and gospel with surgical precision:

> *By the deeds of the law there shall no flesh be justified in his sight: for by the law is the knowledge of sin. Now the righteousness of God without the law is manifested, being witnessed by the law and the prophets: even the righteousness of God which is by faith of Jesus Christ, unto all and upon all them that believe . . .*

Why is this distinction between law and gospel so vital? Simply because the whole message of salvation turns on it. A sinful human race wants above all to prove its worth by saving itself—by demonstrating that it can create and maintain ideal legal and ethical structures and thereby satisfy the most exacting cosmic demands. But Scripture depicts such activity as a Tower of Babel—an impossible effort to scale the heights of heaven: "The fear of the Lord is the beginning of wisdom." Man needs to recognize that the first step in salvation is to admit that he cannot save himself by the deeds of the law—however impressive the deeds or however commendable the law. "No man hath ascended up to heaven, but he that came down from heaven, even the Son of man" (Jn. 3:13).

This endemic fallacy of egotistic fallen man—turning law into gospel—is evident whether one looks back into history or gazes across the expanse of the present. Contemporary political theorist Eric Voegelin, in his epochal series, *Order and History*, has identified the theme of "metastatic gnosis" in the human drama: the Promethean urge to create on earth a millennial perfection which only God is in fact capable of achieving. Voegelin charts the appalling evils produced by this Nietzschean transvaluation of all proper value, and correctly stresses that its result is always the very opposite of true order.[30]

In the Marxist East, one observes a religious conviction (a genuine opiate of the people?) to the effect that if the structures of society are altered, human perfection is attainable: eliminate by revolutionary action the inequities in the ownership of the means of production, recast law so that it no longer favors a ruling caste of capitalists, and a millennial "classless society" will arise.[31] In the Capitalist West, the means of social engineering are different, but the theory is the same: change the structures and you will save mankind. Somehow no one asks the painfully obvious question: how can a self-centered Skinner build a Skinner box that will provide an environment capable of yielding non-self-centered future generations? Our craze for environmental works-righteousness disregards C.S. Lewis' perceptive observation: "Man's power over Nature is really the power of some men over other men, with Nature as their instrument."[32] And in the Third World, whether we observe the lamination of a modern European civil code on a medieval Ethiopia or seek to comprehend mystical socialism in Tanzania, it becomes plain that law is regarded as a prime weapon of social change.[33]

No Christian, much less the Christian lawyer, can justify otherworldly indifference to social amelioration or to the importance of law revision in achieving worthwhile societal goals. But the way of salvation does not lie along that path. Law must be rigorously distinguished from gospel. "The law was given through Moses; grace and truth came through Jesus Christ" (Jn. 1:17).

Confusion of law and gospel is possible in two directions. Law may be invested with the quality of gospel, thereby deceiving men into thinking that they can save themselves through personal or societal efforts. But gospel may also try to replace law, producing what Bonhoeffer has classically phrased "cheap grace." In the one case, law swallows up gospel, and the result is *legalism*; in the other, gospel absorbs law, yielding *antinomianism*. The gravity of dispensing with law for any reason—even on the alleged ground that grace renders it no longer necessary—is suggested by the New Testament use of the Greek word *anomos* ("Lawless one") for the Antichrist (2 Thessalonians 2:8).

In contemporary theology, the antinomian error is rife. Among modern theologians, Paul Lehmann argues that not law or moral rules but rather "believing contexts" should guide our actions; what we should do will be discovered dynamically as we participate in the believing community.[34] A more radical variation on this new morality is Joseph Fletcher's "situation ethics," where we learn that "only one thing is intrinsically good, namely love" and that "love's decisions are made situationally, not prescriptively."[35] Such views fail to recognize that law and principle are unavoidably present—implicitly if not explicitly—in personal and societal decision-making and are far more dangerous when implicit; that love is a motive, incapable of charting specific action apart from a structure of values; and that to depend on situations to yield their own answers is to engage in a most perilous form of magic, since what bubbles up from the caldron of sinful situations has no guarantee whatever of ethical purity.[36]

The late James A. Pike, a lawyer before he entered the Episcopal priesthood, declared in his 1962 Rosenthal Lectures at the Northwestern University School of Law that though the Ten Commandments "give us a very good rule of thumb as to standard situations," they are "pregnable to the assault of a higher claim": "Rules, whether they be traffic regulations or commandments from Mount Sinai, do not exhaust the full moral dimensions of things." And where is the "higher claim" to be found? In the dynamics of the existential situation. "In these pages," wrote Pike,

335

"it will become apparent that I am an existentialist." As an illustration, he commends the heroine of the apocryphal book of Judith for her willingness to operate with a "higher claim" than the Sixth Commandment in being willing to commit adultery so as to kill a political enemy of her people.[37] Here, as in situation ethics, the sinful human existential moment is invested with revelatory quality: immediate, individual situations are naively supposed to be able to "reveal" what neither human law (the product of far wider and deeper reflection) or even Holy Scripture (which claims to be and is the very Word of God) can adequately provide.[38]

The belief that the world of law is capable of being humanistically replaced by a climate of love, peace and joy has been expressed by Charles Reich, formerly of the Yale law faculty, in *The Greening of America*. There he declares that the hippie exuberance of the 1960s heralded the dawn of a new consciousness, i.e., "Consciousness III," representing no less than "the beginning of the development of new capacities in man" and "a community of a very different sort, based upon love and trust." The conquest of scarcity has made literally possible a "change in human nature," since "man no longer needs to base his society on the assumption that all men are antagonistic to one another." As for legal structures, Reich grudgingly concedes that "perhaps democracy, law and constitutional rights will still be wanted in a new society," but quickly adds that, if so, "they cannot be based or justified any longer on assumptions" such as that "man is a wolf to man."[39]

And yet that is precisely what man continues to be. The Christian must never make the mistake of thinking that—in his personal life or in the life of his society—law is dispensable. If he does, the wolf within him (and others) will gnaw away his very soul and that of society. Concretely, the Christian will recognize that Romans 13 makes any violation of positive law an evil, even if in particular instances the law is not wise or just, and even if the subject matter prohibited by it is not *malum in se*. (Thus revolution is always an evil—though in some instances it may admittedly be a lesser of evils—and alcohol or marijuana, even if not inherently harmful to the body, cannot be used with moral impunity where prohibited by law.)

In sum, the Christian will test all positive law by the pronouncements of Holy Scripture, endeavoring by every legitimate means at his disposal to bring man's temporal law into conformity with God's eternal law.[40] Such a practical recognition that law is indispensable will serve the highest purpose of all: it will remind the individual and the society how far short of God's standards of justice they fall, and will as a schoolmaster point them to Christ's perfect salvation.[41]

Endnotes

[1]Carl Joachim Friedrich, *The Philosophy of Law in Historical Perspective*, 2d ed. (Chicago: University of Chicago Press, 1963), p. 8.

[2]W.H. Auden, "Law Like Love" (from *The Collected Poetry of W.G. Auden*), reprinted in John Warwick Montgomery, ed., *Jurisprudence: A Book of Readings*, 2d ed. (Strasbourg, France: International Scholarly Publishers; Anaheim, CA: The Simon Greenleaf School of Law, 1980), pp. 4–5.

[3]Hart has presented his philosophy of law systematically in *The Concept of Law* (Oxford: Clarendon Press, 1961). J.W. Harris offers a helpful interpretation of Hart's ideas, with good bibliography (*Legal Philosophies* [London: Butterworths, 1980], pp. 105–114).

[4]Alan S. Rosenbaum, "Introduction," in his *The Philosophy of Human Rights: International Perspectives* (Westport, CT: Greenwood Press, 1980), p. 33.

[5]Hart, op. cit., pp. 105–106.

[6]For a more detailed treatment of legal positivism, with an examination of the views of Hans Kelsen, Ronald Dworkin, et. al.,

see my *Human Rights and Human Dignity* (Dallas, TX: Probe; Grand Rapids, MI: Zondervan, 1986), chap. 4.

[7]Ch. Perelman, "Can the Rights of Man Be Founded?" in *The Philosophy of Human Rights*, ed. Rosenbaum, p. 47. See also M.J. Detmold, *The Unity of Law and Morality: A Refutation of Legal Positivism* (London: Routledge & Kegan Paul, 1984).

[8]Cf. G.G. Haines, *The Revival of Natural Law Concepts* (Cambridge, MA: Harvard University Press, 1958).

[9]John Finnis, *Natural Law and Natural Rights* (Oxford: Clarendon Press, 1980), p. 3. Finnis' list of human goods is based upon Germain Grisez, "The First Principle of Practical Reason," *Natural Law Forum* 10 (1965): 168–96.

[10]Henry B. Veatch, Review of *Natural Law and Natural Rights* by John Finnis, *American Journal of Jurisprudence* 26 (1981): 253.

[11]Z.K. Bankowski, Review of *Natural Law and Natural Rights* by John Finnis, *Law Quarterly Review* 98 (July 1982): 474.

[12]Veatch, op. cit., p. 250.

[13]Aristotle, *Politics,* 1. 5.

[14]G.E. Moore, *Principia Ethica* (Cambridge: Cambridge University Press, 1903), chap. 1. For a more extended discussion and critique of contemporary natural law theories, including the Neo-Kantian approaches of Rawls and Gerwith, see my *Human Rights and Human Dignity.*

[15]Sir William Blackstone, *Commentaries on the Laws of England*, ed. Stanley N. Katz, et. al; 4 vols. facsimile ed. (Chicago: University of Chicago Press, 1979), 1:39, 42.

[16]On Luther, see Philip S. Watson, *Let God Be God! An Interpretation of the Theology of Martin Luther* (London: Epworth Press, 1947), pp. 73–85, 105–116; and Marc Lienhard, "Luther et les droits de l'homme," *Revue d'Histoire et de Philosophie Religieuses* 54 (1) (1974): 15–29 (English translation in *A Lutheran Reader on Human Rights*, ed. Jorgen Lissner and Arne Sovik: *LWF Report* 1–2 [September 1978]: 66–80). Paul Helm of the University of Liverpool's Department of Philosophy, in delivering the Third Finlayson Lecture, provides an excellent overview of "Calvin and Natural Law:" *The Scottish Bulletin of Evangelical Theology* 2 (1984): 5–22.

[17]See the celebrated debate between Barth and Brunner, *Natural Theology: Comprising "Nature and Grace" by Professor Dr.*

Emil Brunner and the Reply "No!" by Dr. Karl Barth, trans. Peter Fraenkel (London: Geoffrey Bles, 1946).

[18]John Warwick Montgomery, "Karl Barth and Contemporary Theology of History," in his *Where Is History Going? Essays in Support of the Historical Truth of the Christian Revelation*, reprint ed. (Minneapolis: Bethany, 1972), pp. 104–105; and Montgomery, "A Critical Examination of Emil Brunner's *The Divine Imperative*, Bk. III," in his *The Shape of the Past*, rev. ed. (Minneapolis: Bethany, 1975), pp. 358–74.

[19]See, for example, Alan F. Johnson, "Is There a Biblical Warrant for Natural-Law Theories?" *Evangelical Theological Society Journal* 25 (2) (June 1982): 185–99; and Bruce A Demarest, *General Revelation* (Grand Rapids: Zondervan, 1982). Professor Demarest (p. 244) rejects on biblical grounds the entire—predominantly Dutch hyper-Calvinist—tradition which maintains that "no knowledge is mediated by general revelation in nature and providence" (Demarest refers specifically to Abraham Kuyper, G.C. Berkouwer, Cornelius Van Til, Gordon Clark, T.F. Torrance and Donald Bloesch—as well as Karl Barth). Jacques Ellul, as one would expect, follows Barth in unqualifiedly rejecting natural theology. See his *The Theological Foundation of Law*, trans. Marguerite Wieser (New York: Seabury Press, 1969); and cf. John Warwick Montgomery, "Technology and Eschatology," in his *Faith Founded on Fact* (Nashville: Thomas Nelson, 1978), pp. 155–59.

[20]Quoted in Marc Lienhard, "Protestantism and Human Rights," *Human Rights Teaching* [UNESCO] 2 (1981): 30.

[21]D.L. Perrott, "The Logic of Fundamental Rights," in *Fundamental Rights*, ed. J.W. Bridge, D. Lasok, et. al. (London: Sweet & Maxwell, 1973), pp. 13–15.

[22]Friedrich, op. cit., p. 33. See also John Warwick Montgomery, *The Law Above the Law* (Minneapolis: Bethany, 1975), pp. 38–40.

[23]C.S. Lewis, *The Case for Christianity* (New York: MacMillan, 1943), reprinted in his *Mere Christianity* (New York: MacMillan, 1953); and cf. his *Abolition of Man* (New York: MacMillan, 1947).

[24]For a systematic presentation of the scriptural norms governing positive law, see, for example, H.B. Clark, *Biblical Law*, 2d ed. (Portland, OR: Binfords & Mort, 1944).

339

[25]Joseph Stump, *The Christian Faith* (Philadelphia: Muhlenberg Press, 1942), pp. 309–310. This basic conceptualization is found in all the standard works of classical dogmatics.

[26]This theme is further developed in my book, *Law & Gospel: A Study in Jurisprudence* (Oak Park, IL: Christian Legal Society, 1978).

[27]See John Warwick Montgomery, "The Law's Third Use: Sanctification," in his *Crisis in Lutheran Theology*, 2 vols., rev. ed. (Minneapolis: Bethany, 1973), 1: 124–27.

[28]C.F.W. Walther, *The Proper Distinction Between Law and Gospel*, ed. W. Dau (St. Louis, MO: Concordia, 1928).

[29]*W.A.* [the standard, critical Weimar edition of Luther's writings], 36: 25, 29, 30–31.

[30]See Montgomery, *Shape of the Past,* pp. 131–37. Norman L. Geisler has recently pointed out similarly disquieting tendencies in the Calvinist "Reconstructionist" camp ("A Premillennial View of Law and Government," *Bibliotheca Sacra*, July–September 1985, pp. 250–66)—though the true source of the Reconstructionist error would appear to lie, not in their rejection of premillennialism or dispensationalism, but in their acceptance of the Calvinist view that the Pedagogical use of the law is to be subordinated to the Third or Didactic use. Such triumphalism opens the door to postmillennial naïveté.

[31]See John Warwick Montgomery, "The Marxist Approach to Human Rights: Analysis & Critique," *The Simon Greenleaf Law Review*, Vol. 3 (1983–84), *passim*.

[32]Quoted in P.H. Sand, "The Socialist Response: Environmental Protection Law in the German Democratic Republic," *Ecology Law Quarterly*, 3 (1973): 485.

[33]H.C. Dunning, "Land Reform in Ethiopia: A Case Study in Non-Development," *UCLA Law Review*, 18 (1970): 271; R.B. Seidman, "Law and Stagnation in Africa," *Zambia Law Journal*, 5 (1973): 39.

[34]Paul Lehmann, *Ethics in a Christian Context* (New York: Harper and Row, 1963), pp. 159–61.

[35]Joseph Fletcher, *Situation Ethics: The New Morality* (Philadelphia: Westminster Press, 1966).

[36]Joseph Fletcher and John Warwick Montgomery, *Situation Ethics—True or False; A Dialogue* (Minneapolis: Bethany, 1972), pp. 25–48.

[37]James A. Pike, *Beyond the Law* (New York: Doubleday, 1963), pp. xii, 14–16.

[38]For my critiques of Pike's theology, in dialogue with him and in print, see John Warwick Montgomery, *The Suicide of Christian Theology* (Minneapolis: Bethany, 1971), pp. 17–61, 231–32.

[39]Charles A. Reich, *The Greening of America* (New York: Bantam Books, 1971), pp. 379–430.

[40]For guidelines in those difficult situations where the implementation of divine norms in a secular legal climate conflicts with the Christian's primary evangelistic task, see John Warwick Montgomery, *The Shaping of America* (Minneapolis: Bethany, 1976), pp. 152–58.

[41]Noteworthy as contemporary illustrations are Charles Colson and Jeb Magruder, who came to Christ as a direct result of seeing their lives in shambles because of their participation in the Watergate illegalities.

Evangelical Ethics and Public Policy

by Perry Glanzer

*I*n the 1980s, evangelicals raced into the public square like bulls into a china shop. As a result, critics often castigated evangelical political involvement for its absence of intelligent reflection, as well as its lack of civility, gentleness and love. This essay attempts to address the first problem by making some suggestions for developing a more sophisticated evangelical public philosophy. It is also hoped that following these suggestions will help evangelicals demonstrate Christian virtue when participating in the public arena.

In general, I argue that evangelical involvement in the public square is currently hindered by three major problems: (1) A social ethic that is usually underdeveloped both theologically and in church practice; (2) Simplistic methods for moving from biblically derived ethical positions to public policy recommendations; and (3) A lack of reflecting about the moral reasoning evangelicals employ in the public square. Allow me to explain.

First, politically involved evangelicals, especially at the grassroots level, have failed to enter the public arena with a social ethic that is both theologically and practically developed. At the theological level, evangelical Christians

343

often quote a variety of texts from the Old or New Testaments that they claim provide the biblical perspective on various issues. However, they often fail to take into account the whole canon. For example, in regard to social support for the poor, different evangelicals with different agendas will cite laws from the Pentateuch that emphasize Israel's need to care for the widow and orphan, Proverbs about the relationship between poverty and laziness, prophetic condemnations of Israel's injustice to the poor, on the one hand New Testament passages about Jesus' concern for the poor, or on the other Paul's claim that if a man does not work, he should not eat. After citing certain verses to prove their point, all of the individuals or groups claim that they have taken *the* biblical position on the matter.

In addition, evangelicals are usually more concerned with the social practices of America than those of evangelical churches. By not applying their Christian social ethic to church practices, evangelicals often find themselves asking the state to impose penalties on certain behaviors for which evangelicals do not even ask repentance in their own churches. They ask the state to meet social needs the church itself may not even be meeting. For example, evangelicals might ask the state to enforce child support laws and punish dead-beat dads, but fail to rebuke and ask repentance of fathers in their church who fail to pay child support. They are likely to demand laws outlawing abortion, but fail to consider whether or not their church disciplines and asks repentance of women who commit abortions, or of their partners who encourage them to obtain one. In addition, they might demand that the government do something about homelessness, but do little about the problem within their own community. In other words, the witness of the evangelical church has often failed to consider its own practices.

A second weakness with evangelical political involvement is that its spokespersons often fail to clarify the proper responsibilities of the political sphere. In *The Scat-*

tered Voice: Christians at Odds in the Public Square, Jim Skillen persuasively argues that Christians often take different and sometimes inconsistent political stands, because they lack clarity about the appropriate tasks of government.[1] In particular, he cites four types of evangelicals who have insufficient conceptions about the nature, responsibilities and limits of the state. Pro-family conservatives such as James Dobson, Jerry Falwell and Pat Robertson take random moral issues and crusade about them; cautious conservatives such as Charles Colson remind us to be pessimistic about what the state can do; pro-justice activists such as Jim Wallis and Ron Sider use the model of the kingdom of God as the ideal for the state; and Reconstructionists such as Gary North and Greg Bahnsen use Old Testament Israel as the proper ideal. However, each of the groups, Skillen argues, fails to clarify why the government should be concerned with certain responsibilities and not others. The overall result is confusion and inconsistency in evangelical thinking about the proper scope of the state's role in society.

This confusion is apparent in the local church. For instance, a social action committee pamphlet from a large Southern California church I visited cited various Bible verses to support the church's political opposition to pornography, abortion and homosexuality. From the pamphlet and the committee's other literature, it was not clear why these issues were the major political concerns of the church, as opposed to the problems of poverty, urban violence or racism. In addition, it was not clear why Christians who rely upon the Bible for moral guidance should expect someone who does not believe the Bible to agree that these things are immoral or should be illegal. Furthermore, it is not clear why the church should ask the state to address these immoral behaviors and not others, such as wife beating, disobedience to parents or adultery. All of these issues remain clouded because evangelicals have not developed a public philosophy.

Finally, politically involved evangelicals have also failed to reflect about the nature of their witness to the state—especially their moral language. The potential danger this poses to evangelicals is indicated by James Davison Hunter in *Culture Wars: The Struggle to Define America*. According to Hunter, evangelical Protestants, along with conservative Catholics and Orthodox Jews, are in a culture war with a group he labels the progressivists. The battle between these two groups is problematic because each one appeals to different sources of moral authority in speaking about right and wrong. Evangelicals and their partners appeal to transcendent norms. Progressivists appeal to moral "truths" based either on personal experiences or on "self-grounded rational discourse"—the belief that "moral positions and influence are justified solely on the grounds and evidence about the human condition and the coherence and consistency of the arguments adduced."[2]

Who will win this conflict, Hunter believes, is open to question. However, he notes that at one level the progressivists have already won. The knowledge sector, composed of the media, the educational establishment and the government have already defined the rules for moral reasoning in the public square. As a result, one cannot appeal to an authority such as the Bible, the church or tradition to argue one's point in the political sphere. Instead, to muster a legitimate argument one must rely solely upon deductive reasoning or empirical evidence to establish one's position. The end result is that in the public square the orthodox must play by the rules set by the progressivists. Hunter believes that the orthodox use of the progressivist frame of reference in the public square will transform their own moral language through compromise and moderation. In fact, evidence indicates that "orthodox communities may become so assimilated to a progressive political (and linguistic) culture that they will not be capable of offering any effective opposition to the worldview that currently plagues them."[3]

Is this happening? How are evangelicals at the grassroots reasoning about moral issues in the public square? Are they conscious of the moral arguments they are using? In order to gain an answer to these questions, I sought to learn the methods of moral reasoning that politically active evangelical Christians are using in the public square. Thus, I interviewed eleven politically involved evangelicals. Seven of the interviewees were leaders of the social action committees of their church, two were trying to start a committee, and five were leading or involved in chapters of conservative, pro-family organizations in the area.

Not surprisingly, when the activists were asked what their main way of coming to know right and wrong was, they were unanimous. Without exception every respondent affirmed that the Bible was their primary source of moral guidance. All but one of the interviewees believed one could appeal to some sort of common ground to prove one's moral claim. The common ground to which they believed they could appeal consisted either of facts that both they and the non-Bible believer could agree upon or an understanding of the common good at which both could arrive. Usually, the facts to which they appealed referred to certain consequences that they believed would occur if a specific moral view was or was not adopted. One man claimed that he would start by asking, "Why do you feel that way? Taken to its logical progression I see it ending up this way. In your heart do you consider that good or bad? Now if you took this other approach what is the logical ending? Do you consider that good or bad? So it's the questions, questions that lead to a conclusion free of manipulation. Just the facts, please." Other respondents expressed similar beliefs about the use of facts to arrive at some agreement about the common good. The assumption being that an agreement on what consequences are bad or good for society could be reached. Pat, a retired school teacher explained,

I think that we all have things in common, whether we're Christians or non-Christians, and things that work for the good of Christians are things that work for the good of everyone. If we think of it on the level of what is good for humanity, I don't think there is really a difference. People may perceive a difference. For instance murder is bad for everyone. Hunger is bad for everyone. The break up of the family is bad for everyone. Look how that impacts society.

Thus, although the Bible was the source of moral guidance for all those interviewed, they did not believe that dependance on its moral authority would limit their discussion of moral issues in the public square. Rather, they contended that one could use an alternative basis of moral reasoning that led one to arrive at similar moral conclusions. In other words, they believed that Christian moral truths known by revelation were verifiable by empirical methods and reason.

This switch in bases of moral reasoning from divine revelation to empirical evidence and reason was even more apparent when the activists shared how they reasoned about specific problems in the political realm such as abortion, sex education and homosexuality. Interestingly, they showed little consciousness of the switch in the bases of moral reasoning that was occurring. Appeals to the Bible were largely abandoned by the interviewees with few exceptions. Instead, in the public square interviewees often looked to facts and consequences to justify their moral positions. They also appealed to the rights of parents, as well as arguments based on inconsistencies, majority opinion and educational priorities.

Thus, Hunter's claim does appear to be true. Many evangelicals are using a different method of moral reasoning in the public square than in their personal lives. I am not as sure as Hunter that being forced to appeal to moral arguments based solely on rational or empirical grounds in the public square leaves the orthodox weakened in the culture war. From my interviews, it was clear that many found the empirical and rational resources to defend their positions apart from a direct appeal to transcendent authority. However, it remains to be seen whether these reasons will be convincing or find their way into the public debate. Most important was the fact that the interviewees were not very conscious of this transition in moral reasoning. Therefore, one might wonder whether or not a dependence on these forms of reasoning by conservative Christian political activists will eventually mean that they and other Christians are assimilated into a progressivist worldview. In other words, they will no longer think in a theological manner about moral issues. As a result, one may end up with Christian children who will abstain from premarital sex because of AIDS and associated health hazards, but not out of obedience to the Lordship of Christ.

Evangelical Christians and Public Policy: A Three Step Method

How should evangelicals remedy these weaknesses? I suggest a three step process for evangelical communities to consider when they are making public policy recommendations to the state.

(1) Undertake Ethical Analysis within the Context and Practice of the Christian Community Using Christian Sources of Moral Authority

First, before evangelical communities attempt to witness to the state, they should work out their own theologically based ethical positions by drawing upon the whole of the biblical canon. After arriving at their conclusions, they should apply this ethic to their own church practices. In regard to the first part of this step, Christopher Wright has provided a helpful outline for using the Bible in social ethics, one that avoids picking a few biblical quotations to arrive at a "Biblical view" of specific issues. He notes that there are certain major themes in the biblical story: (1) God's creation; (2) humanity's rebellion and the Fall of creation; (3) God's punishment and gracious redemption of humanity in history, beginning with the call of Abraham and culminating with the incarnation of Jesus Christ; and (4) God's promise of the restoration and renewal of creation. These broad biblical themes provide the fundamental framework for understanding specific problems in social ethics. For example, in regard to issues pertaining to sex and marriage such as homosexuality, pre-marital sex and divorce, the church should ask what are the creation order purposes and standards for sexuality and marriage, how the Fall has corrupted those purposes and standards, and how the redemptive communities of Israel and the New Testament church suggested regulating the practices of marriage and sexuality to restore God's creation order purposes. This approach to evaluating issues takes into account the whole biblical canon and provides a biblical context for discussion on social ethical issues.[4]

Does using this approach to issues in social ethics mean that the Bible supplies specific moral norms that are known only to Christians by biblical revelation? Traditionally, a debate has existed between "creationists" and "kingdomists" over whether or not Christians should adhere to an "ethics of creation" or an "ethics of the kingdom."[5] Generally speaking, proponents of an ethics of creation claim that all humans can arrive at knowledge of the divinely established moral order apart from making a Christian commitment. In fact, Paul's discourse in Romans 1 and 2 seems to support this point. However, proponents of an ethics of the kingdom claim that the Fall not only resulted in humans rejecting God's moral order but also altered their perception of it as well. Thus, one only fully knows God's moral order by faithful participation in the Kingdom that Christ announced and revealed.

Both Oliver O'Donovan and Christopher Wright have argued that the polarization between an ethics of Creation and an ethics of the Kingdom is an unhelpful dichotomy. O'Donovan notes that this sharp contrast fails to understand the relationship between the ontological and epistemological aspects of God's moral order. God has created the moral order, and the fact that it exists determines how humans are to behave in the world. Of course, humanity in its fallenness has rejected this moral order. Thus, in regard to epistemology, fallen humans have difficulty gaining a proper perception or knowledge of this moral order apart from God's own disclosure of himself and his works. Humans may have some natural knowledge of the moral order, but only through God's revelation in Christ can one more fully apprehend the moral order in which we are situated.[6] Therefore, in the resurrection of Christ, a new moral order is not created but the moral order of creation is restored and the kingdom of God dawns. In other words, redemption and revelation have their proper theological meaning as the divine *reaffirmation* of created order.[7] Redemption seeks to reverse the effects of the fall. Wright makes a similar point when he notes: "The redemptive work of God, running through both testaments, is a restorative response to the failure of human kind to fulfill God's creative purpose for them."[8]

In sum, Christian communities possess unique epistemological insight into the moral order through Christ, but they also have some points of common understanding with nonbelievers. As a result, the church should justify its moral decisions by relying upon the authority of Christ in the Bible, which provides a fuller understanding of the moral order. Furthermore, the Christian community must realize that communication about the moral order is difficult with nonbelievers who possess a fragmented and less complete knowledge of the moral order.

As noted above, the Christian community's moral perspective should not only be enhanced by the revelation of Christ, but also by its Spirit-filled attempt to live according to the moral order revealed by Christ. The church is not merely a vehicle for evangelism or a fellow-ship of those people who give assent to a system of beliefs, but it is a community where a new form of social existence should take place. Often, evangelicals ignore the fact that the church's social life should be a model to the rest of society in its demonstration of love, holiness and forgiveness, its manner of church government, discipline and accountability, its use of the creative gifts of the congregation and its love and service to the world.[9] Thus, when the church arrives at its theologically-based positions on social issues, it should first apply these positions to the church's own social practice. For example, if Christian communities reach conclusions on social issues such as abortion, homosexuality or racism, they should ask their congregation to acknowledge these as sins and repent of them.[10] Furthermore, they should discipline those who do not repent of these sins. In addition, they may wish to develop new social practices to meet social needs related to these issues. For example, some churches may want to start homes for unwed mothers and pregnancy counseling centers to confront the problem of abortion, or have joint church events with congregations of different ethnicity to break down racial barriers. Through practicing its Christian social ethic, the church may act as a leavening influence in society.[11] Overall, by developing its own theologically grounded ethical positions and putting them into practice, the church sets its own house in order before it witnesses to the state about its messy rooms.

(2) Develop the Contours of a Christian Political Theology

As the church evaluates issues within a biblical framework and attempts to develop practices that help it consistently live out its convictions, it indirectly witnesses to the state. However, a more direct witness requires that the church perform a second task. It must also develop the contours of a political theology—a biblical idea of the proper responsibilities of the state and the standards it should uphold when fulfilling those responsibilities. What is God's purpose and ethic for the state?

Answering this question will require viewing the state within the context of the biblical story.[12] A number of scholars have found that the biblical understanding of "principalities and powers" helps make sense of the place of the state in God's universe.[13] These powers, they suggest, refer to the religious, moral, intellectual and political structures of society as well as the cosmological influences behind them that order human life. They were originally part of God's good creation order, but they share in the fallenness of creation. As a result, the powers became objects of idolatry. They fail to serve humanity and instead "demand from the individual and society an unconditional loyalty."[14] Nonetheless, the powers' sovereignty over humans was broken through the work of Christ, who "disarmed and defeated" the powers and triumphed over them (Col. 2:15). However, although Christ is Lord of the powers, not all powers have been subjected to him. Stephen Mott notes, "The government, like other spheres of social life, is still the scene of the struggle between the fallen worldly powers and the authority of God for control of the human community."[15] Different strands of the evangelical tradition have different ideas about how the Christian community should participate in this struggle.

Traditional Ways of Understanding the Political Order

Traditionally, Reformed thinkers have contended that the political order would have developed in creation without the fall.[16] In other words, it is part of God's good creation order. Since the corrupted powers have been conquered through Christ, Christians are now called to restore the political order in accordance with the state's creation order norm of justice. Of course, the restoration is still a battle, but Christians are to participate in developing a just state.

However, Anabaptist scholar John Howard Yoder disagrees with this depiction. He contends that the necessity of orders and organization based on power in social relations is due to the Fall.[17] The state had no part in God's creation order and has no proper ideal. Therefore, the basis of two levels of ethics—one for the church and one for the state—is not a duality in the creation order. The important duality is between belief and unbelief. Yoder claims,

> Since we cannot say that God has any "proper" pattern in mind to which unbelief should conform, the Christian witness to the state will not be guided by an imagined pattern of ideal society such as is involved in traditional conceptions of the "just state," the "just war," or "the due process of law." An ideal or even a "proper" society in a fallen world is by definition impossible . . . There is no level of attainment to which a state could rise, beyond which the Christian critique would have nothing more to ask; such an ideal level would be none other than the kingdom of God.[18]

Therefore, for Yoder, Christians should be concerned with the state and witness to it, but they should not believe a proper ideal for government exists that is different than the kingdom of God. Nor should they believe that an ethical standard for the state exists, such as justice, that is different from the standard of Christ's love required of the Christian community.

The Practices, Laws and Virtues of Israel and the Church

Besides the two views offered above, James McClendon offers a third way of conceiving the issue, one that offers an analysis of specific social practices, virtues and laws, and which moves beyond broad generalities about the church and state. McClendon makes an important comparison between the "principalities and powers" references and the concept of social practices that Alasdair MacIntyre describes in *After Virtue*. He notes, "The principalities and powers are none other than the social structures we may also identify as (MacIntyrian) practices."[19] What are these practices? MacIntyre defines them as:

> *Any coherent and complex form of socially established cooperative human activity through which goods internal to that form of activity are realized in the course of trying to achieve those standards of excellence which are appropriate to, and partially definitive of, that form of activity, with the result that human powers to achieve excellence, and human conceptions of the ends and good involved are systematically extended.*[20]

Understanding the powers as social practices helps to illumine our social life. As MacIntyre notes, these practices have their specific internal goods or ends and appropriate means (governed by rules or laws) for achieving those ends. Participation in moving towards the end of a practice according to the appropriate means will evoke certain excellences or virtues that are required to perform the practice well. In addition, there may be common virtues of many different practices that are required to sustain the practices.[21] For example, Christians believe the social practice of sex has certain internal goods (physically expressing the spiritual union of man and wife) that are governed by certain laws (no sex outside of marriage). In addition, they believe that proper participation in moving towards the end of the practice will produce certain virtues such as gentleness, patience, self-control and love that are common virtues of other practices.

By understanding the powers and social practices in this way, one can discuss specific governing practices that can be performed within any community—Christian or national—as opposed to making general comments about church and state. For example, both Christian and national communities engage in the specific social practice of shaping and managing the common life of their communities. By understanding this practice within a biblical framework one gains even more insight. One can speculate that the practice of managing a community's common life would have developed in creation if the Fall had not occurred. The internal good or end of the practice would have been managing God's creation for God's glory (Gen. 1:26; 2:15). Goal directed participation in the practice of shaping and managing the common life would have evoked certain excellences such as equal respect for humans as made in the image of God, full participation of all members in the community, consideration of the common good and wise stewardship.

Clearly, humanity's Fall had tremendous implications for the practice of managing and shaping the common life. It brought the need for God's punishment (e.g., banishment from the Garden, the flood, the separate languages resulting from the tower of Babel) and the institutionalization of the social practice of punishment as an important component of shaping and managing the common life. The virtue or excellence of the practice of punishment was retributive justice.

In addition, God's redemptive activity brought further changes. A fracture was created in the common life of humanity. Society was divided into two communities—those who are God's chosen people (Israel and later the church) and those who do not acknowledge Him. After God's direct acts of punishment (expulsion from the garden, the flood, the creation of different languages), He started using His chosen people of Israel as an instrument of punishment on other nations. In addition, He promised to use them as an instrument of redemption for those nations (Gen. 12:3).

Israel's position as a redemptive nation was exemplified in certain redemptive social practices, the laws defining both redemptive and nonredemptive practices and the excellences or virtues of those practices. Israel's major redemptive social practice was the performance of corporate ceremonies whose purpose was the worship of God and the remembrance of His mighty deeds. This practice was regulated by a command to worship no other gods. Its ultimate excellence or virtue was the love of God. In addition, McClendon observes how several of the other Ten Commandments functioned in the Israelites' life as regulations of their already existing powerful practices.[22] Interestingly, the laws of Israel were based on the excellences or virtues associated with creation, such as equality and distributive justice, but also contained provision for the practice of punishment and its associated virtue of retributive justice that were required due to the Fall (Exod. 21:23–25). In addition, Israel was given redemptive laws to regulate nonredemptive practices that attempted to reverse the effects of the fall and restore creation ideals. For example, the economic laws promoted economic sacrifice to deal with undesirable economic forces and allowed for creation ideals to be approached. It is important to note that obedience to the redemptive aspects of the law were motivated by Israel's experience of redemption from Egypt.[23]

Of course, Israel itself was vulnerable to having its own practices corrupted. For example, in its worship ceremonies, it failed to keep the laws associated with that practice (keeping the Sabbath, having no other gods), to adhere to the end of the practice (worshiping God and remembering His mighty deeds) and to exhibit the excellences of that practice (love of God). Furthermore, in the practice of managing and shaping its common life it failed to exhibit the virtues characteristic of that practice, to follow the laws governing that practice, or to move toward the end of the practice—wise stewardship for God's glory. Oddly enough, Israel even failed in the practice of being an instrument of God's retributive justice by not fully punishing other communities (1 Sam. 13). As a result of the corruption of their practices, God used other communities to discipline Israel.

357

With Christ's initiation of the kingdom of God, His death and resurrection and the formation of the church, a new form of social existence came into being. The church was different from Israel in that Christ changed its practice of punishment. The church was not to use lethal violence to achieve retributive justice in the practice of managing its common life or in its relationships with others outside its community (Mt. 5:21f). In Israel, punishment regulated by the virtue of retributive justice was meant to balance the equilibrium of the community. Breaking the law created a debt to God and society which one had to pay through blood sacrifices to God and punishment extracted by society. However, the Christian community sought to deal with repentant individuals' debts to society in a different manner—by canceling or forgiving them.[24] Jesus had announced and demonstrated this new form of social existence by dying on the cross to cancel our debt to God (Col. 2:13–14). This is why the church was a community formed especially around the practice of the celebration of the Lord's Supper in commemoration of Christ's death and resurrection for us.[25]

The church was still to perform the practice of discipline through community accountability, their own "court system" or community review, and if need be, by shunning (Mt. 18:15–19; 1 Cor. 5–6). Yet, the church community practiced these forms of discipline with a view toward forgiveness and restoration to the community. It did not demand retribution for wrong behavior but repentance (2 Cor. 7:8–13). Furthermore, in regard to the outside community, the church was to deal with injustice in a similar manner. Not only were they to forgive others out of imitation of Christ but also because of the eschatological hope that Jesus had affirmed. The church knew that it could patiently suffer injustice, just as Christ did, with confidence that the God of justice would vindicate them in the end (Romans 12:17–21; 1 Peter 2:20–24).

In addition, Christ also demonstrated other virtues such as self-sacrifice, leadership by servanthood and forbearance which the church was to demonstrate in its practices. These virtues were motivated by the community's experience of redemption and its eschatological hope. These virtues, along with the practices of repentance and forgiveness, would seek to reverse the effects of the Fall in the practical life of the Christian community as well as broader society. These new forms of social existence are most fully known and motivated through the acceptance of Christ as Lord and the commitment to live according to the standards of His coming kingdom. Again, as in Israel's case, the experience of redemption is an important motivating factor.[26] Of course, as was also true in Israel's case, the church's practice can and has been corrupted at times.

Israel, the Church and the Modern State

How are Old Testament Israel, the New Testament church and the modern church both similar and different from the modern state? All these communities were or are involved in a similar practice of managing and shaping the common life of a community. Certain virtues, such as justice, equality and consideration of the whole community, are exhibited when this practice is done well. Thus, both the modern state and church should exhibit these same virtues in the practice of managing their communities.

In addition, the state is similar to Israel in that it is used by God to perform the practice of punishment (Romans 13:1–7; 1 Peter 2:14). This specific practice of the state should not be considered as outside the "order of redemption or grace" since the state's role in maintaining order is fundamentally to further the work of the church.[27]

The church has different practices concerning punishment and community discipline than either Old Testament Israel or the state. Thus, the state cannot cancel social debts by forgiveness, use forms of church discipline, or merely ask for repentance without giving punishment. Furthermore, the state cannot enforce certain redemptive

359

virtues exemplified by Christ and motivated by an eschatological hope, such as sacrificial love and servanthood. In other words, it cannot bring in the kingdom of God and enforce the redemptive practices and virtues of God's kingdom.

Finally, there are two other important differences between the state and redemptive communities. First, Old Testament Israel performed, and the modern church continues to perform, certain redemptive practices such as the corporate worship of God and ceremonies to remember God's great acts (e.g., the Lord's Supper). The state, due to the composition of its membership, cannot perform these practices without violating the integrity of the practice.

Second, not only will the modern state and the church have different practices regarding punishment and worship and exhibit some different virtues, but they will also have fundamental differences in their vision of the ultimate good or end for which they manage and shape the common life of their respective communities. This difference also exists between ancient Israel and the modern state. Old Testament Israel sought, and the church seeks, to manage and shape its community so that they will be a holy people who are faithful to God. Most modern western states attempt to govern communities of people without promoting a detailed vision of the good life and society, because they believe such questions are unresolvable in a pluralistic society. Therefore, modern liberal governments do little more than attempt to enforce the virtues associated with managing the common life, such as justice. As a result, modern notions of justice attempt to ensure equality of access and procedure along with protection of freedoms. Yet, it would be a mistake to believe the end of the practice of shaping and managing the common life is justice. That is only a virtue or excellence of this practice.

While encouraging justice will foster equality of access and peaceful public debate, it will not solve legal disagreements that stem from different views of the good that different traditions in the civic community maintain (This is why there are controversies over abortion, economic justice, etc.).[28] In the end, the practice of managing the common life of a community will encourage some substantive views of the good life and society—whether it wants to or not—through the world view undergirding its laws and policies.

Law and the Practice of Managing Communities

In democratic societies such as the United States, different communities within the nation-state attempt to impose their views of the good life and society on others through legal methods. These may or may not coincide with Christian ideals of what laws should govern social practices. Should Christians join the fray and mobilize a majority to legislate their views?

I would argue that the modern church should translate its laws that are based on creation values and that guide its *nonredemptive* community practices into middle axioms the state can apply. In addition, it can attempt to translate its laws based on redemptive values that guide its nonredemptive practices. However, this task will be more difficult. Christopher Wright has noted that the laws of Israel and the teaching on social relationships by Jesus and the church promoted creation ideals (equality, the worth of each individual, mutual love) as well as redemptive values and virtues (self-sacrifice, leadership by servanthood, etc.). For example, Israel had economic laws that promoted creation ideals such as fairness in exchange and equality of opportunity. Plus, they had redemptive laws that attempted to reverse undesirable economic forces and restore creation ideals through material sacrifice and special considerations for the poor.[29] I would suggest that it is certainly possible to translate laws based on creation values and it may be possible to translate laws based on redemptive values into the state's practice. Nonetheless, civil societies will rebel against even having Christian

361

laws passed that are based on creation ideals. For example, one can argue that the Christian's stance against abortion, homosexuality and divorce are all founded on principles derived from creation (human persons are God's sacred creation; males and females are God's creation for each other and are joined in a marriage covenant that is not to be broken). Furthermore, members in the civil community who are not a part of the church will certainly have difficulty sharing the motivation for laws based on redemptive values. Nevertheless, I believe that Christians should focus primarily on passing those middle axioms based on creation values.

First, if Christians adhere to the creation virtues inherent in managing and shaping a community, they will not attempt to pass their middle axioms without considering those outside their community. This adherence would prevent Christians from merely seeking hegemony or getting their views passed at the expense of nonbelievers. James Skillen provides helpful insight in this areas. He notes,

> *The biblical view of justice for every earthly creature will mean that Christians will work politically for the achievement of government policies that will protect, encourage and open up life for every person and community, whatever their religious confession and view of life. Justice in political life cannot be based on biblical teaching about church discipline because earthly states are not churches. The state is not a community of Christian faith; it is a community of public legal care for all people which must not favor or persecute any particular group of society.*[30]

Second, Christians should have realistic expectations about their attempts at translation because they realize that society cannot be coerced into following laws or norms based on creation or redemptive ideals. In fact, they will in all likelihood fail to understand or be persuaded by the theological basis for these laws.

How is this overall understanding of the political order different from traditional Reformed and Anabaptist views outlined above? First, it sees the church and state as participating in the same general practice—managing and shaping the common life of communities. This has some similarity to Yoder's view. However, this view is different than Yoder's in that it believes there are virtues or excellences of this practice that the state can and should be expected to uphold. There is a standard for the state, which is the same as for the church regarding the virtues of managing the common life. In addition, these creation virtues can be expected of the state's other nonredemptive practices.

Yet, this view also acknowledges that there is an important difference in dealing with problems brought about by the fall. Communities of the redeemed will have a knowledge of and participate in redemptive practices and virtues that are informed and motivated by their experience of redemption. These things will be somewhat incomprehensible and unattractive to an unredeemed community and thus cannot be expected from them. However, the laws based on creation values and possibly some redemptively motivated laws governing nonredemptive practices may be applied to those same practices of the state in the form of middle axioms. Of course, the Christian community's witness to the state will always be tempered by the virtues or excellences of managing and shaping society that should prevent them from being unjust to their nonbelieving neighbors in their application of these axioms.

(3) Translating the Christian Ethic to the State

The final step Christians must take in witnessing to the state is translating the norms based on creation and redemptive values that govern their nonredemptive practices so that they are understandable (although they may not be persuasive) to those outside the Christian community. In this process it will use middle axioms that

363

"translate into meaningful and concrete terms the general relevance of the Lordship of Christ for a given social ethical issue."[31]

Two important questions are what can be translated and how should the translation take place. As noted above, forms of moral reasoning that are based on the authority of Christ and the Bible and drawn from the Christian tradition, while binding on and persuasive to the church, will probably not be understandable and persuasive to those parts of a society that have rebelled against these sources of morality authority. To some degree this is not problematic in that I believe there should be two parts to the church's witness to the rest of society. The first part should be its prophetic message.[32] Out of its faithfulness to and love for God, Christians should faithfully and civilly declare their full theologically based norms in the public square.

However, in its public policy arguments, the church will be most effective if it translates its arguments to reasons that are understandable and more likely to be persuasive to those outside the church. Thus, out of love for their unbelieving neighbors the Christian church should sometimes refrain from its prophetic message (not compromise the substance of it) and seek to persuade those in the public square with reasons that nonbelievers can understand. The church can appeal to humanity's innate moral sensibilities when society's conscience is not too seared. Other forms of moral reasoning that are accepted in society may at times be compatible with Christian teaching.

Endnotes

[1]James Skillen, *The Scattered Voice: Christians at Odds in the Public Square* (Grand Rapids: Zondervan, 1990), p. 18.

[2]James Davison Hunter, *Culture Wars: The Struggle to Define America* (New York: Basic Books, 1991), p. 44.

[3]Ibid., p. 306.

[4]Christopher Wright, "The Use of the Bible in Social Ethics: Paradigms, Types and Eschatology," *Transformation* 1 (Jan.–March 1984): pp. 11–13.

[5]Oliver O'Donovan, *Resurrection and the Moral Order: An Outline for Evangelical Ethics* (Grand Rapids: Eerdmans, 1986), p. 15; Wright, p. 19.

[6]O'Donovan, op. cit., pp. 19–20.

[7]Ibid., p. 15.

[8]Wright, op. cit., p. 20.

[9]John Howard Yoder, *The Christian Witness to the State* (Newton, KS: Faith and Life Press, 1964), pp. 16–19.

[10]It is odd that as community discipline is often ignored in the church, secular communities are giving it greater attention. For example, *Christianity Today* recently reported that Antioch College, in Yellow Springs, Ohio, requires students "to agree with the school's policy of step-by-step mutual consent before any act of intimacy—from kissing to sexual intercourse." Violators are subject to expulsion. *Christianity Today*, October 25, 1993, p. 79.

[11]Yoder, op. cit., pp. 20–22; Stephen Charles Mott, *Biblical Ethics and Social Change* (New York: Oxford, 1982), pp. 128–41.

[12]Richard Mouw, *Politics and the Biblical Drama* (Grand Rapids: Eerdmans, 1972); and Wright, pp. 13–14.

[13]Mouw, op. cit., pp. 85–116; Yoder, *The Politics of Jesus*, pp. 135–62; McClendon, pp. 173–77; Mott, 1982, pp. 6–15.

[14]Yoder, *The Politics of Jesus*, p. 146.

[15]Mott, op. cit., p. 194.

[16]Mouw, op. cit., pp. 32–36.

[17]Yoder, *The Christian Witness to the State*, op. cit., p. 31.

[18]Ibid., p. 32.

[19]McClendon, op. cit., p. 173.

[20]Alasdair MacIntyre, *After Virtue: A Study in Moral Theory*, 2nd ed. (Notre Dame: University of Notre Dame Press, 1984), p. 187.

[21]McClendon, op. cit., p. 170.

[22]Ibid., pp. 177–86. McClendon makes an excellent point that the Ten Commandments cannot be abstracted into some general rule such as "be humane" because "such summaries fail to tell us the contents of humaneness; when abstracted from the practices, these 'universalizations' become empty" (181).

[23]Wright, op. cit., p. 20.

[24]McClendon, op. cit., p. 224.

[25]Ibid., pp. 214–19.

[26]Wright, op. cit., p. 20.

[27]Yoder, *The Christian Witness to the State*, op. cit., pp. 12–13.

[28]See MacIntyre, pp. 6–22.

[29]Wright, op. cit., p. 20.

[30]James Skillen, "Public Justice and True Tolerance," in *Piety and Politics*, eds. Richard John Neuhaus and Michael Cromartie (Washington, DC: Ethics and Public Policy Center, 1987), p. 165.

[31]Yoder, *The Christian Witness to the State*, op. cit., p. 32.

[32]O'Donovan, op. cit., p. 21.

Appendix

*T*he following resolution was adopted by the Evangelical Theological Society, November 17, 1993.

Whereas the Evangelical Theological Society is composed of members who believe the Bible to be God's inspired Word to every person and nation, and

The theme of the 1993 meeting of the Evangelical Theological Society was *God and Caesar*, and

Papers were presented addressing the role of the Church and individual Christians in society and in public policy, and

The Bible teaches that God is sovereign over every person and nation, and

Every governmental authority will give account to God for their beliefs and behavior, and

The Bible teaches that, "There is no authority except from God, and those which exist are established by God" (Romans 13:1), and

The Bible enjoins every Christian to pray "for kings and all who are in authority, in order that we may lead a tranquil and quiet life in all godliness and dignity" (1 Timothy 2:2), and

God holds Christians, and particularly their leaders, responsible to be exemplary participants in their society,

Be it therefore resolved:

That we, the members of the Evangelical Theological Society, commit ourselves to pray for the leaders of our government and to participate in the democratic process.

That we remind our political and cultural leaders that they are subject to the sovereignty of God and answerable to His Word and judgment.

That we urge the members of the Church of Jesus Christ to proclaim Him to all people in our society by word and deed with the knowledge that only He can change the hearts and therefore the policies of the American people.

That Christians should not allow the gospel to be the tool of any particular political ideology and Christians should not identify the kingdom of God with the kingdoms of this world.

That we challenge Christians, individually and corporately, to exercise a prophetic role in society, calling people to affirm and follow God's standard of righteousness.

That we encourage the evangelical Church to adhere to the ethical principles of the Bible even when they are in conflict with the policies or ideologies of the government or of the culture as a whole.

That we commit ourselves to redemptive ministries sharing the compassion and power of Christ with people, offering constructive ministries, and eschewing reactive or destructive methods.

List of Contributors

Michael Bauman is Professor of Theology and Culture and Director of Christian Studies at Hillsdale College in Hillsdale, Michigan.

Francis J. Beckwith is Lecturer in Philosophy at the University of Nevada, Las Vegas.

D. Jeffrey Bingham is Adjunct Professor of Bible at Le-Tourneau College in Longview, Texas.

Daniel J. Estes is Associate Professor of Bible at Cedarville College in Cedarville, Ohio.

Daniel J. Evearitt is Professor of Bible at Toccoa Falls College, Toccoa Falls, Georgia.

Perry Glanzer is a doctoral candidate at the University of Southern California.

Ronald N. Glass is Pastor of Wading River Baptist Church in Wading River, New York.

David W. Hall is Pastor of Covenant Presbyterian Church in Oak Ridge, Tennessee.

Richard C. Halverson is Chaplain of the United States Senate in Washington, D.C.

Brad Harper is Associate Pastor of the First Evangelical Free Church in Manchester, Missouri.

Daniel R. Heimbach is Associate Professor of Christian Ethics at Southeastern Baptist Theological Seminary in Wake Forest, North Carolina.

Richard I. McNeely is Presbyterian Campus Pastor at Montana State University in Bozeman, Montana.

John Warwick Montgomery is Professor of Law and Humanities and Director of the Centre for Human Rights, University of Luton, England.

Darius Y. Panahpour is a doctoral student in Renaissance Studies at the University of Iowa in Iowa City, Iowa.

James Alan Patterson is Professor of Church History at Mid-America Baptist Theological Seminary in Memphis, Tennessee.

William G. Travis is Professor of Church History at Bethel Theological Seminary in St. Paul, Minnesota.

Donald T. Williams is Professor of English at Toccoa Falls College, Toccoa Falls, Georgia.